119934

Politics and Poverty
. . . .

WILEY SERIES IN URBAN RESEARCH

TERRY N. CLARK, EDITOR

Resources for Social Change:
Race in the United States
by James S. Coleman

City Classification Handbook:
Methods and Applications
Brian J. L. Berry, Editor

Bonds of Pluralism:
The Forms and Substance of Urban Social Networks
by Edward O. Laumann

Nonpartisan Elections and the Case for Party Politics
by Willis D. Hawley

Politics and Poverty:
Modernization and Response in Five Poor Neighborhoods
by Stanley B. Greenberg

Guerrillas in the Bureaucracy:
The Community Planning Experiment
by Martin L. Needleman and Carolyn Emerson Needleman

The Roots of Urban Discontent:
Public Policy, Municipal Institutions, and the Ghetto
by Peter H. Rossi, Richard A. Berk, and Bettye K. Eidson

Education, Opportunity, and Social Equality:
Changing Prospects in Western Society
by Raymond Boudon

Politics and Poverty
MODERNIZATION AND RESPONSE
IN FIVE POOR NEIGHBORHOODS

· ·

STANLEY B. GREENBERG

A Wiley-Interscience Publication

JOHN WILEY & SONS · New York · London · Sydney · Toronto

Library of Congress Cataloging in Publication Data:

Greenberg, Stanley B.   1945—
Politics and poverty: modernization and response in
five poor neighborhoods.

(Wiley series in urban research)
"A Wiley-Interscience publication."
1. Poor—United States. 2. Political participation
—United States. 3.   Slums—United States. I. Title.

HN59.G75   301.15'43'320973   73-10273

ISBN 0-471-32485-X

Printed in the United States of America
10 9 8 7 6 5 4 3 2 1

To

KATHRYN, ANNA,

and

JONATHAN

WILEY SERIES IN URBAN RESEARCH

. . . .

Cities, especially American cities, are attracting more public attention and scholarly concern than at perhaps any other time in history. Traditional structures have been seriously questioned and sweeping changes proposed; simultaneously, efforts are being made to penetrate the fundamental processes by which cities operate. This effort calls for marshaling knowledge from a number of substantive areas. Sociologists, political scientists, economists, geographers, planners, historians, anthropologists, and others have turned to urban questions; interdisciplinary projects involving scholars and activists are groping with fundamental issues.

The Wiley Series in Urban Research has been created to encourage the publication of works bearing on urban questions. It seeks to publish studies from different fields that help to illuminate urban processes. It is addressed to scholars as well as to planners, administrators, and others concerned with a more analytical understanding of things urban.

TERRY N. CLARK

vii

PREFACE

. . . .

This book is far different from the one I set out to write. In the spring of 1968, under the auspices of the Office of Economic Opportunity, I began grappling with the disparate puzzle pieces that comprise a nationwide attitude survey—the research design, survey instrument, sampling procedure, interviewers, and much more. Before the field work concluded the following summer, I had enlisted in the effort four universities, two research companies, 100 interviewers, 100 poor neighborhoods, and nearly 6000 of the poor themselves. Researchers (myself included) in three cities weathered the winter sifting mounds of data, searching for the statistical relations that would portray the reality of poor neighborhoods. We coded and counted the responses of the poor; we scaled, correlated, and tested them for significance. Based on a large sampling of opinion and confidence in statistical inference, we hoped to reveal contours of politics and change in poor neighborhoods.

But what started with 100 cities and statistical inference became, in this book, both more limited and, paradoxically, more expansive. I relied heavily on a systematic survey of five poor neighborhoods and the analysis of indicators drawn from it. But in limiting the scope of the survey, I sought greater methodological rigor (e.g., a larger sample size in each community) and greater evidential and historical validity. Measures of statistical significance could no longer stand alone untested for historical and political importance. Indicators and correlations remain valuable tools for uncovering the dynamics of belief and politics, but only within a framework that makes demands on political theory, literary and subjective material, and history. My analysis, consequently, required a precarious integration of evidence and method; it paints a picture that cannot stand upon any of its individual elements but only on the impression they give together. This book is not a presentation of data analysis or case histories, nor is it a dialogue with literary and political spokesmen of the poor. It is above all a collage created by the interlocking of alternative approaches and streams of evidence.

Though this book began in survey research it now depends as well on my impressions of five neighborhoods, in-depth interviews with those who would speak for the poor, literary texts written by the poor themselves, the examination of community history, and political and social theory. I have spent five years bringing these elements together. If there is a richness of impression that emerges from this interplay, the time will have been well spent. If there also emerges an appreciation for the rich qualities of the people who live out their lives in poor neighborhoods, then we will have advanced not only social inquiry but the poor's struggle for change as well.

*****

When I think of all the people who contributed in one way or another to this study, the claim of single authorship seems almost arrogant.

The impetus for the survey came largely through the efforts of Diana TenHouten in the Evaluation Division of the Office of Economic Opportunity (OEO). Throughout the difficult process of negotiation and implementation, she remained committed to the survey project. Jonathan Lane, also in the Evaluation Division and project officer for a larger study of community action programs, supported the survey and later participated in its design. Without the continued support and vigilance of Barss, Reitzel and Associates

(B/R), it is doubtful that this survey of poor neighborhoods would have been conducted at all or that project quality could have been sustained. Bruce Jacobs, an employee of B/R and a close personal friend, was largely responsible for my participation in the project; during the two years that I was project director, he consistently offered important insights and critiques.

The research design for the survey was developed at B/R with the assistance of Curt Lamb, Linda Sallop, and Peter Powell, and at the University of California at Los Angeles where Richard Whitney and Joan Laurence spent many a long night preparing the survey instrument. The UCLA group, under the direction of David Sears, also helped supervise the field work. The unique sampling procedures (site and snowball sampling) were developed primarily by Warren TenHouten with the assistance of Gerald McWhorter. Diane Dimperio supervised pretesting in Venice, California, and subsequently directed sampling operations in the five communities. David Sears bore overall responsibility for the UCLA operations; he assisted in questionnaire construction and later prepared a supplementary analysis. He may also take credit for making my trips to the West Coast productive and enjoyable.

Leigh Wessell bore considerable responsibility for the mammoth coding operations and made life in an office tolerable and, indeed, enjoyable. She was aided by a number of diligent coders whose names I have lost in the confusion. Participating in the analysis were David Coleman, Margaret Balch, and Fran Goodman; the latter, over a one-year period, suffered great hardship under my whimsical approach to data analysis. Nancy Rich performed invaluable editorial work on a report for OEO.

TransCentury, Inc. conducted the field operations under the guidance of Bob Burns. Without his good nature and good relations with participants at all levels of the project, it is doubtful whether we could have reached this conclusion without a fatal breakdown of operations. Assisting in the field work were David Coleman, Terry Tiffany, Sue Pogash, Lew Rapacilo, Sharon Costello, Bill King, Chuck Underwood, and numerous interviewers whose names I never learned but to whom I am thankful.

In the past year, Andy Irving conducted invaluable library research and Stan Royal salvaged my computer work.

The data analysis was made possible by generous grants from the

Research Division of OEO, the Harvard-M.I.T. Joint Center for Urban Studies, the Department of Political Science at Yale University, and the Institution for Social and Policy Studies, also at Yale University.

The following people were good enough to speak to me during my own field observation, and their perception of politics in poor communities vitally affected the analysis to follow: Mattie Ansley, Rev. Martha Archer, Faye Baker, Gary Bennett, Mark Bihn, Don Bowder, Otho Boykin, Jr., Craig Burns, Harry Caudill, Jerold Charbonneau, Aleta Custer, Jess Delgado, Stanley DeZarn, Clarence Ezzard, Gene Ferguson, Rev. Austin Ford, Tom Gilhool, Harold Haskins, Ben Hernandez, Fred Jansen, Loyal Jones, Faith King, Mike Kilpatrick, John Luster, Sandra McClure, Micki McCullough, Judy Martin, Felix Matlock, Bill Meek, Mary Ann Mahaffey, Andrew Montgomery, Barbara Moore, George Nelson, Esther Perez, Steve Petkov, Betty Phillips, Billy Reid, Frank Thompson, Ron Turner, Nancy Ward, Conrad Weiler, Jack Welsh, Rosa Williams, Frank Witt, and Ada Wright. Many other individuals not mentioned here spoke to me briefly or indicated a desire to remain anonymous.

James Q. Wilson suffered through three drafts of this book and offered advice and criticism that rightfully altered the direction of this research. The manuscript was read in full or in part by Joel Aberbach, Peter Bush, Terry Clark, Edward Greenberg, Willis Hawley, Bruce Jacobs, Michael Lipsky, John Mollenkopf, John Wilhelm, Herbert Waltzer, and Douglas Yates; by Yale graduate students enrolled in my seminar on political mobilization during the autumns of 1971 and 1972; and by the participants in a research seminar on race and class at the Institution for Social and Policy Studies, including Garvill Booker, Allen Goodman, Judy Gruber, Mike Johnston, L. Charles Miller, David Montejano, Laurie Nisanoff, Phil Singerman, and Jerry Webman. I only wish I had the time and the foresight to benefit fully from their suggestions.

Noreen O'Connor, May Sanzone, Martha Brown, and Sharon Hornberger are responsible for three typed drafts of this book. I shall never understand nor cease to appreciate their tolerance of my time schedules and handwriting.

Sharon Hornberger did a remarkable job of editing and, at times, rewriting the manuscript. To the extent the sentences that follow are grammatically correct and clear in their meaning, the credit should be hers. No other person barring myself, has made so strong a personal commitment to this book.

If the work of the last five years has been successful, it is in no small part owing to the help from my friends.

STANLEY B. GREENBERG

Yale University
New Haven, Connecticut
Spring 1973

CONTENTS
. . . .

Chapter One: Introduction   1

    I   *Approach, 3*
    II   *Data, 5*
    III   *Organization, 8*

    PART ONE   DESIGN AND DISORDER

Chapter Two   The Etiology of Poor Neighborhoods   13

    I   *Three Great Population Movements,   15*
    II   *Rape of the Land,   20*
    III   *The Lure of the Cities,   27*
    IV   *The Development of Poor Neighborhoods:*
        Gardner · Belmont · East Side · Summerhill · North
        Central,   29
    V   *Conclusions,   40*

Chapter Three   The Political Permutations of Poor Neighborhoods   42

    I   *Gardner: The Fractionalized, Nonviolent Style,   43*

II   *Belmont: The Politics of Resignation,   49*
III   *East Side: Ghetto Mood and Political Violence,   53*
IV   *Summerhill: Accommodation and Apolitics,   59*
V   *North Central: Frenetic Politics,   64*
VI   *Concluding Notes,   71*

PART TWO   *BELIEF AND POLITICS IN POOR NEIGHBORHOODS*

Chapter Four   Lower Class Culture and Political Response   75

I   *Concept of Culture,   77*
II   *Lower Class Culture: From Focal Concerns to Time,   81*
III   *Street Corner Society: The Locus of Lower Class Culture:
      The Street • Values on the Street Corner • Isolation of
      the Street Culture • Street and Culture in Poor Neighborhoods:
      A Test,   85*
IV   *The Importance of Lower Class Culture,   96*
V   *Cultural Themes and Political Involvement,   100*

Chapter Five   The Alienated Politics of Poor Neighborhoods   104

I   *Political Alienation: A Model for the Study
      of Political Alienation • Politics, Violence,
      and Culture,   108*
II   *Political Alienation and Political Action: Approach*
III   *The Logic of Alienation • Alienation and Mediation
      in Five Poor Neighborhoods,   128*

Chapter Six   The Politics of Collective Understanding   131

I   *Dimensions of Group Consciousness: Factor
      Analyzing Group Consciousness • Factors in Black
      Identity • Factors in Mexican-American Identity,   133*
II   *Three Meanings of Consciousness: Black Consciousness:
      An Oppositional Response • La Raza: Traditional
      Response • "Hillbillies": A Taciturn Response,   140*
III   *Group Consciousness in Poor Communities,   153*
IV   *The Political Relevance of Group Consciousness: Political
      Estrangement and Group Consciousness • Group Consciousness
      and Political Expression • Group Consciousness and Vertical
      Intrusion,   160*

V   *Conclusion,*   *171*

Chapter Seven   The Politics of Class   173

    I   *Class Organization and the Poor: The Black Example,*   *179*
   II   *Labor and Capital in Five Poor Neighborhoods,*   *185*
  III   *Bases of Consciousness,*   *194*
  IV   *Class Ideology: Estrangement or Solidarity?*   *196*
   V   *Group Consciousness, Class Ideology, and Politics,*   *200*
  VI   *Conclusions,*   *201*

Chapter Eight   Conclusion: Radical and Liberal Political Man   206

    I   *Belief and Politics in Poor Neighborhoods,*   *208*
   II   *Explaining Political Permutations,*   *216*
  III   *The Limits of Explanation,*   *226*

Notes   231

Appendix A   The Data Base   265
Appendix B   Derivation of Measures   271

Index   277

Politics and Poverty

Chapter One

Introduction

. . . .

The poor neighborhoods of America's inner cities are a distinctive phenomenon, a product of common forces in industrialization and urbanization. They drew upon the impoverished hinterlands of North America for their people, from areas still bound in this century by feudal relations with the land and landowners. Out of the marginality, dependency, and instability of rural life were forged great migrant streams. The poor worked their way up the Atlantic coast to the urban centers in Maryland, Pennsylvania, and New York; from the Southern Black Belt and the Cumberland Plateau to the great factories of Ohio, Illinois, and Michigan; from the Central Mesa in Mexico to the railroads, mines, farms, and canneries of Texas and California. The "push" of rural impoverishment and the "pull" of expanding industrialization were the forces that created inner city poor neighborhoods. These neighborhoods grew up in cities across the country at about the same time, created by many of the same forces; the people left their farms or villages for many of the same reasons; they later came to face similar urban settings characterized

1

by accelerating deterioration, crime, and the destructive intrusions of urban development.

The mutuality of forces that created urban poor neighborhoods did not generate at the same time a shared political response among the poor. In some communities, the poor have remained basically accommodating and unalienated; in others they have become noticeably estranged from dominant institutions and life styles, preferring to view politics more in terms of struggle than of reconciliation. These contrasts are suggestive of the lack of political design or continuity among poor neighborhoods. The stark similarity of the industrial and urban experiences have given birth neither to a political movement among the urban poor, nor to a compatible orientation toward political expression.

This seeming paradox of politics and origins is particularly perplexing for a perspective that expects, or at least hopes for, a radical response to oppression. In this view, poor blacks, Mexican-Americans, and Appalachian whites are caught in a process, common to all developing capitalist societies, of expropriating the agricultural producer from the soil (1). Without the "freeing" of agricultural labor from "debt peonage" and other forms of bondage, the mass population movements of the twentieth century would not have occurred and capital would not have had available to it a "redundant population of laborers" well suited for exploitation (2). The poor of all colors, no matter how singular their personal afflictions appear, are fulfilling an historic role well played by peasants in all developing societies.

This perspective, simply conceived, anticipates an emergent political response that reflects this shared experience. Radical political man is outraged; his politics are characterized by challenge, confrontation, and rebellion. Although he often includes in his repertoire conventional forms of political expression, he tends to more obstructive acts and higher levels of struggle. He is apt to endorse bizarre forms of political expression, such as sit-ins or marches. On occasion, radical political man resorts to violence, perhaps looting or "trashing," and in extreme cases, bombing and arson.

An alternative perspective, however, might propose an altogether different political man, one who emerges from the processes of industrialization, urbanization, and mass migration, but who is better socialized to conventional expectations and who promises greater social stability. This perspective does not doubt that the poor lived with extreme deprivation in the rural South, central Mexico, and the Cumberland Plateau. It emphasizes, however, that the primary motivation underlying migration is the pursuit of economic opportunities and affluence. The inner city poor seek little more of urban life than did previous migrants — a small share, incremental change, and involvement. The poor, in this view, are anything but radical and come closer to what might be called liberal political man.

Liberal political man approaches political institutions pragmatically and with some confidence in their viability and intentions. Politics is considered a healthy bargaining process whereby each group gets its share if only the effort is made reasonably and forthrightly. Liberal political man, consequently, views the ballot box with some reverence and deplores the actions of those who are disruptive or threaten the civic peace. He votes, seeks favors, joins coalitions, and, if circumstances are favorable, runs for public office himself.

Both views of political man follow logically from the modernizing experience. Both are internally consistent. However, the naked trauma of modernization, we shall see, does not produce an overriding, consistent political style. In some communities the radical political style is ascendant; in others, the liberal political outlook; in yet others, no consistent political man emerges at all. These differences provide the central focus, and reason, for our analysis.

I   APPROACH

Among the welter of forces that determine political expression, belief is the force on which this work relies primarily. Although it might be possible to focus on community history, political institutions, and opportunities or long-standing cultural forces, we have chosen to carve out an area of analysis that is distinct from them, though not removed from them in any causal sense. Our focus in some respects divorces the analysis from history and institutional life and concentrates on the individual and his state of mind. We want to know how he relates to time and fate, how he grapples with forces he cannot control. We want to understand his feelings about political life. Does he identify political institutions and their incumbents as his own, as forces for change or stability that serve his interests and his values? Does he view political life from a distance, removed from the possibilities of personal impact? We need to understand how the poor individual defines his interests. Are they understood within some circumscribed collectivity, defined perhaps by proximate territory or race? Does he establish some transcendent identity which seeks to conglomerate distant groupings around a set of universal values (class, for example)?

In the answers to these questions, we hope to find the clues to political diversity. They pose crucial issues about life, politics, and social interaction that are suggestive, if not determinant, of individual political expression. When we understand the patterns of belief and their relationship to politics, we will make sensible the varying politics of poor neighborhoods.

Without attempting to elaborate in model form the complex causal processes that produce political expression, we can depict an oversimplified, two-part model, whose purpose is to identify a number of bold assumptions and some peculiar biases in this approach.

In Figure 1.1, political expression is a consequence of two broad categories of factors: experience and belief, the former having a causal impact on the latter, and both having a determinant impact on political expression. Experience for our purposes could include kinship structure, the forms of social control in rural areas, the causes of migration, the condition of inner city neighborhoods, the forms of government in both rural and urban areas, the responsiveness of political institutions, the types of work, intergroup conflict, and ob-

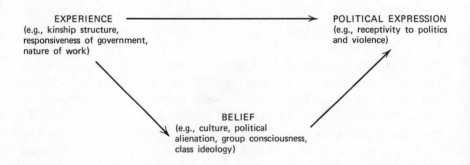

Figure 1.1 A simple model.

viously much more. Attitudes could involve the system of beliefs and mores transmitted from past generations, or culture; feelings of political alienation, involving an evaluation of political institutions, a sense of political effectiveness, and generalized feelings about the political community; a consciousness of a racial or cultural group which stands separate from or opposed to dominant groups in society; and finally, class ideology, feelings of solidarity with other persons subjected to similar work experiences. The model implies, quite plausibly, I think, that traditional life patterns in rural areas, the wrenching of populations from the land, and experience with urban life and institutions are, in large part, determinant of the political attitudes people hold. These experiences, together with generalized norms and values, the evaluation of political institutions, and group feelings, influence the manner and level of political expression.

The model is hopelessly simple, of course, providing almost no insight into the dynamics of political expression, and frankly, it is a bit pretentious. The purpose of the model, however, is to provide not an explanation, but a guide to emphases and limitations.

The emphasis of this work is on the immediate attitudinal determinants of political expression — culture, alienation, group consciousness, and class ideology. Our attention is devoted almost entirely to a formulation of attitudinal concepts, tracing their paths to political action and explaining the variation of politics in poor neighborhoods. But although we are concentrating upon belief and politics, we cannot ignore the life histories that are, in the final analysis, determinant of these beliefs. To ignore them is to place attitudes in a vacuum, as phenomena without cause. Our reliance on attitudes, rather than experience and history, then, must be considered an emphasis, not a preclusion of more general considerations. At no point can we fully separate personal feeling and expression from history.

II DATA

Almost fifteen years ago, C. Wright Mills articulated the promise of social science: to apply a *sociological imagination* to the ostensibly random and highly personal character of social events (3). Mills charged the social scientist with drawing the connections between the personal milieu and the organizational and institutional milieu that make up society, he wanted the social scientist to make apparent "the interplay of man and society, of biography and history, of self and world" (4). The sociological imagination would draw the necessary distinctions between "troubles" that are immediate to individuals and "issues" that transcend the local environment and, at the same time, trace the linkages that bring "troubles" (biography) and "issues" (history) together in society.

Poor neighborhoods can be a personal affliction for those who live in them, and it is possible to dwell on these personal conditions to the exclusion of nearly all other considerations. There is untold anguish for the mother who awaits a welfare check, barely adequate to feed her children, or who must beseech a caseworker for a winter clothing allotment; for the parents who watch their child's cough become a bronchial attack, then pneumonia; for the young man who waits endlessly at a state employment center or who works seemingly endless hours on a production line; and for the elderly couple, evicted from their apartment, who cannot find a home their meager income will support. These "troubles" are commonplace in poor neighborhoods and constitute a large part of their story. But the anguish that surrounds the individual in his immediate relations remains a descriptive essay, not an insight. Their isolated portrayal fails to grasp the social significance of personal troubles or to relate sentiment and emotion to broader patterns of belief.

The study of poor neighborhoods, if it is to transcend personal crises, must make biography tell a larger story. We must explore individual struggle and feelings, but the imaginative pursuit of social knowledge requires that these be understood in terms of shared experience, social structure, or history. In this study, I hope to fuse biography and history, capturing the sense of personal deprivation in poor neighborhoods, while portraying the vital relationship between personal tragedy, patterns of belief, and political response. In the collective political response of a people are merged their history and their individual biographies.

Our primary avenue to personal biography and belief is a survey questionnaire. During January and February, 1969, nearly 1100 interviews were conducted in five poor neighborhoods (5). They include two Northern black communities (North Central Philadelphia and East Side Detroit), a Southern black neighborhood (Summerhill in Atlanta), an urban Appalachian white neighborhood (Belmont in Hamilton, Ohio), and a Mexican-American community (Gardner in San Jose, California) (6). From the standardized information these questionnaire replies provide, it is possible to construct objective indicators for measuring the political discontinuities of poor neighborhoods and measures of belief that might be related to that variation. The survey data enable us to characterize politics and belief in poor neighborhoods and to draw connections between them without relying upon vague impressions and logical inferences. In the final analysis, our dependence upon standardized measures and statistical associations enables us to assess how far we have come in resolving the central issues of this work and what is yet to be explained.

Attitude surveys, however, provide a limited insight into the feelings of the poor and their response as part of a community. The coded categories of an interview schedule grant only a glimpse of the emotions that are involved in urban life — of the struggle for survival, meaning, and political power. Poor people are not characterized simply. They are embroiled in a complex relationship with their past, their neighbors, and political life. A full appreciation of their circumstances requires, in addition to the valuable standardized information of a survey, a knowledge of individuals and a sense of community history.

Our analysis and our understanding rely heavily upon personal contact with these five poor neighborhoods — the people who populate the street corners, playgrounds, stoops, and homes, the community organizations and leaders who claim to aggregate and express their interests, and the city officials who make decisions affecting their political lives. By incorporating our impressions and the reflections of these individuals, numbers and scales that previously related little more than sterile differences or correlations begin to display some of reality's rough edges. The contrasting politics of poor neighborhoods, stark in statistical terms, become stark in our impressions as well. Correlations appear not only statistically significant but also plausible and important. The strength of our analysis, consequently, lies in the beneficent interaction of objective indicators, the feelings and perception of political actors, and our general impressions of reality.

Lest we dwell on problems of belief and politics to the exclusion of broader historical patterns (thus reifying the relationships that emerge), we devote substantial effort to understanding the formation of these five neighborhoods and the political context that surrounds and intrudes on them. The analysis relies on historical material gathered for each community (neighborhood and city) and the impressions of the political actors responsible for the larger political and economic framework (e.g., elected officials, union leaders, and businessmen). In addition, we examine the great trek many of the poor made in this century and the hinterlands from which they came. Essential to this effort are the recollections of the poor, literary material, and my own travels in these areas. Although the analysis focuses on the relationship of belief to political action, the consideration of broader political relations and history adds richness to our discussions; it keeps us from losing sight of the larger context and from forgetting the limits of our own explanation.

III   ORGANIZATION

The analysis follows a simple story line — the apparent paradox, the ingredients of explanation, and finally, the resolution.

In Part One, "Design and Disorder," we pose the central organizing idea of this work. Chapter Two ("The Etiology of Poor Neighborhoods") focuses on the modernizing experience of the urban poor, relating basic continuities of rural life, migration, and urban condition. Using five poor neighborhoods as examples, it seeks to emphasize how much the poor — whether black, brown, or white — share in their experience. The breakdown of these continuities into five distinctive and wholly separate political styles is described in Chapter Three, "The Political Permutations of Poor Neighborhoods." Through five short narrative essays, we sense the differing commitments of the poor to community organizations, politics, and violence.

In Part Two, "Belief and Politics in Poor Neighborhoods," we formulate and develop concepts of belief that are relevant to the social condition and political life of poor neighborhoods. The emphasis in each case falls in three areas: first, the elaboration and measurement of belief; second, tracing the linkages to political expression; and third, the application of these relationships in five poor communities. These results provide a general understanding of belief and politics and a specific sense of the mood and politics of five poor neighborhoods.

In Chapter Four, we pursue differing notions of "lower class" culture to their logical result, showing how specific cultural themes temper the poor's approach toward political institutions. Types of political alienation are described in Chapter Five, emphasizing how evaluation of political institutions and calculations of political effectiveness provide inducements or discouragement to political involvement. Three forms of group solidarity are depicted in Chapter Six, one based on group history and culture, another based on animosity to an oppressive group, and a third that is taciturn; the first fosters intense but peaceful forms of political activity, the second is associated with the resort to violence, and the last suggests political indifference. In Chapter Seven, we assess to what extent the poor have formulated a class ideology congruent with their social and economic position and the importance of these transcendent beliefs for political expression.

In the concluding chapter (and in threads running throughout this work) we grapple once again with our central question: can patterns of political belief make sensible the apparent divergence of politics in poor neighborhoods?

Part One

DESIGN AND DISORDER

. . . .

Our approach to poor neighborhoods is conditioned by the design of
modernization and the disorder of politics. The former emphasizes
the continuities in the poor's experience; it outlines, in effect, the
historical and sociological elements that make the poor distinctive as
a group. The latter highlights the behavioral dissimilarities of poor
neighborhoods, raising the apparent contradictions that underlie this
inquiry.

Chapter Two

The Etiology of Poor Neighborhoods

Poor neighborhoods created newspaper headlines in the 1960s the riots in Watts, Detroit, and Newark, the rent strikes in Harlem and Boston's South End, the violence endemic to all urban ghettos— prompting some of America's most imaginative endeavors in planned social change. We witnessed the President's Committee on Juvenile Delinquency, the Mobilization for Youth Program, the "gray areas" program, the War on Poverty, culminating in hundreds of community action programs, legal assistance offices, and Head Start centers. The Federal Government instituted well-publicized investigations of the national malaise, dealing substantially or entirely with the deteriorating inner city. Reports were prepared for the National Advisory Commission on Civil Disorders, the National Commission on the Causes and Prevention of Violence, and the President's Commission on Law Enforcement and Administration of Justice.

But with the cooling of the ghetto fires and with the institutionalization of community action programs, the air of crisis began to fade. Public officials no longer felt compelled to wage war on the blight and misery of the inner city or to decry the indifference to its deterioration. Of greater salience was the rising cost of meat, polluted skies, "forced bussing," and the war in Vietnam. The agony of being poor and the quality of life in poor neighborhoods had become irrelevant for the politicians and voters of the seventies. The "urban crisis" began to recede from the headlines and from the chronicles of historians and social scientists.

The difficulty, all along, in understanding poor neighborhoods has been this air of crisis—the need for immediate change, the demand for law and order—that has surrounded them. Poor neighborhoods gained sociological and historical prominence because of ahistorical factors that have proved ephemeral, leaving us with little more than the ruin of the riots—the leveled blocks and abandoned stores—as a basis for analysis. Limited considerations of this sort have led some to the facile conclusion that "if these inner districts...were to suddenly disappear, along with the people who live in them, there would be no serious urban problems worth talking about" (1).

But the inner city aggregations of blacks, Appalachian whites, and Mexicans are not simply the focal points for short-term instability or remedial governmental programs. These groups are the first *native American urban poor.* Today's inner city neighborhoods are not the product of a potato famine in Ireland, land enclosures in rural England, unsuccessful political rebellions in Germany, pogroms in Russia, or the extreme poverty of southern Italy. The poor neighborhoods of the mid-twentieth century were created by events largely controlled by this country under conditions nurtured in the rural countryside. The blacks who fled the Black Belt counties of the South, the whites who moved reluctantly out of eastern Kentucky and West Virginia, the Mexicans who escaped the central plain of Mexico and the small towns of Texas and New Mexico lived under strikingly similar conditions, left the land at approximately the same time for many of the same reasons, and moved to neighborhoods suffering the same sorts of economic and political pressures.

The obsessive regard for headline events rather than for history or process has only obscured the role of poor neighborhoods in the most basic social changes of this century. To understand the formation and development of poor neighborhoods is to grasp a fundamental historical process, reflecting a pattern for the exploitation of rural labor and the imperatives of industrial growth.

I   THREE GREAT POPULATION MOVEMENTS

The poor neighborhoods of America's inner cities are a result of three great population movements. One originated in the Atlantic Coastal Plain, the Black Belt and Delta regions of the South, a second in the rich bituminous coal fields of the Cumberland Plateau, and the third in the populous elevated plains of central Mexico (2). It is against this background—millions of displaced persons moving to urban centers—that we begin to appreciate poor neighborhoods, not as "problems," but as the end products of an historical epoch. We cannot understand life or politics in poor neighborhoods, unless we appreciate the experience and the history that created them.

The black population of the United States remained relatively stationary during the half-century following emancipation, confined for the most part to a belt stretching across central South Carolina, Georgia, and Alabama, the Atlantic Coastal Plain, and the Mississippi Delta. From time to time blacks traveled the railroads to the cities of the North. Some went to New York or Philadelphia, others to Chicago or Detroit. Rarely, however, did blacks travel farther north than New York City or farther west than Chicago. Before World War I, few attempted even this distance, with nine out of every ten black persons in the United States residing in the former slave states. This figure had changed little since 1870 (3).

World War I shook millions of blacks loose from their traditional ties to the rural South. The first evidence of systematic decline in the southern black population occurred in Alabama and Mississippi during the teens. Blacks in other sections of the South began to leave for the North, but in most cases, the movement was not sufficiently marked to offset the natural increase in population. By the twenties, however, more easterly states like Virginia, South Carolina, and Georgia were also beginning to experience net population losses. In the twenty year period from 1910 to 1930, approximately one million blacks moved north (4). The blacks of the Delta moved almost exclusively to Illinois; farmers in the central Black Belt crossed Tennessee and Kentucky, then moved in three directions—to Indiana and Illinois, to Michigan, and to Ohio; blacks living in Georgia and the coastal plain moved up the coast to the Mid-Atlantic states of New York, New Jersey, and Pennsylvania (5). Few attempted the trip to California.

Migration was halted for a decade during the thirties, but resumed with much greater force in the forties and fifties. During the two decades following the outbreak of World War II, almost three million blacks fled the South. The small stream that began in Alabama and Mississippi in the teens, then spread to Georgia and South Carolina in the twenties, swelled to a widespread, general migration in the forties and fifties. Blacks followed the traditional routes up the East Coast and along the Illinois Central Railroad line to the Midwestern metropolises, but were increasingly looking to war-boom cities regardless of their location (6). Blacks moved in substantial numbers to the cities of the South (7) and the West Coast. By 1960, the migration of blacks to the West almost equaled that to the Northeast and the Midwest (8).

The most massive internal migration this country has ever witnessed leveled off during the mid-sixties, but only after a remarkable dispersal of the black population. By 1969 as many blacks lived outside the South as in it, and 70 percent lived in cities (9).

The Mexican contribution to poor neighborhoods is, in its initial phases, quite different from that of the blacks and Appalachian whites. The Spanish, Mestizos, and Indians settled the southwestern United States (particularly the area that is now Texas and New Mexico) long before there were any significant English or American settlements. Their entrée into this country was achieved not by the radical transfer of populations, but by American territorial expansion, annexation, and treaty agreements.

This small indigenous population, however, was overwhelmed by the rapid advance of Anglo settlements in Texas and California, and remained small and encapsulated. By the turn of the century, the only significant Mexican urban concentrations were in the stretch of border towns along the line that separates the United States from Mexico (10).

The halting increase of the resident Mexican population, achieved in a half-century by annexation and population drift, became a genuine migration flow during the first three decades of this century. Large numbers of Mexicans began to leave the Central Mesa— primarily the states of Michoacan, Guanajuato, and Jalisco (11)— for the border areas and, eventually, for the large-scale agricultural, railroad construction, and mining areas in the United States (12).

They moved through El Paso to northern New Mexico and southern Colorado, through the Rio Grande River towns to eastern Texas, and to Tucson in southern Arizona. Later in this period, they moved into California (13).

The first major wave of Mexican immigration (1909-1910) coincided with the Mexican Revolution, when most of the immigrants moved to Texas. Of the 200,000 Mexicans living in the United States in 1910, more than half resided in Texas. But during the second major population movement in the twenties—involving almost 500,000 migrants—nearly as many Mexicans went to California as stayed in the more proximate areas of Texas and New Mexico (14).

Very early in this migration it became apparent, despite the association of Mexican labor with agriculture and mining, that the migrants were destined for the cities. Although large numbers sought work in the lower Rio Grande Valley, the Salt and Gila Valleys of Arizona, in the fields around Fresno, and the Central Valley counties of California (15), by 1930 Mexicans had congregated in Los Angeles, El Paso, and San Antonio as well. The 1930 census showed 51 percent of the Mexican population in urban centers (16). Mexicans in New Mexico and Texas were still in predominately agricultural occupations (though many commuted from the cities), but even during this early period, the California Mexican population was represented almost equally in manufacturing and agricultural work (17).

Another migration of Mexicans to the United States came during World War II, but under terms radically different from those of other groups that immigrated in this period. Actual migration, that is, the establishment of permanent residence, continued at a rate only slightly greater than during the Depression. But contract labor was greatly expanded under government auspices, permitting the entrée of 430,000 "bracero" workers between 1942 and 1950 (18). This transient work force was supplemented by a large number of illegal entrées ("wetbacks"), estimated at about 40,000 persons a year, with between 40,000 and 80,000 illegal entrants living in California at any one time (19). The overall impact of this transient work force was to increase the urbanization of the Mexican population; Mexicans looking for contract or illegal work congregated in the border towns of Brownsville, Calexico, and Loredo, and the downward pressure on wages encouraged the resident rural population to seek the more lucrative jobs in the cities. "Braceros" were under contract to remain in agricultural occupations, but many "jumped" contracts and tried to lose themselves in urban barrios (20).

Two important but contrary population movements followed the end of the Korean War. During the immediate postwar recession, the United States Government carried out an extensive program (Operation Wetback) to rid the country of Mexicans residing illegally (without working papers) in the Southwest. More than one million Mexican nationals were deported during the last two years of the Korean War, almost 900,000 in 1953, and more than one million in 1954 (21). But with the passing of the recession, the diligence of deportation authorities relaxed and legal entrées increased substantially (22). The bracero program was terminated in the mid-sixties, but in 1965, 100,000 Mexicans still entered the United States as contract laborers (23).

By 1970, there were five and one half million Mexican-Americans residing, for the most part, in Texas and California. Eighty-five percent of those in California lived in the cities (24).

The third major migrant stream originated in the southern Appalachian Mountains, most noticeably in the coal counties of southern and central West Virginia and eastern Kentucky, known as the Cumberland Plateau. On a scale barely perceptible to the great urban centers of the North Central United States, Appalachian families began to leave the coal fields and the small, unproductive plots of land about the time of World War I. The exodus was small and uneven across the plateau: some coal centers continued to show population increases during the twenties, a few evidenced small declines, and none lost population during the Depression (25).

The great migration began with the bombing of Pearl Harbor. During the next two decades, the entire southern Appalachian region was decimated by population losses: nearly two million persons moved in this period; more than 500,000 left Kentucky alone. During the fifties, the Cumberland Plateau lost one-quarter of its people. This flight continued until 1970, though at a rate only half that of the two pervious decades. By 1970, the great exodus from the Appalachian Hills, if not concluded, seemed near exhaustion (26).

But if the abandonment of the coal fields was no longer important

Table 2.1 Migration and Poor Neighborhoods

Migrant Groups	Principal Migration Periods	Approximate Number of Migrants(i)	Origin	Destination
Appalachian whites	1940–1970	1,600,000	Southern Appalachian Mountains (Kentucky and West Virginia)	North Central United States
Mexicans	1910–1930	700,000	*Mesa Central* primarily, also *Mesa Del Norte*	Texas and south-western United States
	1950–1970	700,000	*Mesa Central* primarily, also *Mesa Del Norte*	Texas and California
Blacks	1910–1930	1,000,000	Mississippi Delta, Black Belt, Atlantic Coastal Plain	Illinois, Michigan, Ohio, Pennsylvania, New York
	1940–1965	3,500,000	Mississippi Delta, Black Belt, Atlantic Coastal Plain	Cities everywhere

(i) These figures are approximate. The data for the Mexican migration, for example, are obscured by contract labor, two-way migration, and illegal entrants.

in the seventies, the Appalachian impact continued in the string of "Little Kentuckies" stretching from a cluster in southwestern Ohio (Cincinnati and Dayton) to Akron in the northeast, to the railroad terminal and hog butchers in Chicago, and to the automotive centers in Michigan. Some of the migrants moved into the growing cities of Kentucky and Tennessee; others moved east into Maryland and Virginia. But the great exodus from the eastern hills and coal fields of Kentucky was directed to the North Central region (27). The concentration of Appalachian whites in the Midwestern urban centers is a direct result of the migration from such coal counties as Leslie, Harlan, Breathitt, and Letcher.

Out of these three migrant streams, originating in the belt of black counties across the deep heartland of the South, the coal counties of the Cumberland Plateau, and the Central Mesa of Mexico, emerge the poor neighborhoods of today. Millions of desperate people followed the railroads and highways of America, hoping to flee what became in the twentieth century an oppressive rural setting. The poor neighborhoods of today are a product of that flight and the life that was left behind.

II   RAPE OF THE LAND

The Black Belt, the Cumberland Plateau, and the plains of central Mexico are superficially distinct areas. Black tenants and farmers in the South picked cotton and tobacco in the sprawling fields of the Black Belt, whereas Mexican labor on the large *haciendas* harvested cereals, maize, and beans. Farmers on the plateau worked small, barren plots of land, usually near a creek bed. Each region displayed its own language or *patois;* each offered its own customs. Yet certain basic social relationships dominated these three areas, overshadowing the striking peculiarities of each setting. These disparate populations all barely subsisted, scarcely able to provide food and shelter for themselves and their families. In each case, rural marginality was exacerbated by the encroachment of large landholders and by the harrassment of their legal and political instruments. The resulting economic marginality and dependency provided the context for the economic and political crises that decimated these areas.

The marginality and dependency of the mass of rural blacks were ensured by a colonial policy that granted large tracts of land for development and by the requirements of a cotton economy. The southern region of the United States provided an ideal climate for the cultivation of cotton: 200 days a year without frost, but with adequate rainfall in the winter, spring, and summer months. The long growing season and the profitability of cotton ensured its agricultural primacy. No subsidiary crop could be grown on the same soil, and during the harvest, all other crops were superseded (28). From these factors—the profitability of cotton, the long growing season, and the nature of cotton cultivation—emerged the system of land concentration known as the plantation economy.

Plantations prospered in the fertile soil of central North Carolina, central and southwestern Georgia, and the Mississippi Delta(29); but their need for extensive labor necessitated the importation of black slaves, most of whom did not prosper. After the Civil War, large landholders adjusted to the termination of "forced labor" by parcelling out the land to tenants or croppers while maintaining a system of unified management (30). The system of control changed as a result, but neither the bare subsistence existence of the black farm workers nor their ties to the land were altered substantially.

Black farm workers, as well as many whites, were bound to the plantations of the Black Belt through ingenious systems for remuneration. Sharecropping was the most common pattern throughout the South, especially in Georgia and Mississippi(31). This system stipulated that the farm worker (the cropper) operate under strict supervision, with no control over the crops and with only a share of the crop as payment. Share tenants were required to provide almost everything but the land and pay a portion of the crop as rent (32). Blacks were kept in a dependent state by the close supervisory system—usually involving the ringing of bells at the beginning and end of each working day (33) and a pattern of intimidation (34)—and by the system of credit indispensable to survival during the long growing season (35). Frequently, the sharecropper had nothing left from his crop after settling accounts, or, more often, had just enough credit to get through the winter months. Moreover, a tenant could not move to another farm without settling his debts in full (36).

The marginality and dependence of sharecroppers were ex-

acerbated by the risks of cotton and tobacco production that fell
disproportionately upon them; their income was virtually dependent
on the yield and the market price. During the Depression, sharecroppers fared badly, particularly those living in the Black Belt and
lower Delta. Predictably, the migrations beginning during World War
II drew most heavily on these sharecroppers (37).

"The Cumberland Plateau," Stewart Udall wrote, is a "mountainous region of flattopped ridges and steep-walled valleys, richly
endowed by nature with dense forests, winding rivers, abundant
game, loamy soils, and thick veins of coal" (38). It bears little
resemblance to the elevated plains of central Mexico or to the flat
expanse of cotton fields in the deep South. Although most of the
Appalachian people came to the United States as indentured servants
for planters on the southern coast, they had long since shed the
mantle of slavery and settled in the interior mountains of Virginia
and Kentucky (39). They were frontier people, crude and independent. Beyond what Toynbee has called their "poverty, squalor
and ill health" (40), their condition had little in common with the
peonage of rural blacks and Mexicans.

Their story, however, begins with the trees. Late in the nineteenth
century, large corporations were organized to exploit the thick
forests on the plateau. They diligently maneuvered among the
overlapping land titles of the highlanders, fostering a process
whereby timber rights passed out of the mountains into the hands of
"foreign" investors. The land that had supported the independence
of the Appalachian mountaineer for so long was now one step away
from his control, and the trees that had protected his frontier were
now reduced to "the pitiful remnant of cull and second-growth
timber" (41).

It was the large veins of coal, however, that ultimately destroyed
the highlander's independence. Coal companies, including such
industrial giants as the Inland Steel Corporation, the Consolidation
Coal Company, International Harvester Corporation, Elkhorn Coal
Corporation, and the United States Coal and Coke Company,
claimed the minerals of the plateau, leaving the highlanders with the
illusion that they still controlled the surface of the land. By 1910
much of that land—three-fourths of the remaining timber, and more
than 85 percent of the minerals—belonged to nonresidents (42).
When the highlanders attempted to prevent the coal companies from

turning the surface into rubble, the courts held (43):

> I deeply sympathize with you and sincerely wish I could rule for you. My hands are tied by the rulings of the Court of Appeals and under the law I must follow its decisions. The truth is that about the only rights you have on your land is to breathe on it and pay taxes. For all practical purposes the company that owns the minerals in your land owns all the other rights pertaining to it.

With the corporations in virtually full control of the land and with mines being sunk throughout the plateau, the highlanders turned to coal for their livelihood. By 1929, one out of every four members of the work force was employed by the coal companies. A small number of blacks were brought into the fields during the boom years, and small groups of Italians, Poles, Slovaks, and Hungarians had come earlier. But even as late as 1930, native Appalachian whites made up three-fourths of the mine employees (44). The Cumberland Plateau and its frontiersmen were now "tied inseparably" to coal, the railroads, and "the colossal industrial complex centering in Pittsburgh" (45).

Occasionally the Appalachian miners returned to the farms that had supported them at an earlier time, but for the most part, they were now controlled by outside corporations and a thoroughgoing system of paternalism. They often were required to live in company towns and to buy their food and supplies at company stores. Sometimes wages were paid in scrip, ensuring that the entire paycheck would eventually come back to company coffers. When company towns were incorporated, the coal companies invariably controlled the tax commissioner, the county judge, the council, the mayor, and the police force (46). The coal companies were assured, consequently, that taxes would not be burdensome, that the schools would not teach "subversive" ideas, and that the work force would remain dependent on the good graces of the company.

The marginality and dependency of rural Mexicans were also tied inseparably to the land. "There is a saying of our ancestors: 'Whoever sells his lands sells his mother,' " a New Mexico farmer declared. "It's a true saying. Land is what keeps you and me and everybody else" (47). But the land failed to keep the peasant population. Some 300 years of Spanish dominion eroded the established system of land tenure defined by the Indians and substituted in its place a pattern of land concentration under the auspices of Spain and the Church. Alienation from the land was most pronounced in the Central Mesa where the sedentary Indians were more vulnerable to Spanish colonization (48). Mexican independence did not alter this pattern of land ownership. The Diaz regime continued to destroy village communal lands, contesting land titles and fostering land monopolization (49).

The process of land concentration was far more advanced in the Central Mesa than in the mountainous and desert regions. For the most part, the land was carved into *haciendas* that dominated the small farms and often surrounded the free villages (50). Only in the mountains were the independent free villages able to escape the encroachment of *haciendas* and *ranchos.* The majority of the rural Mexican population that lived in the central region was, by 1900, forced to live and work on these large estates (51).

The *haciendas* became "feudal patrimonies" where free villagers and farmers were often transformed into *peones de campo,* a rural population tied to the soil on estates owned abroad. This system of domination provided the bulk of the *hacienda's* labor force free of charge, since many peasants were required to work "for the privilege of occupying the place," to pay a "work rental" (52) or to exchange a day's work for a day's ration of drinking water (53). These laborers were tied to the *hacienda* through debts accumulated at the *hacienda* stores, and by money gifts received at marriages—all of which had to be repaid before a worker could move to another estate or to a free village (54). Because the farm workers were dependent on some share of the crop for their subsistence and their ability to make good on debts, they assumed, along with the estate owner, the risk of raising the crops. It was common practice on the *hacienda* to reserve the high risk crops for sharecropping (55).

Yet the marginality and dependency common to these groups did not, in and of themselves, produce the population movements discussed earlier. Poverty had been characteristic of the Cumberland Plateau since its settlement, and the loss of frontier independence evolved for almost seventy-five years before the massive exodus to Ohio, Michigan, and Illinois began. Southern blacks had never lived much beyond the pale of starvation, and their dependency had been complete since they were wrenched from their African homelands. And even though the plight of the Mexican peasants worsened significantly during the nineteenth century, extreme marginality and dependency had been commonplace since the early days of colonization.

Economic and political crises finally forced blacks, Mexicans, and Appalachian whites to reconsider living under the traditional patterns of economic marginality and dependency. Of the three regions the Central Mesa experienced the most severe and thoroughgoing upheaval—one that destroyed the feudal ties to the *haciendas,* plunged the countryside into a quarter of a century of civil war, and precipitated the great Mexican migrations. The bloody Mexican Revolution of 1910 led many Mexicans to move their families and scant possessions to the border areas in Texas and New Mexico, where relative safety was assured. Many more began the trek north when *hacienda* properties were parcelled out to peasants and the free villages, and when debt peonage was abolished, thus cutting the most fundamental ties to the feudal past. Although some redistribution was thereby effected (56), large numbers of peasants used their new freedom to escape the rural areas of Mexico altogether (57).

The bloody campaigns by General Robles aimed at restoring constitutional government in rebellious provinces led to a further rending of the traditional rural society and to a massive depopulation (58). Before the disturbances of the twenties ended (including the De la Huerta rebellion in 1923 and the religious upheavals of 1926) six million Mexicans had been liberated from serfdom (59), and hundreds of thousands of these newly freed men and women sought refuge in the United States (60).

The troubled mining industry created the conditions for the depopulation of the Cumberland Plateau. Depression struck at the coal industry and the timber market as it did industries throughout the country, forcing a large number of camps to suspend operations. In Appalachia, however, there were few alternative sources of employment. New managers, seeking to salvage the mines from retrenchment, acted to recoup their losses at the expense of the miners: they raised commissary prices, lowered wages, and used blacklists and "goons" to fight unionizing efforts. Violence erupted between the workers and the company agents (Pinkertons and the local police), between union miners and those workers who resisted, and between the miners and the black workers who were brought in from the South to break the union (61).

After the war the United Mine Workers began a series of strikes aimed, John L. Lewis declared, at making the operators "come to Carnossa," and in 1948 the first major postwar recession struck at the heart of the truck mining business in eastern Kentucky (62). As a consequence, the six year period between 1948 and 1954 spelled financial ruin for the smaller operators and the small businesses that had grown up around the coal operations. The retrenchment of jobs was further advanced by the introduction of new technology—the "coal mole," the conveyor belt, the "shuttle buggy," and the roof-bolt (63)—that increased the coal producing capacity of the mines while reducing the demand for miners. In 1957 the coal industry was at peak production (233 million tons) though the number of miners (122, 243) had fallen below that of the Depression (64). The mines that had raped the Appalachian frontier, that had created a dependency on the coal companies, were now a dead end. A Chicago migrant summed it up (65):

> But the biggest portion a them [the mines] out there, now, is worked out, shut down, and the people has nothin to do. And the mines what are not shut down, they had men cut off. They got seniority rights there, you see, and you coundn buy a job out there in the mines now. Not a Chinaman's chance a gettin a job out there in the mines.

No revolution kept black field hands from picking cotton, no union came between plantation owners and their labor force, and, in the early twentieth century, no new technology influenced the cultivation of the crops. But before World War I, the boll weevil turned the fields into wastelands and drove both black and white sharecroppers from the land. The devastation of the boll weevil began in southern Texas in the latter part of the nineteenth century and had spread across most of the Cotton Belt west of the Mississippi River by 1908. The pest first entered the plantation country in southwestern Georgia around 1916, and by 1921, had spread through the Georgia Black Belt (66). As a result, plantations cut back on the number of renters and increased the number of croppers, forcing blacks into the least desirable and most dependent systems of remuneration. Some farmers stopped using black labor altogether (67). In the mid-twenties, almost two-thirds of the black farmers indicated that their sole reasons for leaving the rural South were low cotton yield and diminished profits (68).

Economic marginality, dependency, and sustained economic and political crisis are the roots of migration from the rural South, the Cumberland Plateau, and the Central Mesa. Together these forces in disparate parts of the country produced twentieth century rural populations desperate for health and security, ripe for liberation, and susceptible to the lure of the cities.

III   THE LURE OF THE CITIES

It is doubtful that these poor populations would have come to the city (regardless of how severe the rural impoverishment) if there had been no promise of jobs, decent homes, and freedom from oppressive authority. The city represented hope. It represented escape.

The image of the city, however, was not something field hands or men deep in the mines conjured up in their heads. These images were actively planted in people's minds by a variety of sources. In each area, labor agents spoke of the dawning employment opportunities in the new industrial centers. Big city newspapers that circulated in rural areas told tales of migrants who had found jobs and freedom in the cities, as well as a new group culture and social life. Finally, many potential migrants received letters from relatives who had already gone to the city, heralding the prosperity that awaited their cousins and brothers in Chicago, Los Angeles, or Philadelphia. These three streams of communication painted the same picture: jobs, prosperity, and freedom.

If the blacks of the Black Belt and the Mississippi Delta did not already realize that the South was closed to them, the *Chicago Defender* made certain they knew. The *Defender* chided its Southern readers: "Have they stopped their Jim Crow cars? Can you buy a Pullman sleeper where you wish? Will they give you a square deal in court yet?" (69). The questions were rhetorical; the *Defender's* answer included the job listings for northern companies seeking Southern black labor and the not very subtle cry that the "land of hope," the "promiseland," awaited them in Chicago. With a heightened sense of urgency, the paper urged its subscribers to put down their plows before the day of redemption passed them by and join the movement that was going inexorably north. The paper declared (70):

> Some are coming on the passage,
> Some are coming on the freight,
> Others will be found walking
> For none will have time to wait.

Joining the beseeching of the *Chicago Defender* was a flood of labor agents who gave personal witness to the opportunities available in the North and who, on occasion, provided job guarantees and railroad tickets. Many Southern blacks answered the call of the Erie or Pennsylvania Railroads or the steel mills, though many used these first job offers as a vehicle for escaping the South. The Erie Railroad experienced a full turnover of 9,000 workers every eleven days and one steel plant was forced to hire 2500 to 2800 men a month to maintain a work force of 5500 (71). The response to recruiting was so great that almost every Southern state, fearing the loss of its cheap labor force, began registering labor agents. In Georgia, for example, the city of Macon required agents to pay a license fee of $25,000 and to supply recommendations from ten local ministers, ten manufacturers, and twenty-five businessmen (72).

After the initial wave of migration, relatives proved as important as any other factor in encouraging migration and facilitating the transition to the city. When the city was not far from the rural homestead—as in Savannah—many potential migrants first made temporary visits, then acquired temporary employment, and gradually increased the length of their visits (73). Sometimes migrants used a whole string of relatives to work their way up the coast from a Southern town to a border city (like Baltimore), finally seeking out relatives in New York. Employers in Ohio were very conscious of the strong kinship network that bound many migrants to their families still living in the Kentucky hills. Rather than send agents wandering around the creek beds or advertising in newspapers, employers usually passed word of jobs in the plant; they depended on the kinship network to communicate the information to relatives living in the city and, via letters or weekend visits, to friends and relatives still on the plateau (74).

What was a haphazard process of labor recruitment in the deep

South and the Cumberland Plateau (involving newspaper advertising, itinerant labor agents, and kinship networks) was a highly formalized procedure in the Southwest. The initial bracero agreement between the United States and Mexico made during World War II arranged for Mexican nationals to enter the United States to work in agricultural occupations, provided there were written contracts, a guaranteed minimum wage, decent housing and sanitation, and round trip transportation expenses (75). Under the more formalized agreement following the war (Public Law 78) the Secretary of Labor was authorized to "recruit such [agricultural] workers, establish and operate reception centers, provide transportation, finance subsistence and medical care in transit, assist workers and employers in negotiating contracts and guarantee the performance by employers of such contracts" (76). This policy was supported by the growers' associations (such as the Central Valley Empire Association), and "agribusiness" in California came to depend on the cheap labor pool it provided (77).

The Atlantic Coastal Plain, the Black Belt and the Mississippi Delta, the Cumberland Plateau, and the Central Mesa were volatile areas in the twentieth century, ready to loose their impoverished and desperate populations on proximate regions. The large cities in the United States (like Philadelphia in the East, Detroit in the Midwest, Atlanta in the South, Cincinnati, Dayton, and Hamilton in Ohio, and San Jose in California) viewed these strangers with suspicion, but also with a sense of need. European immigration had been reduced to a trickle by the war, and immigration restrictions had created a heightened demand for cheap labor. Industry, Chambers of Commerce, business boosters, and governments turned to these impoverished regions and welcomed their people yearning to be free. Blacks, Mexicans, and Appalachian whites came to the cities of the United States not simply out of a desire to escape the marginality, dependency, and crisis of their homelands, but because jobs were available to them in the cities and because labor agents, newspapers, relatives, and governments encouraged and facilitated their migration.

IV   THE DEVELOPMENT OF POOR NEIGHBORHOODS

When America's poor, rural peoples came to the cities, they sought out the neighborhoods that would least tax their limited resources and that would provide the most secure entrée to the city. They looked for inexpensive housing. They sought out their relatives and friends. They chose to live with people who understood their way of life, who spoke their language, and who had come to the city for many of the same reasons.

What the migrants did not seek, and what they certainly did not foresee, was the permanency and deterioration of these first settlements. In most cases, the poor moved into the worst housing, buildings that deteriorated further as poverty-stricken migrants from the South, Appalachia, or Mexico continued to arrive. These tendencies were exaggerated at first by the inclination of these peoples to live together and by severe housing discrimination in surrounding parts of the city. With the coming of freeways and superhighways and the advance of urban renewal, these poor neighborhoods were placed under even greater pressure. Homes were demolished. Highways, public facilities, and high rises created segregated, walled-in cities for the poor. Public parks and services were allowed to fall into disuse. When the upwardly mobile of the first generation migrants began their exodus to other parts of the city, the now ghettoized first settlements faced accelerating problems in housing abandonment and crime.

Contemporary poor neighborhoods, the repository for the massive migration from America's rural areas, are segregated, often physically marked off from the rest of the city, include the worst housing, and suffer from the most violent, entrenched crime. The cities have given up on them or actively seek to destroy them; many of their long-term residents have abandoned them.

This, at any rate, is the situation in five poor neighborhoods.

A   Gardner (78)

Gardner is a small residential community in San Jose, California, one of a string of eighteenth century Spanish settlements that stretched along the coast from San Diego to San Francisco. The city began in 1777 as a Franciscan mission, nestled on the banks of the Guadalupe River (79) at the southernmost tip of the San Francisco Bay. The slopes of the Diablo Range rise on the east and the Santa Cruz Mountains on the west, placing San Jose in a valley no more than twenty miles wide, but endowed with some of the richest farmland in the world. Over the years, the Santa Clara Valley has provided a rich crop of fruits and vegetables; it has supported a large number of canneries, packing houses, and frozen food plants, many of which are located in San Jose. Principal concerns still operative include the California Canners and Growers with four plants in San Jose, Del Monte with three, and the Dole Company (80).

San Jose is a growing city. New tract housing is expanding as far as the eye can see and the hills will permit, destroying vineyards and orchards in its path. Within the last two decades, city officials have moved the boundaries out from the original seventeen square miles to include a sprawling 137 square miles of farm land. The population has risen from 95,000 in 1950 to an incredible 437,000 in 1970 (81). Lost in this expansion are some 16 percent of the population who are Mexican-American.

Many *barrios* are simply absorbed by cities that reach out for more land, creating pockets of impoverishment within a new suburban prosperity. There are such pockets in San Diego and the San Fernando Valley (82); small agricultural labor communities have certainly been overrun by San Jose. But that is not the situation with Gardner, nor with most core city Mexican-American neighborhoods. The Gardner neighborhood is an old inner city community, one of the principal areas for twentieth century Mexican settlement. Its homes are predominantly single family, single story stucco houses. They are generally in good repair. Many have been newly painted. All have small yards and some are a testimony to careful attention and thoughtful landscaping. Gardner's housing, however, despite its relative adequacy (compared to Harlem, for instance), is the oldest, cheapest, and the most deteriorated in the city.

Gardner's residents responded to the call of the Progressive Growers Association of Santa Clara, coming to work in the thriving orchards and processing plants in and around San Jose. But few still work in the fields except on a seasonal basis, and in recent years, the canners and packers have begun to move their operations to other parts of California. At the time of the survey, 20 percent of the sample were out of work and an additional 10 percent had given up the search. In 1971, more than half the residents, because of old age, inability to find employment, or apathy, were outside the labor force (83). The residents of Gardner are poor—in fact, the poorest in the city, with almost 50 percent of the population living on incomes under 3000 dollars (84).

Urban renewal and highways have devastated Gardner. The Park Center urban renewal project carved a fifty-five acre patch out of the northeastern section of the Gardner neighborhood. This section remained vacant and desolate for years for want of a developer, but now houses a new city library, a civic auditorium complex, and a host of banks. More than 20 percent of the people living in this area have been forced to move and the housing surrounding the project has deteriorated appreciably in recent years (85). In the very core of the neighborhood, the city has constructed a gigantic freeway interchange, although the two intersecting highways have yet to be built. When they are completed, the neighborhood will be chopped into four distinct and wholly separate pieces (86). In the midst of this dissection and demolition, settlement of the soil around the river is causing foundations to break up and sidewalks and streets to crumble.

Although many Mexicans continue to come to Gardner for its cheap housing, it has been abandoned by the city and by many of its former residents. Gardner has been losing population for the last ten years to the Mexican-American concentrations in the southern and more westerly sections like Olinder, Mayfair, and Tropicana.

B.   Belmont

The Belmont neighborhood in Hamilton, Ohio, is a loose association of blocks made discontinuous by large highways, railroads, a river, and the city boundary. Its poorest section, commonly called "Peck's Addition," is set off from the central part of the city by a park and the Great Miami River and from the rest of the neighborhood by the Baltimore and Ohio Railroad and a major north-south highway. Peck's Addition contains twelve blocks of some of the worst housing available in America. Many of the buildings are without adequate flooring, and perhaps a third of them have only one room. Several of the nearly 100 structures are renovated chicken coops; only one of the eighty-seven housing units listed by the 1960 census is considered "completely sound." The area is pocked by would-be junk yards, strewn with rusting, abandoned automobiles and a great variety of trash (87).

The largest section of Belmont is, except on its northern boundary, completely removed from the other residential areas of the city. To the south is a large shopping area and the small Hamilton airport. Erie Boulevard, the north-south artery, forms the western boundary and is surrounded on either side by small manufacturing concerns, hamburger stands, motels, automobile showrooms, and the like. Tylersville Road and the city limits enclose the area on the east. The houses are small, frame, and often in need of paint. They are sometimes "substandard"—a number still have outhouses. But they are not the work of "squatters." Each house has a small yard, often converted into a marginal corn patch, and although the roads are hardly equal to those in the rest of Hamilton, they are at least paved.

To the south and east of this area are scattered homes in a similar state of disrepair, but which fall within Fairfield Township and outside the jurisdiction of Hamilton. This area is rural in tone, although the residents are very much a part of Belmont.

Scattered groups of Appalachian migrants began arriving in Belmont before World War I, responding, at least in part, to the recruiting efforts of Champion Papers. It was rumored, a Champion employee remarked, that the president of the company went into the hills of eastern Kentucky to look over the area and to talk to the highlanders. Full-scale migration did not begin, however, until after 1940. Pausing only for the recession of the late fifties, migrant families came to Hamilton, sought jobs at Champion Papers, Fisher Body, Beckett Paper, and other plants. They settled, for the most part, on the east bank of the Great Miami River.

Hamilton and the entire Ohio Valley region (including Cincinnati, Dayton, and Middletown) have long enjoyed a reputation as an industrial center and attracted settlers from New Jersey and Pennsylvania (who came down the Ohio River through Marietta) as well as miners from Kentucky (88). The opening of the Miami and Erie Canals in the 1820s and the construction of a "hydraulic" plant on the Great Miami River fostered industrial development in Hamilton, particularly the paper mills that depended upon local timber, waterpower, and water and rail transportation (89). In 1940, almost half the work force in Hamilton was engaged in manufacturing, compared to a national average of 23 percent; in 1960, 46 percent were still employed in industry. At least half the industrial employment was in paper and paper products and in auto-body stamping (90).

The fate of Belmont and Hamilton is unclear. Although no superhighways are expected to further separate Belmont from the more affluent west bank of the river and no major interchanges are planned in Belmont, urban renewal will certainly have an impact in the next few years. A Miami University extension campus is expanding along the east bank of the Miami River and all the houses in Peck's Addition will be leveled. They will be replaced by a school board site, a new high school, and a 500,000-dollar covered ice rink (91). No new housing is planned in the Belmont area. Moreover, in-migration from Kentucky had practically ceased by 1969, underscoring Hamilton's decline as a manufacturing center. The paper industry has stagnated locally, and companies with antiquated physical facilities are moving to new locations (92). The 1970 population was 67,865 down 6 percent from 1960.

C East Side

Beginning with a dozen sawmills, Detroit drew upon the Erie Canal, Lake Michigan and an extensive railway network to develop a vast nineteenth century industrial complex. The carriage, wheel, and marine engine companies blossomed by the turn of the century into a mammoth automotive complex under the leadership of Henry Ford, Ransom E. Olds, and Charles Brady King (93). By 1926, 77 percent of the work force in Detroit was employed in manufacturing (94).

Automobile companies, particularly Ford, were quick to exploit the large pool of Southern black labor. Recruiters were sent to the Black Belt and the Delta, flyers were distributed, and trains were chartered to carry the teeming black population to "Michigan City." Blacks fleeing the devastation of the boll weevil hailed the L and N Railroad to Cincinnati, then the M. C. Railroad to Detroit. By the beginning of World War I the surge of migration had made the work of labor agents superfluous. Blacks were coming to Detroit by the thousands from Georgia, Alabama, Tennessee, and Mississippi (95) to cash in on the "Ford Bonanza": a guaranteed minimum wage of 5 dollars a day in 1914, 6 dollars a day a few years later (96). By the mid-twenties, 10,000 Black men were employed at Ford, comprising 10 percent of their work force.

From the time Detroit served as a center for the underground railroad to 1910 (97), the city's black population remained small and stable: a mere 6000 people, representing 1.2 percent of the total population (98). But during World War I, the black population increased sevenfold, reaching 41,000 by 1920 (99). After the war, blacks continued to congregate in Detroit, and by 1930 the black population had increased to 120,000 (100). The most sustained in-migration came in the forties, however, when the massive industrial complex was straining to meet the demands of wartime production: more than 100,000 blacks between the ages of 24 and 40 came to work in the Detroit automobile plants (101).

When blacks first came to Detroit in large numbers (1910), they settled close to the factories in an area east of Woodward Avenue and south of Grand Avenue known as "Paradise Valley." They lived with the noise of the factories, the smoke, and the fumes. By 1920 many were moving east toward Gratiot Avenue. Blacks infiltrated only a few pockets on the West Side; most remained, crammed into the already deteriorated East Side. In 1919 the Associated Charities reported(102):

> There is not a single vacant house or tenement in several Negro sections of the city. The majority of Negroes are living under such crowded conditions that three or four families in an apartment is the rule rather than the exception. Seventy-five percent of the Negro homes have so many lodgers that they are really hotels. Stables, garages, and cellars have been converted into homes for Negroes. The pool-rooms and gambling clubs are beginning to charge for the privilege of sleeping on pool-room tables over night.

The Housing Commission reported at the height of the Depression that 85 percent of the houses east of Woodward Avenue were unfit for human habitation (103). During the continuing migration after the war, blacks moved south to the river and east across Gratiot to Mt. Elliot Avenue (104). Not until the fifties, however, did large numbers of blacks move across Woodward Avenue to the better housing on the West Side.

During the fifties, Detroit began to encroach on the East Side. The

Edsel Ford Freeway cut across its northern boundary; the Chrysler Freeway formed a new western boundary; and their intersection in the northeast sector of the East Side obliterated what remained of "Paradise Valley." The Gratiot Redevelopment Project, a modern upper middle-income housing complex, replaced some of the neighborhood's oldest housing (black housing) (105). What remains on the East Side is a mixture of industrial plants, older, dilapidated housing (particularly in the areas nearest the Chrysler Freeway) and some decent one and two family homes (in the areas nearest Grosse Point) (106). The East Side is now subject to frequent muggings, armed robberies, larcenies, and murder, with a fifty square block section in the neighborhood's center singled out as one of the highest crime areas in the city (107).

D   *Summerhill (108)*

More than any other neighborhood we consider, Summerhill is being traversed, strangled, and demolished by the progressive development of Atlanta. The principal east-west expressway passes through what used to be the northern part of Summerhill and intersects with the primary southbound expressway in a maze of ramps, bridges, and underpasses right in the center of the neighborhood. Route 75 South cuts through the center of Summerhill as well. At least a thousand black families were displaced by these roads (109). Forty-three acres of Summerhill homes—5500 buildings—were razed to make room for the 18 million dollar Atlanta Stadium. Surrounded by acres of open parking lots, the stadium reigns over Summerhill as Mt. Vesuvius looms over Pompeii, seeming to defy the highways, deteriorating housing, and abandoned stores that make up Summerhill.

In addition to this frontal assault there is the petty harrassment that further accelerates the deterioration of the neighborhood. The expressways, for example, serve primarily as feeders for the stadium and as commuter routes, causing a double-edged problem. First, the scarcity of local ramps makes it very difficult for Summerhill residents to use the highways, thus causing considerable traffic congestion within the neighborhood. Second, during stadium events, the local streets are clogged by overflow parking and traffic tie-ups. Consequently the Model Cities board devotes more of its time to

facilitating traffic flow than it does to planning housing construction
or to maintaining neighborhood facilities (110). The old warehouses
and abandoned stores on the north end, large truck storage facilities,
and the scrap metal and junk yards along the railroad line in the
south simply add to the blight that surrounds these "public
improvements."

Summerhill, now the oldest black community of any size in
Atlanta, was not the first black settlement. The early migrants
clustered primarily in the "Old Fourth Ward" just to the north of
Summerhill. In the 1880s and 1890s blacks congregated around the
railroad tracks on Decatur Street, Ellis Row, Fuller Row, Edgewood
Street, and Houston Street. Many came to work for the railroad and
settled near it (111). Decatur Street, now a shell of deteriorating
warehouses and empty stores, was at the center of black business and
cultural life before the turn of the century. Its western end no longer
exists; it has been replaced by new construction in the downtown
area. Auburn Avenue is still a substantial commercial area housing
some of Atlanta's most important black businesses (including
Citizens Trust and Atlanta Life) (112).

During the twenties, when the great in-migration of blacks began,
the migrants moved beyond the "Old Fourth Ward" to Summerhill
and the neighborhoods immediately west (113). By 1940, the black
population of Atlanta was distributed almost equally between the
West Side, the "Old Fourth Ward," and the Summerhill area (114).
Since World War II, however, only the West Side has escaped the
consequences of progress. The "Old Fourth Ward" was the victim of
downtown expansion; Summerhill was devastated by highways and
the stadium. The collapse of the "Old Fourth Ward" shifted the
population to the West Side, and the rape of Summerhill displaced
blacks to the far West Side (West Adamsville and West Center Hill),
the southwest (Southwest Ben Hill and Southwest Adams Park), and
East Atlanta (115).

In the face of aging, urban development, and the movement of
blacks to more affluent areas in the east, west, and southwest,
Summerhill has become a haven for poverty and crime. Almost half
the houses suffer from minor deterioration and an additional third
show signs of major deterioration or dilapidation. Fifty-four percent
of the residents lived on poverty incomes in 1966, the number re-
ceiving AFDC payments having increased 36 percent since 1963 (116).

The census tracts that comprise the Summerhill neighborhood rank second, third, fourth, fifth, eighth, and tenth out of a citywide total of 112 on delinquents per 1000 population. One tract ranks in the top six on both day and night burglaries and on murders (117).

E.   North Central

W.E.B. DuBois called Philadelphia "the natural gateway between the North and South." For a hundred years, "there passed through it a stream of free Negroes and fugitive slaves toward the North, and of recaptured Negroes and kidnapped colored persons toward the South" (118). The black population of Philadelphia had been sizable since the Revolution, reaching a pre-twentieth century peak in 1810 when almost one out of ten residents was black. Before 1900, Philadelphia had the largest black population of any Northern city (including New York and Chicago) and of any Southern and border city except Washington, Baltimore, and New Orleans (119).

The first substantial wave of black migration came during the last decade of the nineteenth century, increasing the black population in Philadelphia by 60 percent (120). The influx of Irish immigrants slowed this pace in the first decade of the twentieth century (121), but the massive flight from Maryland, Virginia, North and South Carolina, and Georgia in the next twenty years pushed the black population beyond 200,000 by 1930 (122). Rural blacks were reluctant to enter the tight urban labor market during the Depression. Consequently Philadelphia, like most other Northern cities, witnessed no appreciable change in the black population in the decade preceding World War II. The war, however, renewed black interest in the city. The black population increased by 125,000 in the forties, and by an additional 153,000 in the fifties. More than 500,000 blacks lived in Philadelphia in 1960—almost ten times the number there in 1900 (123).

Before Philadelphia felt the full impact of mass migration, most of the city's blacks were servants or domestics; a sizable, though smaller, group were common laborers (124). Increasingly, during the period preceding World War I, blacks came to Philadelphia to work on the railroads, in the refineries, and in the steel mills. The Midvale Steel Company, for example, which employed 200 blacks in 1896, had 400 black employees in 1917 (125). Other companies brought blacks to Philadelphia as strikebreakers (126). By the time World War II broke out, the principal employers of blacks were the Pullman Company, the Pennsylvania and Baltimore and Ohio Railroads, the Philadelphia Transportation Company, the Philadelphia Electric Company, and the New York Shipbuilding Corporation (127). The black population of Philadelphia, which began as a servant class, is now primarily an industrial population centered in the large manufacturing plants along the Schuylkill River (128).

Before 1920 blacks settled around Sixth and Lombard Streets, an area south of present downtown Philadelphia (129). This restricted slum community, however, could not accommodate the large number of rural blacks who came to Philadelphia seeking industrial employment. Blacks began to settle across Broad Street and as far north as Susquehanna Avenue (now the principal commercial center in North Central). Others moved immediately to the west, across the river from downtown (130). Although the black neighborhoods of South Philadelphia remained relatively stable after 1900 (about 20,000 people), the North Central and West Philadelphia communities continued to grow until 1960. By 1950 the peak of black migration, almost half the black residents of Philadelphia lived in North Central (131). The great in-migration of blacks from the Atlantic coastal region and the Black Belt had shifted the core area of Negro life in Philadelphia from a small area in South Philadelphia to the sprawling slums of North Central.

North Central, like the other poor neighborhoods we have discussed, suffers from deteriorating housing, a high crime rate, and abandonment. The homes in North Central are brick row-type structures, almost all built before World War II. In 1960 one-quarter of the housing units were deteriorating or dilapidated; the substantial efforts on the part of the city to do scattered site renovation and to build public housing (132) have failed to keep pace with the accelerating rate of home abandonment. Almost 24,000 houses have been abandoned in Philadelphia, most of them in North Philadelphia (133), leaving many structures with boarded windows and glass and brick-strewn streets. Deterioration and home abandonment also contribute to the high rate of residential fires (134).

The deterioration of North Central is partially the result of code enforcement policies during the sixties, the encroachment of middle class renovation on the southern borders of the neighborhood and the expansion of Temple University. However, North Central has not been encircled by a freeway system as have other poor neighborhoods; nor have its homes been demolished to make way for a stadium or civic center. At the root of this neighborhood's decline is abandonment of North Central by upwardly mobile blacks. For the first time in fifty years, North Central lost population during the sixties (135). Its residents moved north to Mount Airy and Germantown, across the river to West and South Philadelphia. In their wake they left the poorest black residents of the city, the least stable families, and frequently, houses that could not be sold or rented (136).

Adult crime, juvenile delinquency, and street gangs are more widespread in North Central Philadelphia than in any other police district in the city. In 1968 there were 35 homicides, 71 rapes, 652 robberies, and 1570 reported burglaries. In every conceivable crime category, North Central ranks number one in the city; overall, North Central accounts for one out of every ten crimes committed in Philadelphia (137). Territorial conflicts between street gangs accounted for more than 200 killings in the past seven years.

V CONCLUSIONS

The etiology of poor neighborhoods reveals, above all else, how much the urban poor share in their experience. The poor of these five neighborhoods are subjected to a similar pattern of encirclement, intrusion, and abandonment. Expansive highways traverse poor communities, chopping them into unconnected pieces or skirt their borders, hiding and segregating them from their more affluent neighbors. These highways often converge in the very heart of poor neighborhoods in a great catharsis of overpasses, underpasses, ramps, and offshoots. Urban and civic improvement (e.g., dormitories, community theaters, parking lots, and football stadiums) intrude on the neighborhoods' fringe areas, razing block upon block of housing and abetting deterioration and land speculation. While highways and public improvements continue to be built without regard to established communities, the upwardly mobile flee these areas of first settlement in favor of new housing opportunities elsewhere in the city. Poor neighborhoods stand forsaken as a consequence, faced with accelerating problems of crime and home abandonment.

These present difficulties emerge from a shared experience with the past. The residents of each of these neighborhoods trace their roots, either directly or through their parents, to the hinterlands of North America. Although their origins are disparate (the Cumberland Plateau, the Atlantic Coastal Plain, the Black Belt, the Central Mesa of Mexico), they share a fundamental relationship with the land and with authority. The rural poor—brown, black, or white—were denied title to productive property and stood helpless before the will of large landowners, plantation masters, and mine bosses. Their economic marginality became intolerable under the added pressure of revolution, recession, and natural disaster.

The poor first came to these neighborhoods looking for jobs and freedom. They went to work on the assembly lines at Ford, in the canneries and packing houses, in the paper mills—anywhere they could find work and earn a decent wage. Two twentieth century wars brought hope of prosperity and a steady stream of new migrants, interrupted only by the Depression. They came because industry needed them and recruited them, because newspapers and relatives foretold a better life in the cities.

The etiology of poor neighborhoods is a story of modernization and urbanization, where each community plays a role reminiscent of all the others. The story portrays common threads of historical development, indeed, the constituent parts that make these neighborhoods distinctive. It is inevitable that we ask, therefore, why the politics of poor neighborhoods do not follow the lead of their origins.

Chapter Three

The Political Permutations
of Poor Neighborhoods

. . . .

Poor neighborhoods in America emerge out of an historical epoch involving a pattern of rural oppression, the imperatives of industrial growth, mass population movements, and the concentration of a redundant and impoverished work force in the inner cities. Their residents find themselves abandoned by the cities in which they live and, in some respects, by those who have shared their experience but have achieved relative affluence. This shared experience, however, does not appear to have dictated a mutuality in the political response of the poor. No singular political tactic or goal, tone, or style has emerged comparable to the historical movement that created these neighborhoods. The politics of poor communities are remarkably varied. Some neighborhoods display persistent violence and are highly assertive about their political autonomy. Others appear resigned, inactive, and politically subservient. The politics of poor neighborhoods provide a range of political response, their extremes representing more an opposition than a mutuality.

candidates. But in recent years, it has forsaken these roles to pro-
mote mutual aid (4), education programs, information and referral,
and United Fund work. The Mexican-American Political Association
(MAPA) has maintained its explicit political origins, publicly en-
dorsing candidates for elected office, leading voter registration drives,
and through litigation, eliminating literacy tests and other impedi-
ments to Mexican-American political involvement (5). The local San
Jose chapter, however, has proved to be largely a "paper organization," using the media extensively to further the group's goals, but
doing little voter registration or membership recruitment. The United
Farm Workers Organizing Committee maintains an office near the
Gardner neighborhood and draws support from Gardner residents for
its grape and lettuce boycotts, but focuses primarily on the agricultural areas near San Jose.

The organizational energies of Gardner residents have been di-
verted in recent years to the more turbulent politics of government
poverty agencies. Beginning with the first OEO programs (the Area
Service Centers) Mexican-American groups have fought for control of
the local poverty agencies. Residents found themselves embroiled in
struggles to elect "interim" and "permanent" representatives of the
poor (6), advisory boards of various sorts, and the Gardner Assembly
(a local governing board for Model Cities). The politics of government programs, although responsible for a heightened attention to
public matters and an increase in community involvement, has sup-
planted the traditional concerns of neighborhood politics. CSO
(Community Service Organization), MAPA, and the *Confederation
de la Raza Unida* (an umbrella organization in Santa Clara County)
spend more time and energy dealing with poverty boards than exe-
cuting the normal work of their organizations. Many community
groups have found, moreover, that with increasing federal involvement in community politics, only delegate agencies have the funds to
support full-time organizational work. A former activist noted (7):

> There was a time when everybody had to have community organi-
> zers—church groups, CSO. But there was problems with the money
> to keep them out there. The only people in the field in the last year
> are ESO people.

The backdrop for organizational politics in Gardner is the multiple image residents have of themselves and their community. One facet of that image involves "a group of loyal Mexicans and their children and grandchildren, who for various reasons have not been able to return to their own country" (8). They are as likely to look to the Mexican consul in San Francisco for help as to any of the service organizations in Gardner. Other residents "see the colony as an American ethnic community of Mexican origin that, like Italian, Irish or Scandinavian immigrant groups, will eventually be absorbed into the pattern of American life" (9). Their concerns are integration, nondiscrimination, and respect; they have long been represented by the Community Service Organization, the G.I. Forum, and the United Latin-Americans of America. A third and more recent facet of the image involves a minority of Gardner's residents. Though increasingly important to community politics, this group is less concerned with absorption and more concerned with reaffirming traditional lower class, Mexican values in an American context (i.e., reacceptance of the Mexican heritage, the language, and the celebration of Mexican National Holidays). Politically, purveyors of this view are not likely to look to assimilationist organizations such as CSO or MAPA, and are registering with the *la Raza Unida* Party in increasing numbers.

This confusion of images is reflected in a terminological conflict: how to identify Gardner residents. Some prefer to be called Mexicans; others refer to themselves as Mexican-Americans or Americans; still others proudly call themselves chicanos, a term many Mexicans consider derogatory. The difficulty can be seen in the following group discussion as described by an Anglo community worker:

> I was with a group of community people and naturally spoke in Spanish. Someone asked me whether I was a chicano because I spoke Spanish so well. I said, "No. I'm an American." Well a brown women stood up and said, "I'm an American." Another fellow said he was a Mexican-American. Another man said he was neither an American nor a Mexican-American but a chicano.

These terminological differences often seem trivial to an outsider but are heartfelt and reflect very real differences in perspective, values, and political behavior. They have led one community worker to conclude that a group of ten Gardner residents randomly sampled "will agree on nothing political."

The division of the Gardner community, reflecting contrasting images of the group and its relation to the dominant Anglo society, carries over into the politics of government programs and the consideration of electoral strategies. In the initial struggle for Mexican -American control of the Area Service Centers, eight organizations formed an uneasy alliance, but their unity was short-lived and collapsed when the EOC was reorganized (10). The contention persisted on the ESO board, a reorganized EOC. At one point the *Confederatión de la Raza Unida* withdrew from the board, stating that it "could not afford to have member groups fighting other members on ESO" (11). The election to the Gardner Assembly was also bitterly contested. The two factions were the Mexican-American Community Organization (MACO) and the group controlling the Gardner neighborhood center (ESO). MACO was, from a biased perspective, a "little Mafia" which controlled the EOC and subsequently Model Cities when it lost control of the poverty program. When MACO was defeated in the Assembly elections, it splintered, with some of its leaders returning to Mexico. Residual divisiveness persists, reflected in the contention over acceptance of Assembly minutes and in the court challenges on the conduct of Assembly elections. The seemingly endless struggle in ESO and the Gardner Assembly has led some community leaders to despair, claiming that federal "pennies" have "forced brother against brother," until "we don't know who our brother is."

Electoral politics in Gardner does not command the same attention that the plethora of community organizations and the struggle for control of government programs do. (Only in Summerhill is voting turnout lower than in Gardner.) Nonetheless, the same pattern of intracommunity conflict dominates here. The Mexican-American community in San Jose, consequently, has had little success in city elections. Two, three, sometimes four Mexican-American candidates run for the same office, reflecting distinct segments within the Mexican-American community. Mexican-American electoral strength is further diluted by an at-large system of representation (12) that effectively precludes segregated, minority communities from electing their own representatives and by the unwillingness of many Gardner residents to be bound by feelings of "racial solidarity." Gardner voters overwhelmingly rejected the candidacy of a Mexican-American who challenged the liberal congressman, Donald Edwards, and gave only lukewarm support to Mayor Norman Mineta, a Japanese-American who was supported by the established Mexican-American leadership (13). Even Al Garza, later named by Mayor Mineta to fill a vacancy on the Council, was defeated by the San Jose electorate in April, 1971.

Gardner's politics are highly divisive: there is little consensus on the group's relation to Anglo society (e.g., assimilation vs. separation) and little agreement on the meaning to be given to the Mexican-American heritage. Community groups act out these cleavages daily, investing the struggle for leadership with an acrimony uncommon in poor neighborhoods. But the push and pull of Mexican-American politics, despite its intensity and divisiveness, is played out within a context that abhors violence and physical abuse. When presented with three questions regarding political violence, two-thirds of the Gardner residents proved receptive to violence on *none* of them. Less than 1 percent affirmed all three violent responses.

Despite the widespread use of protest as a political tool—EOC offices were picketed in their early days (14), employees have picketed the ESO office in Gardner, and students have struck at an elementary school and Wilson Junior High in Gardner—rarely has protest generated into political violence, nor has it contemplated violence. Physical conflict erupted between demonstrators and police at the *Fiesta de las Rosas* parade in June, 1969, but there have been no instances of political violence reported in the subsequent three years. More characteristic of the community's mood has been Cesar Chavez's fast or the fast of a local leader protesting the disparaging remarks of Judge Gerald Chargin. "At his bedside," wrote a reporter from the *San Jose Mercury* (15),

> were copies of the New Testament, the *Life of Mahatma Gandhi*, and *Among the Valiant*, a book on Chicanos serving in World War II and Korea by Raul Morin. Two flags depicting a crown of thorns and a cross, symbolic of oppression, were on the walls.

Almost all community workers believe that the violence of an East Los Angeles or a Watts is ineffective, destructive of their own movement, inappropriate, given their goals and their sense of community sentiment, and finally, a violation of good moral sense.

II   Belmont: The Politics of Resignation

Political concern is barely discernible in Belmont. One can walk the dirt paths of Peck's Addition, across the railroad tracks and Dixie Highway, buy a bottle of pop at the Five Points Market, gaze over the apparently rural Fairfield Township, and not hear a murmur about politics. Probably no one would mention that Frank Witt was elected Mayor. Mention of a sit-in or a protest demonstration would be met with an uncomprehending goggle. There has never been a protest demonstration in Belmont—or Hamilton, for that matter— except by the "niggers." The men at Fisher Body were on the picket line last year, but that was different: they were there to gain strike benefits. The only community organizations mentioned are the Catholic Charities ("they gave out clothes last Christmas") and the center in an abandoned elementary school ("they have sewing classes, don't they?"). A few indiscreet women might talk of the Planned Parenthood group.

The facts confirm this impression of political indifference. Organizational activity is extremely limited in Belmont. Only 12 percent of the residents belong to any kind of organization (Table 3.2) and these are, for the most part, social or service-oriented. The most frequently cited organizations are church groups, school-related activities (PTA), fraternal orders, and civic groups. Only four people (3 percent) claimed membership in more than one organization. In a survey of ninety-nine low income people in the Belmont area conducted by the Butler County Community Action Commission, only three respondents indicated any organizational activity: one belonged to the PTA, one was active in a church, and the third was a member of the Veterans of Foreign Wars (16). The *Hamilton Journal* reported only one instance when Belmont residents had banded together to press a common cause: the formation of a multiple purpose neighborhood center to assist area residents with neighborhood organization, health services, welfare coordination, home management, and job opportunities (17). But even then, there was little indication that the program involved many people in Belmont.

An official at Planned Parenthood was frustrated in almost every attempt to involve Appalachian whites in the program, as OEO directives required:

Table 3.2.   The Belmont Political Record

	Belmont	Average Percentage for Five Neighborhoods
1. Electoral participation		
Registration–1970	59%	61%
Congressional election–1970	32%	35%
Presidential election–1968	55%	49%
Municipal elections–1971	27%	31%
2. Organizational participation		
Belong to community organization (i)	12%	16%
Belong to three organizations	1%	1%
3. Political participation		
"High" receptivity to politics (i)	–	65%
4. Violence		
"High" receptivity to violence (i)	–	51%

(i) See Appendix B.

> I just don't know how you do it. There is just no way and I don't know why.
>
> We sent letters to all the individuals who had anything at all to do with the association. We told them that OEO demanded—insisted—on community participation. And we told them that OEO regional was sending three representatives to be at a community meeting.
>
> Do you know that not one person showed up? Not one. The only people that were there were the employees of Planned Parenthood and three regional officers. . .
>
> We tried to form an advisory committee but the same sort of thing happened. I contacted 24 of the people most closely tied to the association. I mean, these were the people I really knew. But when we had the meeting, only four people showed up.

One organization that has grown to mammoth proportions throughout Ohio is O'Tuck—Kentuckians in Ohio. It sponsors an annual festival noted for "down home" entertainment and has provided relief for flood and mine victims in Kentucky. Few Belmont residents, however, were involved in its founding or administration. An O'Tuck leader observed:

> When I first went into Belmont, no one was interested. When I went into other areas, the Kentuckians had already gone underground. So I struck out, got a leading realtor and an insurance man. Men who had money and who could help me raise money. With this help, I was able to get in with the founding fathers. We just couldn't make it with this class of people [the people in Belmont]. What they have is in hand. They don't try to build up anything. They want it right now.

The organization has yet to provide a center for political expression, either for the Appalachian whites in Belmont or in Ohio generally. Its leader stated:

> I felt we had to build an image around the rich qualities of our people. Do you understand? Out of this will come political power.

If the poor whites of Belmont have had little to say about politics, the political concerns of Hamilton have, in their turn, been indifferent to Belmont. The Democratic Party in Hamilton is organized at the ward level (rather than at the smaller precinct level), thereby minimizing grass roots involvement. The Republican Party is organized on a precinct basis but has made no sustained effort to develop precinct organizations in Belmont (18). The depth of the political indifference to Belmont is reflected in the virtual exclusion of the east side of Hamilton from any representation in electoral office. None of the members of the Board of Education live on the east side; neither do any members of the City Council. The closest Belmont residents have come to electing one of their own is Frank Witt (the Mayor) who lives on the affluent west side, but owns and operates a store in the midst of Belmont. When he ran for the City Council in the fall of 1971, Frank Witt was the leading vote getter in four of the city's six wards, running strongest in the Fifth Ward (which includes Belmont).

Even the poverty program—whose purpose is to ameliorate conditions in the Belmont neighborhood and in similar areas throughout the city—neglects the neighborhood's worst poverty. The Chicago regional director for the Office of Economic Opportunity criticized the Hamilton program for failing to delve into the most fundamental problems of poverty. "The army of the poor keeps growing," he declared, "and your concern has been aimed at people who are not poor" (19). The entire program was at one point jeopardized for lack of a quorum of trustees at CAC meetings (20). While other local poverty agencies have organized the poor, brought pressure on city and state agencies, and begun to administer substantial service programs, the Belmont Center's principal concerns have involved a Boy Scout troop, a sewing and nutrition class, and a "learning about alcoholism" organization (21). The Head Start and housing programs and the Second Ward neighborhood center are intended primarily for the small black community in Hamilton.

Estrangement from politics is part of a more general estrangement from the city and urban life. The Appalachian migrant in Belmont often makes a distinction between his "house"—which is in Hamilton—and his "home"—which is in Harlan, Clay, or one of the other counties in the Kentucky coal region. His parents, or brothers or sisters, probably still live on Stinking Creek or Red Lick Road, or in one of the thousand other hollows in the Kentucky hills. Whenever they can, the Belmont poor go "home." A store owner remarked:

> A lot of Appalachians see Hamilton or Fairfield Township as a temporary headquarters to mass their fortune. Then they sell out lock, stock and barrel. I see it all the time. A man comes into the store, announces he has made his fortune and is going home.

Even when they cannot move back to the hills permanently (and most cannot) Belmont residents use every available opportunity to renew their traditional associations with Kentucky. When asked to comment on the crime problem in Belmont, a police officer responded, "Yes, they do have an effect—on holidays and weekends they go home and we sit around and play cards" (22).

For the thousands of Belmont residents who make their life in the city—the men working in the paper plants along the river or at Fisher Body, and the women frequently surrounded by children—living within the city limits of Hamilton is a burden. Most live in Belmont and use whatever services are available (the schools or the Belmont

Center, for example), but prefer to live in Fairfield Township. Fairfield Township has no kindergarten and schools frequently hold half-day sessions, but it lacks some of the trappings of the city, including blacks. "Appalachians find prestige or something up in Fairfield Township," the director of the Belmont Center remarked.

> There's no blacks there. No black would be safe going in there alone. They won't let Hamilton incorporate them because of the colored. They figure the blacks will move in, their kids will have to go to school with them.

In this separate but contiguous area, Appalachian whites can find at least superficially some of the isolation of the hollow, can set up a vegetable patch, and can find some of the homogeneity still preserved in the Kentucky hills. Although only a small percentage of Belmont residents move into Fairfield Township, it remains a symbol of the desired disjunction from the politics and tensions of urban life.

III   EAST SIDE: GHETTO MOOD AND POLITICAL VIOLENCE

The East Side of Detroit is a stable black community, protective of its own interests, suspicious of the intentions of whites, city government, unions, and other outsiders. Within its walled boundaries (dominated by the Detroit River, the Chrysler and Ford Expressways, and the Gratiot Redevelopment Project) lives a community long segregated from the rest of Detroit. The flood of black job hunters that came to Detroit during and after the two world wars crowded into the rooming houses east of Woodward Avenue. They faced a larger community that eyed them with hostility. On a hot, muggy Sunday evening in 1943, fighting broke out between whites and blacks at the Belle Isle Park, followed by days of rioting and assaults that both physically and psychologically quarantined the East Side from the white community in Detroit (23).

The East Side is the womb of black politics in Detroit. Within its walls, blacks began to formulate their politics and build their defenses. "The lower East Side is the core of Detroit's black community," a resident and candidate for public office observed.

Table 3.3. The East Side Political Record

	East Side	Average Percentage for Five Neighborhoods
1. Electoral participation		
Registration–1970	77%	61%
Congressional election–1970	45%	35%
Presidential election–1968	60%	49%
Municipal elections–1969	51%	31%
2. Organizational participation		
Belong to community organization (i)	17%	16%
Belong to three organizations	0%	1%
3. Political participation		
"High" receptivity to politics (i)	60%	65%
4. Violence		
"High" receptivity to violence (i)	71%	51%

(i) See Appendix B.

> It is not only where the blacks were first located, but the home base of almost every first for black people in this city. Most black professionals come from the area. Also the black union officials. The fraternal organizations which lace the black community originated on the East Side. The first black principal of a school is from there.
>
> The East Side is a very tight community. It's well integrated, highly organized, together.

From this integration of forces and sense of self came a unity which "could support public officials whom the whites would have eaten up."

> They [the East Side] produced Judge Crocket and Coleman Young. They were red-baited. But they had the community behind them.

That the East Side represents a base, a home for blacks that is united in support of its own, is a theme repeated throughout the East Side by militants and conservatives alike. An aide to the congressman from the area observed that Adam Powell "forgot that the most dangerous man was the Man"; and the converse of that lesson: the only secure base for black people is the black community.

> In these urban centers, we are very much aware of reconstruction. A hundred years ago we thought we had made real progress. We had two black senators. Some representatives. Black judges. This is what happened one hundred years ago. . . But we lost all of those things. We lost them because the carpetbaggers and others were able to divide us.
>
> So today we are cautious. When a white man comes into this community, we want to know just how honest are the meanings. . . When we go out of this community, we can't be divided by the forces that divided us one hundred years ago.

The solidarity of the East Side community and its concern for its "own" are evident in the electoral struggles that have brought blacks to the City Council, a black congressman who remains independent of the state Democratic party, and a selective response to a black candidate for mayor. Through these struggles, the East Side has developed an unusual political sophistication: it votes black, seeks an autonomous political base, and insists that blacks who choose to represent the black community remain true to these tests.

The first black councilman, William Patrick, emerged from a precarious alliance of white trade unionists, liberals, and blacks. The alliance became increasingly unstable as Polish and Italian workers failed to support UAW-endorsed candidates and as blacks, beginning to sense their own power, became more demanding of the coalition and more selective in their voting (24). In 1965 the AFL-CIO and the *Detroit News* opposed the candidacy of Jackie Vaughn, a black man, producing a serious rift between black union leaders and the churches on one hand and the labor-liberal alliance on the other (25). In the council runoff election, many ministers urged their parishioners to vote "four and no more"—the number of blacks seeking office (26). East Side Blacks have lent their support in increasing numbers to black candidates; by 1969 black candidates ran at the top of the ticket in the East Side, followed by UAW-backed white liberal candidates. It is estimated that black candidates for the council received somewhere between 73 and 96 percent of the vote in black areas, and leading white liberals received approximately half of the votes (27).

The cornerstone of black electoral strength in Detroit is the sustained support of indigenous and independent black political institutions, particularly those in the area of first settlement, the East Side. The ministers of the large black churches (e.g., Macedonia, Mt. Zion, and Christ Baptist) have for a long time supported unified black political action; sometimes supporting black, sometimes white, candidates who are responsive to the desires of the church. Candidates and their workers greet worshippers as they leave the church on Sunday; frequently the minister endorses candidates from the pulpit. Whenever possible, the UAW, the Democratic organization, and the church work together to support liberal and black candidates. But the church has not hesitated to support independent black candidates such as Coleman Young (state senator and national committeeman) and Judge Crocket. An aide to the local congressman remarked on the impact of the black church:

> Local churches are more important in Detroit than in any town I know. There is really nowhere like here. A lot of people look to those churches. We've always maintained a good rapport with the churches. The congressman is one of the best church-goers in the state.

Congressman Diggs maintains a cooperative, working relationship with the local Democratic organization and the UAW, but his incumbency rests on factors wholly independent of them. First, the Diggs family is well remembered for its commitment to black politics; many East Side residents recall the racial turmoil during the 1930s provoked by the jailing of the congressman's father. More important, perhaps, is the "House of Diggs," a mammoth funeral home in the midst of the East Side. Beginning with a small florist shop, the Diggs family built up a substantial business ("everyone has a policy with Diggs") which now serves in a dual capacity. In half of the house, Diggs's courteous morticians, chauffeurs, and pallbearers attempt to cope with the mortality of East Side residents; in the other half, Diggs's political operatives run a district headquarters that processes complaints and serves community needs.

Although institutions indigenous to the East Side supported the growth of a black council and a congressman, they declined to lend their full weight to the candidacy of Richard Austin, the first black candidate to run for mayor. East Side voters as a rule turn out for elections in numbers comparable to those for the rest of the city. For the Austin-Gribbs race, however, (when they might be expected to respond to the call of "black power") black voters made a correct but unimpressive showing, falling eight percentage points short of the citywide turnout of voters (59 percent). Austin did not come from the East Side; he was not part of the black community—at least in the sense of a Diggs or the ministers or officers of the NAACP who had "paid their dues" to the community. The Congressman's aide felt Austin was unfamiliar to the "important black families." A worker at the Human Relations Commission expressed a similar sentiment.

> Black leaders were suspicious of Austin so his campaign wasn't able to generate much interest, and he only got lukewarm support. People were asking, "Where was he for the last 40 years?"

Many black leaders declined to support Austin's candidacy, leaving him in some respects isolated from the traditional assurances afforded by the ghetto.

The independent, defensive quality of politics on the East Side has created considerable tension in relations with the United Automobile Workers, who control the district Democratic organization. This tension grew initially out of the arrangement between many important black ministers and the Ford Company. During the 1941 strike, the Interdenominational Ministers' Alliance extolled the virtues of the corporation and urged black workers not to side with the UAW (28). The distrust of unions gradually faded, however, as black ministers came to see the union as a possible avenue for black advancement. They have since forged an alliance with political representatives from the UAW in the thirteenth district. UAW officials control the chairmanship of the district Democratic organization, easily dominate the endorsement meetings held at the Prince Hall Masonic Temple (sometimes bringing in their own members, sometimes with the help of "little old women, sitting with fans"), and on election day, pay precinct workers to bring out the vote. But what has proved to be an effective political instrumentality—helping to elect black and liberal officials—is also a source of uneasiness. The UAW cannot always get the ministers or the leaders of other organizations to affirm their decisions (as with Judge Crocket, Coleman Young, and Jackie Vaughn) and many blacks consider UAW community action work "plantation politics."

Defensive, and in some respects self-contained, the East Side has developed a rich organizational life that includes the normal array of government programs (the Mayor's Committee for Human Resources Development and Model Cities), block clubs, tenants' organizations, militant youth organizations, and revolutionary self-defense groups (e.g., the Black Panthers, the National Committee to Combat Fascism). The Model Neighborhood board put out a directory of "Community Leaders and Organizations" with approximately 150 listings. They include organizations like the Ralph Bunche Community Council, the East Side Chamber of Commerce, the Central East Side Property Owners' Association, and the Gratiot-Mack-Boulevard Area Council. Most organizations on the East Side are affiliated in some way with a church, a block club, a government program (like Model Cities) or the local arm of the poverty program.

The Ralph Bunche Community Council is one of the most important organizations on the East Side. It began as a federation of block clubs, but grew in scope and import when it received substantial funding from the New Detroit Committee after the riots. The Council has also garnered funds from federal agencies and from the mayor's office; it is now in charge of a large housing program that includes both the Ralph Bunche and the Martin Luther King Homes. Other housing needs are met by the United Tenants for Collective Action, a group that organizes tenants into collective bargaining units, and by block clubs comprised primarily of home owners who want to stem the tide of deterioration (29). The Tenants Association received financial support from the Archdiocese of Detroit, from New Detroit, Inc., and from a group of young, white bankers (30); the block club phenomenon is encouraged and directed by the Neighborhood Conservation Section of the Detroit Housing Commission (31).

Even the militant East Side Voice for Independent Detroit, which sponsors a community watchdog on crime and police brutality, a mock city government for children, and Project Pride, relies on noncommunity support for its existence. The organization leader, Frank Ditto, was brought to town by the Churches on the East Side for Social Action (CESSA) in the hope that he would kindle a militant spirit in the community. His organization was well financed and able to maintain a full-time staff of seven members. In 1968, his organization received 60,000 dollars from CESSA and 50,000 dollars from the New Detroit Committee, an organization of businessmen established after the riots (32). ESVID publishes a newspaper, *The Ghetto Speaks,* which has a circulation of 3000 to 5000. A full-time editor was made possible by a grant from the Archdiocese of Detroit (33).

The tension between a defensive black community and the larger white society was made explicit and in some respects tragic by the civil disturbances of July, 1967. Violence first developed on the West Side (the bulk of the devastation was confined to that area), but some of the worst shooting exchanges took place on the East Side around Mack and St. Jean (34). Two years after the riot, almost two-thirds of the East Side residents thought the riots had been helpful to the cause of black people and more than one in five expressed a willingness to participate actively if such a disturbance should occur again (see Table 3.3). East Side residents, it would seem, are more receptive to violence than the poor of any of the other five neighborhoods.

IV   SUMMERHILL: ACCOMMODATION AND APOLITICS

Summerhill is a quiet neighborhood. Few political or social events disturb the calm since Summerhill is a neighborhood without organizations, without institutions, and without its own politics. Its residents do little to interrupt the even pace of inactivity, playing out the roles of coalition and accommodation established twenty-five years ago—roles that blacks elsewhere in Atlanta have since forgotten. The few notable political events—small civil disturbances in 1966 and 1970, intermittent protests by the Welfare Rights Organization—stand in sharp relief against the drab background of apolitics.

Summerhill politics takes its cue from a tradition of block voting calculated to ensure "progressive" city leadership that is dependent on black neighborhoods, though not recruited from them. From the third day of April, 1944, when the courts declared the white primary unconstitutional, blacks in Atlanta began to reassert an electoral role denied them by Hoke Smith and Tom Watson at the beginning of the century. Between 1946 and 1948, 25,000 new black voters joined the rolls (35) whom the Atlanta Negro Voters League, organized in 1949, urged to vote en masse. Under the leadership of black ministers, newspaper editors, the president of Atlanta University, businessmen, and the executive secretary of the YMCA, the Voters League molded the growing mass of black voters into an essential element in the precarious balance of power (36) that would dominate Atlanta politics for a score of years.

The bloc of black voters formed one leg of a "three-legged stool" that supported Mayors Harsfield, Ivan Allan, and to some extent, Sam Massell. The other legs of the stool were the Atlanta press and the business elite (including "the heads of three principal department stores, the three or four biggest real estate firms, the utilities, manufacturing companies, and major banks. . .") (37). Black leadership throughout the fifties and early sixties calculated that black voters could not seriously contest the at-large Atlanta elections but, allied with "liberal" forces, could ensure receptive public officials at the highest levels and a number of black officials at lower levels. A black candidate for the board of aldermen outlines his strategy (38):

> But I can tell you this: My analysis of the political situation in Atlanta is that there have always been three huge groups of voters in Atlanta, and the combination of any two of them means election. One huge group is the segregationists, the other huge group is the Negro, and the third huge group is the people that the power structure influences in the white community. And these are usually your "liberals."
>
> Unfortunately, in Atlanta, the Negro groups has always had to align with the power structure. Some of us refer to it as the "unholy alliance." But the Negro group is not able to ally with the white segregationists because their views are too diverse, so this was the only other group they could ally with. And in my election, what I did was put the power structure with the Negro group.

Studies have established that throughout the fifties, under the prompting of the Atlanta Negro Voters League, black registrants

Table 3.4.   The Summerhill Political Record

	Summerhill	Average Percentage for Five Neighborhoods
1. Electoral participation		
Registration–1970	66%	61%
Congressional election–1970	27%	35%
Presidential election–1968	34%	49%
Municipal elections–1969	25%	31%
2. Organizational participation		
Belong to community organization (i)	11%	16%
Belong to three organizations	0%	1%
3. Political participation		
"High" receptivity to politics (i)	70%	65%
4. Violence		
"High" receptivity to violence (i)	47%	51%

(i) See Appendix B.

voted with greater unity of purpose and in larger percentages than either lower or upper income whites (39).

The coalition upon which black power rested crumbled before the sixties were out, in large part because blacks were no longer able or willing to respond to the Voters League endorsements. The sit-in movement created the initial discord that destroyed the coalition. Student groups led a citywide protest to integrate lunch counters that grew into a highly successful black boycott of Rich's and other large downtown department stores. The older leadership of the Voters League was unenthusiastic about the arrests, the disruption, and the rancor—all of which threatened the working relationship with the power structure (40). When the city leadership sought negotiations with members of the League rather than with students, the black leadership of Atlanta split wide open (41). In the 1961 elections, the Voters League endorsed the President of the Chamber of Commerce while student groups supported another candidate. Although the League was successful in this first challenge (their candidate got 73 percent of the black vote) (42), by 1965 they lost control of the aldermanic elections (43).

The Atlanta black community abandoned the Voters League, rejected the previous balance of power, and turned to black power. But Summerhill to a large extent still plays traditional black politics: the old alliances have not been forsaken; residents have yet to insist that the highest political offices be held by blacks, but are satisfied to provide the margin of victory in a precarious balance. In the Atlanta municipal elections in 1969, Dr. Horace E. Tate, a black educator, sought the mayor's office. His candidacy was endorsed by Coretta King, Dr. Ralph Abernathy, and Julian Bond—the established progressive black leadership in Atlanta (44). But Summerhill blacks did not heed the call, "Brother Tate for Mayor Now This Time." They cast a majority of their votes (57 percent) for either Sam Massell, a Jewish, liberal candidate, or Rodney M. Cook, the heir to Ivan Allan's coalition. They responded similarly in 1970, casting a smaller percentage of their votes for the black candidate, C.B. King, than did the more affluent black neighborhoods of Atlanta. When Governor Carter, the most conservative of the gubernatorial candidates, came to speak at a Model Cities meeting (after his election), Representative Clarence Ezzard, legislator from Summerhill, pledged his "100 percent" support (45).

Whether united or divided on a particular strategy, blacks have played a vital role in Atlanta politics for twenty-five years. Their votes have been decisive in electing three progressive mayors, their leaders gained entrance to the highest councils, and by 1970 Atlanta had a black Vice Mayor, five black aldermen, and three black members of the Board of Education. Black candidates had run for mayor, congressman, and governor. But the great majority of Summerhill residents were uninvolved. Nearly two-thirds of the Summerhill residents are registered voters, but only one-third voted in the 1968 presidential elections, just over one-fourth in the 1970 congressional elections (involving civil rights activist Andrew Young), and one-fourth in the 1969 mayoral race (see Table 3.4). Whatever black politics may become in Atlanta and in Summerhill, they are apparently unimportant now to those who remain in Atlanta's oldest black settlement.

Summerhill is a community without institutions. There are few churches, no YMCA, and no political clubs. In sharp contrast is the rich organizational life of Atlanta: the Odd Fellows (46), the Hundred Percent Club of Shiloh Baptist Church, the Gold and Silver Social and Savings Club, the Eastern Star, NAACP, SNCC, and the Southern Christian Leadership Conference. But these groups, even those most dedicated to civil rights, look to the blacks around Atlanta University, to the spreading black settlements to the west and south, or to a national constituency, rather than to Summerhill (47). The survey confirms the low level of organizational participation in Summerhill, as did a local minister who believed that Summerhill residents had "a great many beliefs and a warm sense of God," but described their "connections with organized religion. . .(*as*) tenuous" (editor's note in italic).

The only protest organization of any import in Summerhill is the Welfare Rights Organization with a membership of approximately 150. Recently the group "slept-in" at the Model Cities office, insisting on housing construction that had been delayed since the inception of Model Cities. Their demands read, "We demand that you make the Model Cities program a program to help people instead of what it is now, a program to clear land." The Mayor promised 108 temporary mobile residences immediately and 500 permanent homes within the year (48). He has since denied this commitment. Ethel Mae Matthews, WRO chairwoman, led a contingent to the statehouse to meet with members of the black caucus to discuss a five point program for welfare reform (49). But the WRO, vocal and sometimes committed to direct action, remains a minor force in Summerhill. Its membership is small, given the potential constituency, and the organization depends on one dynamic leader. Summerhill residents remain committed to political protest activity, however, even if that commitment is a reminiscence of the civil rights struggle (53 percent supported the boycotts and 25 percent joined a picket line) rather than actual participation in ongoing organizations (see Table 3.4).

There have been two civil disturbances in Summerhill, one in 1966 and one in the summer of 1970. By the standards of Harlem, Watts, or Detroit, neither could be considered major riots. Rocks and bricks were thrown; looting and some fire bombing occurred, but did not approach the intensity characteristic of major Northern disturbances. Few residents or policemen were injured as a result of the violence.

The city newspapers and public officials claimed that the Student Nonviolent Coordinating Committee sought to politicize and spread the violence. A SNCC pamphlet read:

> They were also SICK AND TIRED of seeing white cops mess over black men and women, as they have been doing for over 300 years. The crowd knew that Harold Prather was only one of thousands of black men and women in Atlanta who have been brutalized and shoved around by white cops and their bosses.

Mayor Ivan Allan appeared on the hood of a car, beseeching the crowds to disperse, to ignore the incitement of "SNCC provocateurs." He was hooted; the press of the crowd against the car forced him to the ground. It is hard to imagine Mayor Cavanaugh of Detroit trying a similar ploy and escaping with his life.

The most prominent institution in Summerhill—but not *of* Summerhill—is Model Cities, a large new office complex that includes a branch of the Atlanta Public Library, the Atlanta Housing Authority, the Board of Education, and Planned Parenthood. Model Cities sponsors a shuttle bus that runs throughout the Model district and has implemented a few educational and recreation programs. Most of its other endeavors, including new housing construction, are in the planning or proposal stages. Its efforts to establish a mass-based organization, the Mass Convention, has proved no more successful in piercing the wall of apolitics than other organization efforts. Early in the Model Cities program, more than 500 people attended meetings of the Mass Convention, but recent decentralized elections involved only 230 people in the Model Cities area, including Grant Park, Pittsburgh, Peoplestown, Summerhill, and Mechanicsville (50).

V   NORTH CENTRAL: FRENETIC POLITICS

Politics has an insane quality in North Central Philadelphia. Every day great reserves of energy are expended in a vast range of political outlets: large, active community organizations, electoral organizations and campaigns, boycotts and demonstrations, and even violence (see Table 3.5). North Central has several vital tenants' organizations that represent resident interests before the Housing Authority and private tenants; one of the largest and most active welfare rights organizations in the country; large churches and comprehensive church-sponsored social welfare programs; an active Model Cities program; a strong city-based electoral organization; frequent pickets, marches, and boycotts; and violent, though sometimes constructive, street gangs.

Table 3.5.   The North Central Political Record

	North Central	Average Percentage for Five Neighborhoods
1. Electoral participation		
Registration–1970	64%	61%
Congressional elections–1970	35%	35%
Presidential elections–1968	55%	49%
Municipal elections–1971	39%	31%
2. Organizational participation		
Belong to community organization (i)	22%	16%
Belong to three organizations	0%	1%
3. Political participation		
"High" receptivity to politics (i)	74%	65%
4. Violence		
"High" receptivity to violence (i)	52%	51%

(i) See Appendix B.

Yet North Central residents are as far from wresting political control from the city as are the residents of Summerhill. Recent mayoralty elections demonstrate that the black vote, concentrated in North Central, cannot block the election of a "racist" administration. North Central residents do not control Model Cities, nor have they ever seriously challenged the leadership of the community action program. They are impotent in the face of Temple University's expansion. Throughout all these struggles—against the municipal political organization, Model Cities, OEO, and Temple University—North Central residents have been active and involved, but have failed to develop an articulate, visible community leadership cadre.

Consequently political involvement in North Central has a haphazard quality. Politics is intense, involving a plethora of political outlets. But it is also unfocused and in many respects ineffective. Residents move from one conflict to another, waging a seemingly continuous battle against the forces that make life precarious in North Central. But in the end, others somehow remain in control.

Important to the regularity of resident electoral participation, and also important to understanding the lack of political autonomy on nearly all fronts, is the strength of the citywide political "machines." Both parties have operative organizations in every ward of the city, though the Democratic party is particularly strong in North Central. The Sixteenth, Twenty-eighth, and Thirty-second Wards (which make up North Central) each have a ward leader and two representatives for each of the seventy-odd divisions in these wards. The party organization has the power to deliver patronage (much of it through the absence of a state civil service law), correct minor traffic violations, and facilitate other matters. Those who make their way up in the organization can expect a reasonable return for their time investment. Of the sixty ward leaders in the city in 1960, half held elective positions: six were congressmen, thirteen held state jobs, and six had city jobs (51).

Until the last mayoral election, the Democratic organization proved effective in delivering the vote for its designated candidates. Although Mayor Tate barely defeated a liberal Republican challenge in 1967, he received 68 percent of the ballots cast in North Central. A black third party candidate, Cecil B. Moore, head of the rebellious North Philadelphia branch of the NAACP, carried only 5 percent of the black vote. In the 1970 congressional race, Robert Nix (a black selected by the party some twelve years ago over the opposition of much of the black party organization) defeated his Republican challenger by a four to one margin. Only when the party endorsed Frank Rizzo, "tough cop," did the black community defect—though one in five still voted Democratic in the 1971 general election. Even this did not destroy the Democratic organization, however, and no autonomous black organization has arisen to challenge it.

High levels of political involvement are not confined to conventional electoral politics. Twenty-two percent of North Central residents belong to at least one community organization, few of them church or church-related groups. Two of the most important organizations in North Philadelphia, the Philadelphia Welfare Rights Organization and the City-Wide Tenants Council, draw most of their active membership from North Central. These groups, often working together, were able to involve large numbers of poor blacks and whites in protests at the United Fund office and at the State Office Building. A community organizer described one of these actions:

> We got 1800 people down to the United Fund office. We wanted more of that money spent on the people who needed it. All of the people there were welfare recipients with their children. I mean, we had welfare mothers in that office at 8:00 A.M. That means women were getting together at 6:30. We had eight or nine hundred people in there before they knew what was happening.

And the organization that supported it:

> We got this large turnout through local committees and organizations. There are a lot of local housing groups, like block clubs. Maybe 10 or 20 members in each. We hold meetings of the Chairmen and they get information down through these channels. It's all private.

The Philadelphia Welfare Rights Organization claims a series of accomplishments that affect sizable numbers of welfare recipients in North Central. Largely through their efforts, they claim, the number of welfare recipients in Philadelphia was raised in one year from 110,000 to 185,000; the poor had been granted credit at downtown stores; and the telephone, gas, and electric companies were granting services without a deposit. They conducted a Christmas grant sit-in at the State Office Building, with well over 1000 participants, waged a campaign against rotten meat, and fought discrimination by local real estate offices against welfare recipients.

National civil rights groups that remained inactive at the community level in other cities became involved in the politics of North

Central. Cecil Moore headed the North Philadelphia branch of the NAACP, developing a militant style atypical of the organization's national leadership. The local chapter joined with some of the North Central gangs in disruptive demonstrations at Girard College (52). Moore estimated his membership at 20,000 to 30,000, but his active support was considerably smaller. He himself was unable to generate substantial support for his political campaigns. By the mid-sixties, CORE showed more of a concern with North Central blacks and less interest in the Southern civil rights struggle. They moved their offices to North Broad Street and concentrated on North Central's housing problems. In the summer, street corner meetings and rallies were organized. CORE supported a trash "dump-in" and the picketing of landlords who owned slum tenements (53).

Gangs play an important role in North Central's organizational life. There are almost seventy-five active gangs, each with a membership of between 250 and 400 young blacks. They come to citywide attention when conflicts over territory result in a mutilation or killing (a frequent enough occurrence to arouse city and community concern), though their daily operations are usually devoid of serious violence. Gang members now publish a newspaper, *Dig This Now,* that has a publicized circulation of 40,000 copies; many gangs engage in cooperative programs with Temple University. On occasion, other groups have successfully involved gangs in political action. Several gangs, particularly the Moroccos, joined the NAACP demonstrations against Girard College's discriminatory admission policies. In November, 1967, gangs participated in a black power demonstration involving 3500 students (which ended with a brutal police charge against chanting and singing participants).

The examples of the City-Wide Tenants Organization, the Welfare Rights Organization, the NAACP, CORE, and the gangs are a large part of North Central's political life, as are the churches and the store boycotts. But they are ingredients of politics, not the context. Without a sense of the citywide political agencies that diffuse this political explosion, we cannot appreciate the frenetic quality of the political life in North Central.

In North Philadelphia, black voters were wedded traditionally to the Republican Party, even during the depression when many other oppressed groups flocked to the New Deal banner. Not until the scandals of 1949 and the Democratic reform administrations of

Joseph S. Clark and Richard Dilworth did blacks become a mainstay in the Democratic political organization (54). Congressman Green and a succession of Democratic mayors have since built the Democratic party into an effective electoral organization predicated on favors, patronage, and loyalty. An aide to Congressman Nix commented (55):

> Negroes with political ambitions should know two vital facts. . . . Fact One: If you're endorsed by Bill Green (then Democratic City Committee Chairman) for the elective office in Philadelphia, you can rear back and say, I'm on my way. . . . Fact Two: If you're seeking a Federal appointment and can't get Green's endorsement, your chances of succeeding are slimmer than the thread that links the buttons to your coat.

The black community has in effect lost its prerogative to choose the elected officials who will represent them, black or otherwise. No competing organization has been able to offer a substitute nomination process or provide concrete opportunities for electing independent black politicians. But although the Democratic organization commands the loyalties of North Central residents, few of the traditional rewards have been offered in exchange. White Irish politicians have resisted the movement of blacks into the party hierarchy; they allow blacks to attain district committee positions, but not ward leadership positions. Blacks have successfully penetrated civil service and municipal employment under Democratic administrations, but few have jobs that pay more than 7000 dollars annually. In the Fifty-second Ward, west of North Central, 53 percent of the registrants are black, but blacks have received only five of thirty patronage positions (56). The strong black representation on the Council—three from North Philadelphia—is diluted by the two older black councilmen who remain creatures of the machine.

Federally funded antipoverty programs in North Central such as the community action program (PAAC in Philadelphia) and Model Cities have remained under the control of the Democratic mayors and party organizations. To thwart pressure for community participation, the PAAC provided predominant representation for city and welfare agencies and drew district boundaries that ignored traditional neighborhood divisions (57). Despite these obstacles to participation, community groups took PAAC seriously in the beginning. The North City Congress, a federation of civic, recreation, and neighborhood improvement associations, even recruited a slate of candidates and campaigned for them. Some 8100 people in poverty areas throughout Philadelphia attended town meetings organized to support the 1965 poverty elections. In the end, however, only 13,000 people, 2.7 percent of the eligible voters, participated in the elections (58). The elections were terminated after 1967 for lack of funds. Community participation in PAAC programs has since proved minimal. Officially sanctioned community organizations have been discouraged and many programs, at least according to many North Central political activists, have become patronage centers for a Mayor's office short of patronage positions.

The Model Cities program also began with a spurt of citizen involvement. It incorporated the Area Wide Council (AWC) into the active management of the program as the citizen participation component (59). In 1969, however, the Department of Housing and Urban Development objected to the plan, stating that the program had "insufficient involvement of the city. . .and established institutions" (60). Bound by this ruling, the city administration constructed a substantial program—including medical services, training programs, a tenant union, modular housing experiments, and cultural arts programs—tied directly to the Mayor's office. Neighborhood Councils were established to ensure community involvement in the Model Cities program, and AWC people have often used these opportunities to reintroduce their influence. Council elections in 1971 produced a 6 percent turnout, significant when compared to the participation in PAAC elections. In 1971 the Area Wide Council won its suit before the Federal Court of Appeals that ordered the Model Cities Agency and the Neighborhood Councils to bargain in good faith with AWC. The city has resisted both the ruling and AWC, however, and is making a concerted appeal of the court decision.

Agencies of control and co-optation (the party apparatus, Model Cities, and PAAC) have fostered substantial community political involvement in some ways, but they have at the same time assured a mildness and lack of focus. Few organizations have managed to avoid the lure of municipal jobs and city funding, leaving North Central without a leadership of its own and a political direction defined by the community. An architect of an incipient community development corporation summarized the frustration of black politics in North Central:

> The black leadership in this city is always picked off by the white political machine. They are simply bought off into government agencies. And what we get is an institutionalized black middleman. We get no black leaders who are doing anything. The PAAC's aren't doing anything. Model Cities isn't doing nothing.
>
> These cats are out of the market. Any movement finds itself pitted against other blacks. Even with the vote, there is no way to deliver the vote.

VI   CONCLUDING NOTES

These five neighborhoods provide five unique political responses, as evident in Table 3.6. Gardner is a community divided against itself by various conceptions of group interest, but bound by an overriding commitment to nonviolence. On the other hand, solidarity and mutual defensiveness characterize the politics of the East Side, unbridled by the aversion to violence evident in Gardner. Belmont residents demonstrate only the most tenuous connection with political life, seemingly uncommitted to political organizations of any sort or to the neighborhood itself. Summerhill residents display a similar disregard for political strategy and organizations. Electoral involvement is extraordinarily low, as is membership in community organizations. North Central is a unique neighborhood and its residents demonstrate a unique commitment to political participation in a plethora of organizations and institutions (the church, electoral politics, Model Cities, tenants' organizations, and welfare rights groups). Their participation is unfocused, however, and has thus far been ineffective in achieving neighborhood autonomy.

There is little mutuality in these narratives, little that would suggest a shared approach to politics. It is difficult to imagine black residents of the East Side convincing Mexican-American activists in Gardner that they share common tactical concerns, or discussing the utility of political violence with Appalachian whites in Peck's Addition. Such communication would be marked by uneasiness and lack of comprehension, and probably by outright hostility. The political concerns and the political manifestations of these communities are distinct and somehow removed from what was a shared modernizing experience.

This paradox leaves us with two questions: why did a profound historical process fail to produce a common political orientation? What accounts for the variability of politics in poor neighborhoods?

1. Average Voting Turnout Percentage (i)

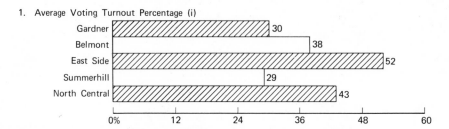

2. Percentage Belonging to Community Organization

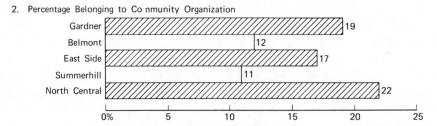

3. Percentage "High" Receptivity to Politics

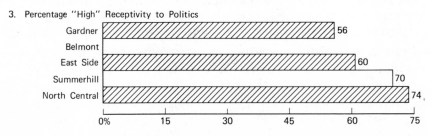

4. Percentage "High" Receptivity to Violence

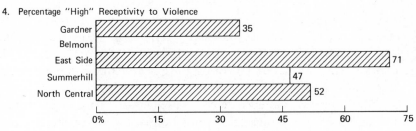

Part Two

BELIEF AND POLITICS
IN POOR NEIGHBORHOODS

· ·

Beliefs are the basis of our explanation. The poor's sense of time and fate, their assessment of political institutions and opportunities, and their sense of group identity and class interests are formative states of mind. They pose fundamental calculations about life, identity, and politics. In the four chapters of this part, we develop these beliefs. First we establish the integrity of a belief system (conceptual coherence and operational clarity); next we determine the relation of the belief system to political expression; finally, we assess its importance in specific neighborhoods. Through an appreciation of beliefs and politics, and a sensitivity to their interaction, we expose the roots of political contradiction.

Chapter Four

Lower Class Culture
and Political Response
. . . .

Our analysis of belief and politics is predicated on variability—the presence in poor neighborhoods of distinctive political styles, of differing commitments to community organization, conventional political involvement, and violence. But "lower class" culture, the single attitudinal concept in social science with exclusive application to low income communities, denies this apparent political disorder. It assumes not a variability of political expression but a uniformity of response derived from an integrated system of beliefs. Specific institutions (e.g., family and peer groups) and behavior (e.g., crime and politics) are part of a cultural system that is internally consistent, each part explicable in terms of the whole. Consequently the relationship of specific beliefs to politics becomes sensible only in the context of the whole that creates and maintains it. In this view, the political life of inner city neighborhoods is fostered by a cultural system characterized by fatalism, personal impotence, limited time perspective, disorganization, and apathy that combine to suppress any collective political urge. These basic beliefs forestall a political movement based in poor communities and even mitigate against a range of political approaches. They suggest, instead, a shared inability to conceive of politics.

We shall discover in this chapter that the concept of "lower class" culture is supported by a literature that draws upon a great variety of national and institutional settings. Herbert Gans' survey of cultural research confirms a pattern of lower and working class behavior and beliefs in the West End of Boston (a low income neighborhood comprised primarily of Italians, Poles, and Jews), in the barrios of Mexico City, and among Puerto Ricans in both New York and San Juan (1). Field work in a number of Spanish-speaking communities has led Oscar Lewis to the conclusion that "lower class" culture—or "culture of poverty"—transcends ethnic, regional, urban-rural, and even national differences (2). Although American social patterns— highly industrialized, affluent, technologically advanced, literate, and aspiring—are destructive of a "lower class" culture, Lewis suggests that core beliefs survive as relics among "very low-income Negroes, Mexicans, Puerto Ricans, American Indians and Southern poor whites" (3).

Our analysis lends further credence to this concept, but at the same time questions its relevance for the urban poor. It will become apparent that "lower class" culture is not so much an attribute of poor communities as a characteristic of a particular group within them, that is, the "street corner society." The men who congregate on street corners, outside bars and carry-out shops, are perhaps the most visible of the poor; in an important sense they create the cultural milieu that dominates the outsider's perception of poor neighborhoods. Many of the recent works on delinquency, crime, and community pathology have dwelt on gangs and street corner populations, drawing inferences from them to the larger neighborhood. This data analysis demonstrates the importance of "lower class" culture among these groups, confirming much of the previous research, but it discourages the extension of these findings to the urban poor in general.

Furthermore, our analysis fails to establish a strong bond between the politics of poor neighborhoods and a broader cultural context. "Lower class" culture tends to suppress the urge toward political involvement, though its impact is at best marginal on organizational participation, demonstrations, and even acts of violence. For some groups the cultural setting of poor neighborhoods may affect family stability, the nature of friendship groups, and attitudes toward work. But the global nature of culture—the primary questions of fate, time, and human nature—translates only indirectly into conceptions of politics. In most neighborhoods, the decision to participate in a demonstration, to attend a community group meeting, or to throw a brick is controlled more by immediate political concerns, opportunities, and experiences than by the influence of a "lower class" culture.

The tenuous connection between cultural context and political expression is evident in the weak, overall impact of "lower class" culture indicators on political activity and, perhaps most significantly, in the uneven effects of these measures in a number of the neighborhoods studied. Conceptions of culture have little importance beyond the street corner milieu in Gardner, the East Side, and North Central. Only in Belmont and Summerhill can the tone of neighborhood politics be traced plausibly to a "lower class" cultural context. Even in these two neighborhoods, however, the implications for politics are contradictory.

I CONCEPT OF CULTURE

The apparent utility of "culture" in the examination of poor neighborhoods emerges almost methodically from a broad range of cross-national research. In *Political Man,* Seymour Martin Lipset uncovers a common cognitive framework among working class groups throughout Europe and the Western Hemisphere that involves an incipient anti-intellectualism and a demand for concreteness in politics (4). Edward Banfield describes an attitudinal complex in southern Italy, "amoral familism," that encompasses a personalization of politics and a limited trust of anyone outside the family. Finally, Oscar Lewis finds *machismo* and cynicism prevalent in Mexico City's *Casa Grande.* From these and comparable studies, social scientists have traced a uniformity and a logic suggestive of a broader and a more profound attitudinal context.

The emerging pattern of belief reflects more than simply repetitive (though disjointed) observations; the pattern, its advocates argue, is

internally consistent, describing what is more accurately called a
"lower class" culture—a design for living that is persistent, stable,
widely accepted within a community, and passed on from generation
to generation (5). This "lower class" culture (or "culture of
poverty") provides answers to essential questions about life, speci-
fying the facts: what is real, what behavior or acts are approved, and
which are to be admonished (6). It provides a philosophy that sets
the bounds of legitimate behavior and predictions that describe the
existing opportunities and the eventualities to come. For marginal
populations the culture as a total system dictates certain patterns of
sexual behavior, family structure, life goals, and collective expression.

A culture does not emerge in determinant or mechanical fashion
from common conditions of marginality; it represents, instead, a
shared groping for order and predictability in precarious surround-
ings. Initially it is an adaptation and a reaction to what Lewis
considers the poor's "marginal position in a class-stratified, highly
individuated, capitalistic society" (7). Out of despair and hopelessness, the poor develop defenses against their failure, means of coping
with their situation, and a justification of their plight. These
adaptations are particularly pronounced where the economic context
includes a cash economy, wage labor and production for profit, a
high rate of unemployment, few social or political organizations, a
bilateral kinship system centered on a "nuclear progenitive family,"
and the assertion of wealth and property as overriding values by the
dominant class (8).

Though Edward Banfield argues in a recent work that there is a
phenomenon called the "cognitive" lower class—a group that is
simply psychologically incapable of acting providently (9)—his
earlier, more credible work outlines a notion of culture that is bound
up with the vicissitudes of circumstance. He observes, for example,
that the fear of premature death (infecting life with feelings of
anxiety and despair) is explicable in light of objective conditions in
southern Italy—principally the high death rate and the lack of an
extended family. Parents who expect to die before their
children reach maturity are understandably fearful that their
children will end up as orphans, wards of the state, or perhaps
beggars. Because the farms in southern Italy could support
little more than the nuclear family, parents faced these fears

unsupported by extensive family bonds (10).

This stark association of circumstance and belief suggests that the attitudes and behavior, some have taken for culture, may prove little more than an immediate response to situations, without regard to some overriding system of thought. Charles Valentine's critique of Lewis notes, for example, that hostile sentiments toward dominant institutions, negative feelings about one's own group, "spatial and temporal provincialism," and other elements of "lower class" culture are "strikingly consistent with objective situational factors" (11). That societal institutions are perceived as inimical to the interests of the poor may reflect a "cultural paranoia," but it may also reflect reality. The self-indulgence of "temporal provincialism" may stem from an inability to defer, but it might also derive logically from an objective assessment of opportunities (12). Nor do the suspicion and hostility toward government officials and bureaucrats, apparent in Boston's West End, necessarily reflect an inability to evaluate political institutions and officials. Gans notes that, no matter how irrational the West Ender's attitude toward the middle class appears, there is considerable congruence between the factual situation and the attitudes expressed. West Enders watched a new expressway sweep through the North End—the childhood home of many West Enders—and the demolition of their own homes in anticipation of a new high rent apartment complex (13). Although their cynicism and hostility are consistent with a larger system of thought (or life view), they are not devoid of evaluations that accurately reflect social reality.

Also detracting from a rigid "lower class" cultural perspective is the idea (implicit in Lewis' analysis of Mexican and Puerto Rican groups, and explicit in Robert Merton's work) that the poor, even in their aberrant behavior, are demonstrating acceptance of society's norms. The feelings of despair and hopelessness the poor express in the face of limited opportunities for success are plausible only if the poor accept society's definition of success. The poor would not despair of having failed to achieve status and wealth if they were not concerned with these rewards (14). This discrepancy between the success goals of the society and the opportunities for achieving them, Merton argues, is the root of "lower class" deviance or "innovation." He writes, "It is when a system of cultural values extols, virtually above all else, certain *common* success-goals *for the population at large* while the social structure rigorously restricts or completely closes access to approved modes of reaching these goals *for a considerable part of the same population,* that deviant behavior ensues on a large scale" (15). The distinctive behavior of the poor, evident to the general public as crime and welfare payments and to the social scientists as expressions of social deviance and despair, may reflect an undistinctive conception of values and norms. In this view, it is the general acceptance of social standards that is responsible for what society considers characteristically bizarre, and sometimes unacceptable, behavior.

The dependency on circumstance and the derivative aspects of belief among marginal populations should not leave cultural perspectives in disrepute, however. No belief system, including culture, is cerebral or devoid of social roots. Cultures are adaptive and responsive to the circumstances that force people to cope or adjust (16). Adjustment to historical forces, climate, and institutional factors does not warrant the conclusion that a cultural system is undeveloped or unimportant to the thought and behavior of a group.

Persistence, salience, and acceptance are the core attributes of a cultural system. Though responsive to circumstances, does the belief system maintain its integrity over time? Is it important to a group in facilitating its adjustment to adverse circumstances? Are the beliefs widely shared? As Gans points out, it is not adequate for a belief system to represent an "ad hoc reaction to a current situation" (17). Beliefs must be internalized by large groups of people living in common circumstances; though possibly adaptive, they must not be dislodged easily by a change in situation. The norms comprising the system may vary in salience: "at one extreme, there are norms that are not much deeper than lip service; at the other, there are norms that are built into the basic personality structure, and a generation or more of living in a new situation may not dislodge them" (18). The critical test is whether, in their entirety, these norms exert a substantial influence on the attitudes and behavior of a group and whether they remain important even when circumstances change. The fact that a cultural system may originate in an adaptation to limited opportunities, in modification or extension of dominant values (19), or even in the formulation of a counter-cultural system, does not detract from the possibility or importance of "lower class" culture.

II LOWER CLASS CULTURE: FROM FOCAL CONCERNS TO TIME

A picture of values and beliefs in poor neighborhoods has emerged from the substantial literature on "lower class" culture (and from authors of widely divergent biases) that is striking for its internal logic, comprehensiveness, and uniformity. The conception in some cases reflects disparagingly on the poor, accepting almost without question the judgment of dominant classes; the data employed are often inadequate to demonstrate that behavior is a consequence of a coherent system of thought. The internal logic of culture, evident particularly in its persistence and adaptive qualities, is often ignored in favor of a facile listing of attributes or "focal concerns." When considered together, however, the studies reveal, despite their limitations, a picture that is quite uniform: the emergent culture of poor communities provides for conceptions of time and fate, feelings of competence and control, evaluations of institutions and people, and predictions of behavior and nonbehavior.

For Walter Miller, a substantial segment of the population in America shares certain focal concerns, derived from a distinctive "lower class" cultural system. These attributes fit comfortably with a picture of low income neighborhoods as dangerous, violent and gang-ridden (not surprising, given Miller's preeminent concern with delinquency). Culture adherents are seen as frequently preoccupied with "getting into" or "staying out of" trouble; with demonstrating "toughness" (personified in the movie gangster, private detective, or cowboy), with a capacity to "outsmart, outfox, dupe, 'take,' 'con' another or others"; and with the sense to "avoid being outwitted, 'taken,' or duped oneself." They also avoid the routine in favor of excitement, a "thrill," a "night on the town." They represent caricatures of "toughs," thoughtless, reckless teenagers, drawn perhaps from *Blackboard Jungle* or *Rebel Without a Cause. Fate* is a principal concern in this cultural perspective—the feeling that people's "lives are subject to a set of forces over which they have relatively little control." "Luck" or a "big killing" provides the breakthrough. There is little calculated activity that is likely to alter the dull regularity of impoverishment. Work, saving, planning, and politics are difficult, long-term investments apt to yield little more than frustration. The more likely route to change involves the "lucky break," or the "big haul" realized in gambling or crime. Related to this belief in fate is a faith in *autonomy*. People should be independent, able to pursue excitement, and act out their toughness free from institutional restraint and extrinsic norms. This sense of autonomy is sometimes expressed as "I don't need *nobody* to take care of me. I can take care of myself." It finds specific expression in hostility toward police, social workers, and politicians (20).

These latter concerns—fate and autonomy—are extended and elaborated upon in Oscar Lewis' portrayal of the "culture of poverty." At the individual level, the defining characteristics of this culture are a "strong feeling of marginality, of helplessness, of dependence and of inferiority." These are reflected in the poor's isolation from the larger society and, above all else, in their minimal commitment to organizational life outside the nuclear family. The life of the poor, consequently, seems anachronistic in an industrial society, peculiar in its organization, and in many respects, lacking the spirit for change. "People within a culture of poverty," Lewis notes, "are provincial and locally oriented and have very little sense of history. They know only their own troubles, their own local conditions, their own neighborhood, their own way of life" (21). Their hopelessness, isolation, and disorganization, evolving from their condition and their culture, offer little prospect for an emergent "participation or civic political culture" (22).

Miller and Lewis arrived at similar conclusions from different approaches: Miller's approach is largely descriptive of a difficult environment; Lewis' is in some sense drawn out of the logical necessities of capitalist development. A similar coincidence is achieved in the work of Herbert Gans and Edward Banfield, though they rely on a more circumscribed context, the family structure. Intrigued by the prevalence of a female-based family and the "superfluous" male, Gans describes a life style characterized by sexual segregation, formation of peer group societies, and unpredictable male behavior (23). Important to this pattern is what Gans calls a strong "person-orientation," marked by immediate aspirations. The overriding concern of lower class individuals "is the desire to be a person within a group; to be liked and noticed by members of a group whom one likes and notices in turn" (24). It is an immediate, personal concern that has little reference to group goals or purpose. Consequently, the lower class finds itself unable to express itself collectively on subjects of common interest. Gans observes, "To the object-oriented (*the converse*), person-oriented people seem to be without aspirations, to lack ambition, and to be unable to defer gratification" (25) (editor's note in italic). Group interests and goals go unrealized and probably unnoticed.

In southern Italy, the focus on the immediate interests of the nuclear family produces a similar result, what Edward Banfield calls "amoral familism." Participants in this culture find little reason to consider the well-being of the entire community, and in turn, are assured that their fellow citizens cannot be trusted to serve *their* interests. Collective endeavor is consequently remote, unless its connection to the short-term advantage of the individual is glaringly obvious. These beliefs have important implications for politics (26):

- In a society of amoral familists, no one will further the interests of the group or community except as it is to his private advantage to do so.

- For a private citizen to take a serious interest in a public problem will be regarded as abnormal and even improper.

- In a society of amoral familists, organization (i.e., deliberately concerted action) will be very difficult to achieve and maintain.

- The amoral familist who is an office-holder will take bribes when he can get away with it. But whether he takes bribes or not, it will be assumed by the society of amoral familists that he does.

- No one will take the initiative in outlining a course of action and persuading others to embark upon it (except as it may be to his private advantage to do so) and, if one did offer leadership, the group would refuse it out of distrust.

Emerging as the pivotal aspiration in "lower class" culture is a demand for immediacy, concreteness, and conversely, beliefs that are not abstract, remote, or future-oriented. This conception is evident in Miller's discussion of fate and autonomy and in Lewis' formulation of "culture of poverty," removed from a historical sense and from a faith in the future. Gan's concept of "lower class" culture centers on the rewards of immediate person-to-person contact and the inability to comprehend long-term or collective goals. Finally, Banfield has described a pattern of peasant life that spurns notions of collective good, future rewards, and public interest, relying instead on short-term gain and family interests. Although other factors associated with lower class culture remain important (feelings of powerlessness, helplessness, and distrust, for example), they are either subsumed under notions of immediacy or are logically derived from them.

Perhaps the most extreme statement on "lower class" culture as immediacy is found in Banfield's *The Unheavenly City*. All elements of culture are consumed in a single overriding framework based solely on the lower class's inability to imagine or discipline itself for a future. The present-oriented individual, Banfield writes (27),

> lives from moment to moment. If he has any awareness of a future, it is of something fixed, fated, beyond his control; things happen *to* him, he does not *make* them happen. Impulse governs his behavior, either because he cannot discipline himself to sacrifice a present for a future satisfaction or because he has no sense of the future. He is therefore radically improvident: whatever he cannot consume immediately he considers valueless. . . .
>
> The lower-class individual has a feeble, attenuated sense of self; he suffers from feelings of self-contempt and inadequacy, and is often apathetic or dejected. . . . In his relations with others he is suspicious and hostile, aggressive yet dependent. He is unable to maintain a stable relationship with a mate; commonly he does not marry. He feels no attachment to community, neighbors, or friends (he has companions, not friends), resents all authority. . . . He is a nonparticipant: he belongs to no voluntary organizations, has no political interests, and does not vote unless paid to do so.

"Lower class" culture centers primarily on the marked tendency of the poor (at least as observed in these works) to demand immediate returns and to think in concrete terms. Their behavior consequently tends to be calculated in terms of immediate satisfactions, with little regard for community or for persons outside the family. Without benefit of an overarching evaluative framework, poor individuals find themselves embroiled in a series of spontaneous encounters, seemingly bounced from one circumstance to another. Their sense of helplessness in this situation leaves the poor isolated and without apparent recourse.

The individual sees little he can do to change his circumstances. He cannot get a better job; nor is he likely to remain in his present one. The union, he believes, does little except line the pockets of its own officials. Politics remains a remote avenue for change. In fact, the "lower class" person has no conception of collective action, nor does he perceive a set of values that might be served by such action. Except when the possibility of immediate personal benefit is present, the "lower class" person would probably not vote, participate in a community organization, or demonstration. Public life- including local and national politics—is a foreign land in which few "lower class" people would invest their meager personal resources.

III   STREET CORNER SOCIETY: THE LOCUS OF LOWER CLASS CULTURE   *Sub-culture not culture,*

"Lower class" culture is epitomized in the street life of poor neighborhoods. Every day young men gather on street corners, on stoops, outside carry-out shops, and in playgrounds to discuss women, their "phantom successes," their brothers, and other "street business." In almost every respect these men fulfill the requirements of the culture: they show little regard for the pace and style of "mainstream" life, preferring to live from day to day as sometime husbands, fathers, or workers. Needless to say, they have almost no interest in the community, the future, or politics.

The street life is the most visible aspect of poor neighborhoods, catching the eye of police and casual passersby alike. It epitomizes the notion of "lower class" culture and leaves outsiders with the impression that all the poor live by these standards and values. Unanswered, however, is the question whether "lower class" culture, demonstrated on the street corner, is also confined to it.   *Sub*

A.   The Street

Unlike many suburban developments where homes are set off by yards, the demands of privacy and tradition; unlike middle and upper-middle income neighborhoods where lot size and trees keep people apart, low income communities are structured to encourage high levels of interaction between neighbors. In North Central, for example, Susquehanna Avenue runs the full width of the neighborhood, leaving in its path a great variety of establishments that cater to low income needs—Army-Navy stores, storefront churches, religious articles stores, bars, luncheonettes, takeout shops, and snack bars. Day in and day out these stores are crowded with North Central residents, mostly young men who use them as vehicles for friendship and continuing social contact: they tarry over a sandwich, a beer, or a cup of coffee; they often linger outside or on the corner. In the summer, the street life of commercial areas is transferred to many of the residential blocks in North Central. Residents of all ages use stoops to escape the heat inside the row houses and to view other residents on their stoops or in the streets. All year, especially after school or at night, small groups of male youths crisscross the community, sometimes using the streets, sometimes vacant lots and back yards.

In Summerhill, much of this kind of street life takes place just outside the neighborhood, to the north, where stores in the downtown area cater to a low income clientele. The street people are largely teenagers (both male and female), and there is a younger appeal in the stores (in addition to the usual snack bars, there are also several record shops). Downtown street life is active and vital; people are animated, talkative, and boisterous. The street life within Summerhill itself is made up, to a much greater extent than in communities elsewhere, of older men. They tend to congregate around liquor stores and many of the small grocery stores that pepper the neighborhood. Unlike street gatherings elsewhere, the men are noncommunicative and inactive, as if made mute and lethargic by liquor, hunger, and increasing years.

Belmont has an undistinguished street life, confined largely to a pool hall, a grocery store, and a few bars outside the neighborhood. The nearest commercial development is comprised almost entirely of auto parts stores, car dealers, and a few motels, not the type of establishments that cater to a young, low income clientele, and that would welcome the gathering of young men inside or outside their stores. Even during the summer, there is little street life in Belmont, though people use their yards for play or gardening. This comes no closer to a street life than farming would in a rural community.

The street life characteristic of North Central, Summerhill, the East Side, and to a lesser extent, Gardner seems to prosper in black communities. Elliot Liebow's description of social relations in and around the New Deal Carry-Out Shop in Washington, D.C., is remarkably similar to those observed, with much less precision and insight, in North Central. The shop is on a corner in downtown Washington, sharing the intersection with a liquor store, a dry cleaning plant, and a shoe repair shop (28). The Carry-Out is open seven days a week, serving the special needs of its clientele. There are no tables or chairs to accommodate the customers, but there are considerable wall space and "leaning facilities" (29). The men who come here form the street life of Tally's Corner (30):

> Some are close friends, some do not like others, and still others consider themselves enemies. But each man comes here mainly because he knows others will be here, too. He comes to eat and drink, to enjoy easy talk, to learn what has been going on, to horse around, to look at women and banter with them, to see "what's happening" and to pass the time.

An outsider would gain the impression that in Tally's Corner, large groups of young men prefer standing around to working. But most of the men on the corner do hold jobs, however intermittently. Some work on construction where the demand for their skills (or lack thereof) varies by the day, the season, and the weather. Others simply work odd hours: they are garbage collectors, janitors, or truck drivers. "But since, at the moment," Liebow writes, "they are neither working nor sleeping, and since they hate the depressing room or apartment they live in, or because there is nothing to do there, or because they want to get away from their wives or anyone else living there, they are out on the street. . . " (31).

Facilities for a street existence can be found in nearly every low income black community. Bronzeville (St. Clair Drake and Horace R. Cayton's black belt in Chicago) is a "world of store-front churches, second-hand clothing stores, taverns, cheap movies, commercial dance halls, dilapidated houses and overcrowded kitchenettes" (32). In Harlem 27 percent of the 1617 businesses listed in the telephone directory are barbershops, beauty shops, cleaning establishments, or similar services; a remarkable 35 percent involve the consumption of food or drink (33). Together these kinds of establishments form the physical nucleus of low income street life (34).

B. Values on the Street Corner

The men who populate the street corner have failed by the standards of the dominant society. Their marriages often end in separation or divorce, leaving many low income families without a male head. When able to find employment, street corner men rarely pursue job opportunities that lead up some "occupational ladder," or that can provide an adequate and steady income. The men of Tally's Corner, for example, remain in a pattern of occupational failure centered around unemployment insurance, unskilled and undependable construction work, and odd jobs (35). What value they find in life emerges from the loose pattern of interaction on the street and the "excitement" of its day to day conflicts, minor happenings, and tall tales.

The street corner man, Liebow writes, "puts no lower value on the jobs available to him than does the larger society around him" (36). Rather than face these personal failures alone, street corner men turn to others faced with similar difficulties and structure an environment "where failures are rationalized into phantom successes and weaknesses magically transformed into strengths" (37). They engage in what a Swedish anthropologist calls "collective street corner mythmaking" (38,39).

> The men seem preoccupied with creating and maintaining a definition of natural masculinity which they can all share. By seizing on individual experiences of kinds which they have all had, they "talk through"and thereby construct the social reality of the typical Ghetto Man, a fact of life larger than any one of them. This Ghetto Man is a bit of a hero, a bit of a villain, and a bit of a fool, yet none of them all the way. He is in fact a kind of a trickster—uncertainty personified, a creature fluctuating between competence and incompetence, success and failure, good and evil.

This mythmaking provides a rationalization for their failure (by conventional standards) and a folk hero who makes sense of lives dependent on intermittent employment, transient sexual relations, and street corners. Mythmaking not only provides the individual with a tangible model, but also, in some sense, with a collective rejoinder to the judgments of the dominant society. The dominant society proffers a male model committed to a family, a better job, more money, and planning and scheming for an education for his children; the street offers a model based on alternate, oppositional values. Ghetto Man is forged out of a "mini-memory," incorporating chance, excitement, hunting women, sociability, and getting into and out of trouble (40).

There is considerable disagreement in the literature on the extent to which the street corner represents an alienative system of thought. Albert Cohen presents one of the more forthright positions, indicating that the culture of the delinquent gang is an oppositional one. The delinquent subculture in Cohen's analysis is not too different from that discussed in the preceding section. Because many individuals cannot meet the criteria for success established by schools and settlement houses, they turn to groups that can provide criteria for success that are attainable (41). The essential difference between this formulation and the one developed previously is the oppositional nature of the subculture. Cohen writes, "The hallmark of the delinquent subculture is the explicit and wholesale repudiation of middle-class standards and the adoption of their very antithesis" (42).

Very little research supports Cohen's idea that street youth or delinquents hold values that stand in sharp contrast to those held by the larger society or the rest of the poor population. Doc of *Streetcorner Society* was disgusted with himself because he had failed by standards that, to a large extent, he accepted. Failing to find a job, Doc turned to the street corner for support (43):

> It wasn't until a little while before you came down here that I began hanging on Norton Street again. Now I don't go anywhere else. I'm always on that corner. I'm too disgusted with myself to go any place else.

There is also no indication that the men on Tally's Corner are radically opposed to the social order that oppresses them. In fact, it was their recognition of failure that drove them to the company of the carry-out shop. If Cohen's view is correct, we would expect delinquents to value their deeds. But in fact, very few consider their acts praiseworthy (44).

Out of the self-disparagement and mythmaking surrounding street corner life emerges a variety of social behavior—often unnoticed outside the slum—that is frequently "socially deviant," sometimes subjected to institutional control, and that is almost never political in the conventional sense. These relationships are evident in the strong association made in the minds of social scientists and the lay citizenry alike between the functioning of an extensive street life and

the commission of criminal acts, especially by juveniles. The street
life is viewed not so much as a mechanical determinant of delinquent
behavior, but as a relatively unstructured environment that permits
(and to some extent, fosters) the violation of the value system of the
dominant culture. Thrasher observed in Chicago that "in this ubiq-
uitous crowd of children, spontaneous play groups are forming everywhere—gangs in embryo" (45). Gangs are not a structured criminal
element, but groups in "continuous flux and flow" (46); they do not
form a delinquent subculture, as some have suggested, but a subculture of delinquency. The commission of unlawful acts is intermittent; it is not necessitated by any coherent group or value system,
but is tolerated by custom and the neutralization of prevailing
norms (47).

Street corner men become involved politically, previous research
suggests, only in a most erratic fashion. No instance of political
participation was reported by Liebow in his discussion of Tally's
Corner; Saul Bernstein's examination of youth in the streets found
no important instances of young blacks joining with the Black
Muslims or with civil rights organizations like the NAACP (48). Political action to prevent the redevelopment of the West End proved
futile in part, because the street culture was not receptive to the
exigencies of community organization. Only Whyte discusses political involvement, though political participation in the street corner
society reflects only a periodic involvement of a few individuals. It
does not represent a persistent form of political activity.

The general lack of commitment to community politics was foretold by the concept of "lower class" culture and the values of the
street. Street corner groups, isolated by their failures and thrown
together by their need for a sense of personal worth, have abandoned
the community for mythmaking and what is in effect self-renewal.
The thrust of street life turns its participants away from community
goals and extrinsic social standards. There is little room for political
endeavor and little sense of political community. Rather, these avenues to change or social identification, if perceived at all, are apt to
be viewed as futile exercises or as someone else's "thing." Street
corner society, like "lower class" culture, views politics with cynicism and at a distance.

C.   Isolation of the Street Culture

For the young men on the corner, in the bar, or on the stoop, "lower class" culture plays an important role in their thoughts and deeds. But the street corner society, though a significant element in the interpersonal networks of poor neighborhoods, is not all of it. Based upon two years of participant observation in a black ghetto of Washington, D.C., Ulf Hannerz writes that in addition to the street corner men, there are the "mainstreamers," "swingers," and "street families" whose commitments to this cultural perspective are less pronounced. The mainstreamers —much less visible than the men on the street—can be identified by "the new metal screen doors, the venetian blinds, and the flower pots in the windows," absent from most of the houses in the neighborhood. For most Americans, the mainstreamers remain the refuge of the "normal life." They include all white-collar workers and a good percentage of those holding stable, blue collar jobs. Most mainstreamers are married and live in stable homes (49).

Besides the mainstreamers, there are groups of young people "flitting" around the city and the neighborhood in search of a "good time" whom Hannerz calls the "swingers" (50). Though committed to parties, movies, and a good time, many swingers are sons and daughters of mainstreamers or become mainstreamers after marriage. Others join or form street families like those they belonged to as children. The swingers as a group represent a stage of adolescence apparent in every community regardless of economic composition. Although they seem to adopt "action-seeking" values, it would be premature to assume the integration of these values into a more far-reaching cultural system.

Street families are a principal child rearing institution in the slums. They exist under conditions that outrage the sensibilities of outsiders and, perhaps, many mainstreamers: children are often born out of wedlock and raised in the absence of a resident father; sexual relationships are not restricted by rigid, consensual marriage. Though street families are viewed, along with street corner men, as primary contributors to a lower class culture, it is not apparent that such a categorization is accurate. Much of the behavior that seems morally reprehensible to the outsider is intermittent, reflecting only a casual commitment to values that would justify the behavior. Perhaps most

important and often unnoticed is the fact that many members of street
families attend church on Sunday, play bingo during the week (51),
and express puritanical judgements on the life around them.

But it is the absence of women from the ranks of "lower class"
culture that most forcefully limits the street perspective in poor
neighborhoods. The streets of Boston's North and West Ends, Winston Street in Washington, D.C., and Tally's Corner belong to
men (52). Women assume importance in this environment only in the
most peripheral way—drawing men out of the culture or becoming
the objects of male exploits. Contact between the Nortons and the
Aphrodite Club in the North End highlighted the exclusion of
women from the concerns of the street culture and the differing
aspirations that motivated the two groups. "Association with the
girls was," Whyte noted, "like bowling, a means of gaining, maintaining, or losing prestige in the group" (53). The men of Tally's
Corner, though involved in a complex relationship with the women
of the neighborhood, "saw themselves as users' of women as sex
objects as well as objects of income" (54). Though women had a
considerable impact on the street corner men, they never directly
entered their society.

In slum communities of both ethnic and black origins, women are
socialized in a manner that precludes full participation in the "lower
class" culture. Frederic Thrasher's classic study of Chicago gangs was
one of the first works on deviance and street life to take note of
these differences. There are two reasons for them, he states (55):

> First, the social patterns for the behavior of girls, powerfully backed
> by the great weight of tradition and custom, are contrary to the gang
> and its activities; and secondly, girls, even in urban disorganized
> areas, are much more closely supervised and guarded than boys and
> are usually well incorporated into the family group or some other
> social structure.

This conforms with what Herbert Gans calls the differential access of
men and women to "action-seeking" values. "As children reach
school age," Gans writes, "the boys are allowed to roam the streets
and to look for childhood adventures . . ." (56). The girls, however,
are expected to stay home and internalize the security of a "rou-
tine-seeking" adult and family existence. These expectations lead
many women to a model of female behavior that contradicts the

mythmaking of the street corner and that approximates the role defined by mainstream society. Hannerz writes (57):

> While a woman's life in the ghetto is certainly far from easy, at least she has the satisfaction of living up to her mother role—defined the mainstream way—rather fully. Under the circumstances she has to face, it sometimes comes easy for her to define the ghetto woman as heroine—or as a martyr when things go wrong. This self-typing is shared and talked about among women; between mother and daughter, talking in the kitchen while preparing dinner, as well as among friends and neighbors.

This exclusion of women from the street culture, therefore, represents more than a segregation of peer groups. In some sense it also represents an adherence to oppositional values.

"Lower class" culture can be a valuable concept in the consideration of belief in poor neighborhoods, if we keep in mind that more than half the residents—women—have been socialized to different values, that many of the residents live their lives by standards well accepted outside poor neighborhoods, that many residents whose life styles bring them in contact with the street are simply passing through as adolescents on the way to more mainstream behavior, and that a large percentage of the men of middle age no longer live by the standards of the street. Only in the street corner society—perhaps the area of greatest visibility—do behavior and beliefs substantiate a notion of "lower class" culture. Although the concept is apparently epitomized by the street, it may well be limited to this small path.

D. Street and Culture in Poor Neighborhoods: A Test

The types of individuals who comprise the street corner society are often excluded or underrepresented in surveys of low income communities. The 1960 census, for example, underenumerated the proportion of young, black males living in center cities (58). Most systematic samples, whatever the neighborhood, rely upon the selection of homes or apartments, thus excluding individuals who either do not reside in a residential dwelling unit or only infrequently visit one (59).

We attempted to avoid some of these underenumeration problems in this study by employing an unorthodox form of cluster sampling called "site sampling" (60). A neighborhood was divided into eight sampling sites, hopefully exhausting the areas habituated by the neighborhoods' populations. These sites were created by the possible value combinations of three dichotomized variables—commercial or residential establishments, inside or outside these establishments, and daytime or nighttime interviewing. Respondents were selected within sampling sites to reflect the actual distribution of the neighborhood population. (See Appendix A.) Although some groups certainly remain underrepresented in the study—particularly younger, more militant members of the community—the approach probably minimizes this exclusion.

The by-product of this sampling procedure is a unique population of residents who spend a large part of their time outside the home, particularly in commercial centers. There are 222 respondents who were located in sampling sites other than those considered residential inside, day or night, the conventional locations for sampling. Two-thirds of the respondents interviewed in these remaining six sites were men, compared to 40 percent of those interviewed in their homes. Sixty-four percent were under 36 years of age. Of those found at home, only 47 percent were under 36. Fewer than 4 percent of the respondents outside the home considered themselves housewives. These data give us every reason to believe that we have sampled a portion of the street corner population in these communities. Respondents were all found outside the home and in the locations that form the physical plant for street corner life. The respondents were overwhelmingly male and young and very few were housewives, indicating that the women who appear in the sample are not, for the most part, transient to the street corner society (61).

Respondents were asked to answer two questions posing central issues in "lower class" culture. First, "Would you agree or disagree, 'The wise person lives for today and lets tomorrow take care of itself'?" This question raises what Banfield considers the focal point of the culture, the tendency of lower class people to pursue immediate interests and think in concrete terms. Second, "Do you think people who live in this neighborhood can generally be trusted?"—thus playing up the detachment of lower class individuals from any social commitments and their cynicism about life and

people. Although these two questions do not capture the richness of
the cultural concept, they appear, at least superficially, to consider
some principal concerns in the literature, without which no coherent
conception of "lower class" culture would be possible.

The responses to these two questions suggest that the street corner
society is indeed set off from the remainder of the population in
poor neighborhoods; they demonstrate a much more limited time
horizon and express low levels of interpersonal trust. Precisely half of
the street corner group indicate that the wise person lives for the
present, ignoring what future consequences there might be. Only
one-third of the residential population give a similar response.
Though the differences are not as marked on the second question,
respondents located in the "street" are more distrustful of their
neighbors than those respondents interviewed in their homes. Identical results are achieved on both questions even when these comparisons are made only among males under 36 years of age, assuring
that these differences are not simply a consequence of sex and age
distributions.

Street corner society in many respects epitomizes what has been
called "lower class" culture. Its membership is cynical about a
variety of institutions and, as these data suggest, about the people
with whom they live from day to day. In contrast to the society's

Table 4.1. Comparison of Street Corner and Residential Samples

	Street Corner	Residential	Probability
1. "The wise person lives for today and lets tomor- row take care of itself."			
□Agree	50%	32%	.000 (i)
	(214)	(695)	
2. "Do you think people who live in this neigh- borhood can generally be trusted?"			
□No/don't know	53%	41%	.004
	(213)	(709)	

(i) T-test computed on difference of means.

Table 4.2. Comparison of Street Corner and Residential Samples for Men Under 36 Years of Age

	Street Corner	Residential	Probability
1. "The wise person lives for today and lets tomorrow take care of itself." □Agree	52% (89)	28% (128)	.000
2. "Do you think people who live in this neighborhood can generally be trusted?" □No/don't know	57% (89)	46% (129)	.09

emphasis on saving, planning, and investment, street corner groups seem radically improvident, concerned primarily with the concrete happenings of the present. They stand apart in their realization of the culture—not only from the dominant society, but also from the bulk of the people who live in poor neighborhoods.

"Lower class" culture is part of the reality of poor neighborhoods, but only a *part*. Consequently, it is from a limited rather than a general application of cultural themes that we examine the peculiarities of politics in poor neighborhoods.

IV   THE IMPORTANCE OF LOWER CLASS CULTURE

Even the most cursory consideration of politics in these five poor neighborhoods would confirm that a "lower class" culture does not provide a framework that uniformly depresses political expression. The behavioral implications of "lower class" culture (including a cynical detachment from politics in any form, except violent expression and deviant acts) are not borne out by the widespread organizational politics of many communities and the trenchant electoral participation in others. In Gardner, though plagued by a persistent divisiveness, and North Central, though laboring under an attenuated leadership network, participation in community organizations is extensive, running the gamut from church-related groups to militant protest organizations. Politics in Belmont and Summerhill evince a certain reserve, but even here large numbers of residents have expressed at least a limited interest in electoral politics (three out of five residents are registered to vote) and a somewhat smaller number have given attention to the earliest organizing activities of Model Cities or community action programs.

In none of the communities is there a consistent lower class response to these questions (see Table 4.3). The cultural context of the street corner, encompassing notions of immediacy, concreteness, and interpersonal distrust, is distinct from the patterns of belief in poor neighborhoods generally. The minimization of cultural themes is most pronounced in Gardner and North Central—the two communities with the highest organizational involvement—and in consistent patterns are apparent in the remaining three neighborhoods. Preoccupation with the present is most obvious in Belmount and Summerhill, the neighborhoods of political ebb tide; expressions of interpersonal hostility are much more apparent on the East Side than in the other neighborhoods. Although aspects of cultural expression sometimes reach the plateau of cultural response set on the street corner (half the Belmont residents and half the entire street corner sample express agreement with a statement of immediacy, for example), no coherent, pronounced cultural system emerges. A common network of beliefs that transcends the parochialism of particular neighborhoods and asserts their common origin and plight does not fit the political reality of poor neighborhoods. Each neighborhood displays its own unique combination of cultural attributes and, as we shall see later, its own response to social conditions and history (62).

The feebleness of "lower class" culture, however, should not lead us to wholly disregard cultural themes, for *elements* of "lower class" culture may prove important in specific neighborhoods. A pronounced distrust is apparent on the East Side and present-orientation in Summerhill; though Gardner residents are not noticeably bound by the present, earlier work on Mexican culture suggests a pattern of distrust and a detachment from time and scientific principles (63). Belmont, however, gives a singular plausibility to cultural themes, even if, at the same time, it confirms the limited applicability of "lower class" culture. In a fashion reminiscent of a still vital

Table 4.3. *"Lower Class" Culture in Five Neighborhoods*

	Neighborhoods				
	Gardner	Belmont	East Side	Summerhill	North Central
1. "The wise person lives for today and lets tomorrow take care of itself."					
□Agree	25%	50%	31%	53%	30%
	(153)	(178)	(280)	(250)	(250)
2. "Do you think people who live in this neighborhood can generally be trusted?"					
□No/don't know	36%	26%	60%	37%	34%
	(153)	(178)	(280)	(250)	(250)

Appalachian heritage, Belmont residents personalize community life and seek immediate returns from it.

The Appalachian migrant relies upon a Church and a faith that urges him not to grapple with his fate but, on the contrary, to accept it. Man lives in original sin; he is fallible and prone to failure. Only presumption would lead him to begin "pretending to be what he is not, pretending at times *he* is God" (64). Whereas Nikos Kazantzakis would have man emulate Christ's struggle and become God himself, the Appalachian religions (Methodist and Baptist, for the most part) insist that man reject a "struggle between the flesh and the spirit," between "reconciliation and submission" (65). They insist only that man accept Jesus Christ.

The real life analogy of this Fundamentalist faith is the acceptance of suffering as part of the Christian fate. Rather than looking to the future for some distant achievement and improvement of conditions, the mountaineer relies on the present or turns with nostalgia to the past (66). This fatalistic resignation to the present protects him from disappointment and discourages speculation in new ideas, new experiences, and new achievements (67). Although these tendencies are most pronounced in the Appalachian hills, surveys confirm their impact in Appalachian communities in southern Ohio as well (68).

In addition to this unwillingness to consider future rewards (except salvation) the mountaineer is reluctant to employ universal values or abstract ideas in interpersonal relations. Political problems, social conditions, and life itself are seen as a series of personal encounters, determined by motivations no more complex or abstract than personal gain or emotion. This personal orientation is reflected in the animosity many mountaineers felt for Herbert Hoover, who was perceived as singularly responsible for the deadening depression in Kentucky. It is also apparent in the sentiments expressed by migrants in Chicago who saw Lyndon Johnson "making millions of dollars off this war, billions of it, right in his pocket," and Martin Luther King as a "rich man" who "owns a couple of buildings in slum areas" (69). Social workers and chroniclers of Appalachian life lament, to the point of triteness, the influence of family and friendship in church life (70) and community organizations (71). In Hamilton, the Mayor reflected on his inability to pierce the wall of personalization.

There are great vestiges of mistrust. They see everybody in City Hall as crooked. How else can you explain why somebody like myself does all this work for $300? There must be some explanation. They have to make sense of it. What they can't understand is self-satisfaction in a job. It's what you get.

In the Appalachian milieu, nearly all social relations—from church to politics—are structured by personal and immediate desires, with little thought given to general principles, "objective goals," or the "public interest." The survey results and these impressions provide the primary, if isolated, substantiation *at the community level* for a notion of "lower class" culture.

V CULTURAL THEMES AND POLITICAL INVOLVEMENT

The assertion of nonpolitics in lower class culture is, above all else, a logical proposition derived from the disorganization and cynicism in the culture. A man who is radically improvident, is disorganized in his personal approach to family and work, is distrustful of his fellow slum dwellers, and fails to recognize any collective or long-term principles is not a man to evaluate political candidates or enter a voting booth on election day. His response to politics is more distant. He does not perceive how politics can or will affect him; he fails to see how it can be used to his advantage or to enhance some principle. The politics of "lower class" culture is nonpolitics.

The comprehensive denial of politics is presumed, in the first place, because the culture itself is a total system, encompassing nearly all important social behavior. But as our analysis shows, "lower class" culture is limited conceptually and in its constituency. Thus its relation with politics is less profound, influencing its expression, certainly, but not consuming it, as we might have anticipated. The absence of a cultural hegemony further implies that other beliefs not related to cultural themes may affect the level and mode of political expression.

It is not surprising, therefore, that cultural themes do not have a marked impact on political activity in poor neighborhoods (see Tables 4.4 and 4.5). "Lower class" attributes generally depress the level of organizational involvement and receptivity to politics; but

Table 4.4.   Correlations Between Cultural Themes and Political Expression

Cultural Themes	Organizational Membership	Receptivity to Politics	Receptivity to Violence
1. Present orientation	-.095**	.058	.012
2. Distrust	-.039	-.205**	-.066*

  * Significant at .05 level.
** Significant at .01 level.

Table 4.5.   "Lower Class" Culture and Political Expression

	Lower Class (i) Present-Distrust	Ambiva-lence (ii)	Upper Class (iii) Future-Trust	Probability (iv)
Belong to organization	13% (182)	15% (478)	21% (400)	.133
"High" receptivity to politics	66% (157)	62% (402)	72% (339)	Not significant
"High" receptivity to violence	54% (157)	53% (402)	55% (339)	Not significant

(i) Answered "agreed" to present orientation statement (Appendix B) and "no" or "don't know" to trust statement (Appendix B).

(ii) Answered "agreed" to present orientation statement and "yes" to trust statement, or "disagreed" to present orientation statement and "no" or "don't know" to trust statement.

(iii) Answered "disagreed" to present orientation statement and "yes" to trust statement.

(iv) T-test computed on the difference of means between respondents in "lower class" and "upper class" groups.

the two cultural themes taken together account for only 1 percent of the variance in organizational participation and receptivity to violence, and only 5 percent of the variance in receptivity to politics. The combination of "lower class" themes into an apparently coherent, cultural format (Table 4.5) reveals an interesting relationship only with organizational membership, but even here the differences are hardly significant.

Perhaps more interesting for our analysis are the contradictory findings for Belmont and Summerhill in Table 4.6. In Belmont, where "lower class" cultural themes are most pronounced, the present orientation tends to depress political involvement; in Summerhill a similar orientation has the opposite effect. These results further underscore the weakness of the relationship between "lower class" culture and politics. Only in Belmont is there a significant and consistent relationship between cultural themes, community belief, and apolitics.

Table 4.6.   Time Perspective and Organizational Membership in Belmont and Summerhill

"The Wise Person Lives for Today and Lets Tomorrow Take Care of Itself"

	Belmont		Summerhill	
	Agree	Disagree	Agree	Disagree
Belong to organization	8%	17%	15%	8%
	(89)	(81)	(131)	(115)

Culture, concerned primarily with questions of fate, time, value, and meaning, is in the final analysis far removed from politics. The translation of these concepts into political expression (especially where their integration seems highly undeveloped) is indeed a difficult process. Charles Valentine, perhaps, led us to this conclusion when he wrote (72),

> What is prized and endorsed according to the standards of a cultural system is not always manifest or practically available in the exigencies of ongoing existence. Anthropologists therefore do not expect to find all the values that lend inner coherence to a way of

life directly or overtly expressed in everyday life.

Even if "lower class" culture were a salient and well integrated ideological construct in poor neighborhoods, we could hardly expect its logic to be fully executed in the political sphere. There is considerable room for illogic, random behavior, and outside influence in the playing out of cultural influences. But when the culture seems to lack salience for a large portion of the population and the separate strands of that culture remain amorphous, the impact on politics is distorted by other interpretations of events and other factors of greater force and salience.

Chapter Five

The Alienated Politics
of Poor Neighborhoods
· · · · · · · · · · · · · ·

The poor have not been served well by politics, either in their present communities or in the rural hinterlands from which they came. In the Black Belt counties of the South, serious political involvement by blacks was precluded before the mass exodus to the North. The years of tumultuous competition for black support after Reconstruction, plagued by the widespread fear of "Negro domination," in the end led to the complete exclusion of blacks from politics in the South. They were purged from the coalition with the landlords and businessmen of the "New South," as well as from the considerations of the "People's Party"—developments that ensured the separation of Southern agrarianism from national progressivism (1). Southern blacks were not part of politics, merely the object of it. Though local businessmen and political leaders established regular ties with accommodating black church leaders, the great mass of black people saw little of politics and had little concern for it (2). The law (which blacks had almost no role in writing) and public officials (whom blacks had no role in electing) served the interests of plantation owners and merchants. Politics helped ensure the dependence of rural blacks on the plantation, narrowing their rights as debtors and buttressing the plantation owners' control over tenants and farm laborers (3).

The frontiersmen on the Cumberland Plateau had long sought to minimize the role government played in their lives. But while the highlanders remained hostile or indifferent to government, private investors—in mining and lumber in particular—were not similarly unconcerned. Tax commissioners and local courts became indebted to the large companies that owned the wealth of the plateau. Rarely did these companies find themselves burdened by confiscatory taxes; rarely did the courts challenge their title to the plateau's resources. Underfinanced local governments, symbolized by the "crumbling, dilapidated" county courthouses (4), provided inadequate libraries, paltry school budgets and, before the Depression, few roads. Questions about popular control and government services were exacerbated by the corruption and nepotism that plagued local governments from the beginning. County governments paid no heed to strictures of efficiency, hiring relatives whenever possible and supporting hordes of officeholders in "near idleness" (5). At election time, state jobs were particularly plentiful and salaried government employees frequently found their paychecks shrunk to support an election fund (6).

The Mexicans of the Central Mesa knew government through the repressive military policies of Diaz and the legal support provided to land enclosures and the destruction of free villages. The landed gentry fared extremely well under the regime of General Porfirio Diaz, seizing water, timber, and pasture rights, forcing many peasants into an increasingly dependent position on the haciendas. Ancient claims to the land fell away in the face of gentry-controlled courts and government sympathy for landed interests (7). Under Diaz and later "reformed" regimes, the peasant population witnessed the ruthlessness of central and state governments, evident in the bloody and nearly genocidal campaigns of General Robles and other military leaders (8). Some peasants acceded to "resettlement"; others joined guerrilla movements in defense of the "pueblos"; still others simply fled to northern states or to the American Southwest. Even with the enactment of the *Ley de Ejidos* (restoring communal ownership of the land and effecting some redistribution) internal political rivalries continued, as did the periodic violence and the migration to the United States.

The politics of the cities was no more responsive to the poor than were governments in Appalachia, the Black Belt, or the Central Mesa. Until recently the residents of the five poor neighborhoods examined in this study were unable to elect any of their own to public office. Belmont and Gardner are still without any effective representation; what successful political intrusions emerged in the other communities came through protracted struggle. In North Central, the city political organization determined which blacks were to assume responsible positions in the organization and later in city poverty programs. Civic leaders in Atlanta initially chose to deal with the established Negro Voters League rather than the more militant and younger civil rights leaders.

Public policy and public officials have uniformly supported the devastation and abandonment of poor neighborhoods. Superhighways and massive interchanges displaced thousands of families in Summerhill, Gardner, and the East Side. Public improvements—city stadiums and cultural centers—brought land clearance policies to Gardner and Summerhill. Urban renewal programs facilitated the expansion of universities and the construction of office buildings and high rent apartments in North Central, Gardner, Belmont, and the East Side. Overall, it is fair to say that the minimal representation of the poor's interests in municipal governments has been matched by a minimal concern for their welfare in public policy. Moreover, little positive action has been taken in any of these communities to improve the condition of housing, to deter crime, or to improve local roads. The few programs designed to benefit the poor (i.e., Model Cities and the Poverty Program) are overshadowed by the belief, shared by liberal and conservative administrations alike, that these neighborhoods are "problem" areas, the roots of lawlessness, pathology, and inner city blight. The thrust of government policy has been directed more toward their encirclement, isolation, and elimination than toward their rehabilitation and growth.

Political marginality would seem to occupy a pivotal position in the poor's more generalized marginality. Whether in the rural hinterlands of North America or in the inner cities, the poor fare badly in public policy deliberations. Basic public services—schools, roads, and police protection—are inadequate to what is often a desperate need. Rather, political authorities have consistently supported policies that deprive the poor of stable moorings, sanctioning the seizure of communal lands and mineral rights, or implementing land clearance and relocation programs. Given the accumulated misdeeds of political authorities, it is hard to imagine the poor not viewing them as distant, unresponsive, and perhaps in the service of other more powerful interests.

The inattention to, or detachment from, political life fostered by "lower class" culture pales when compared to the estrangement apparently necessitated by the poor's experience with politics. The emphasis on immediacy and concrete experience (important themes in "lower class" culture) translates weakly into apolitics, and only consistently in the Appalachian white community. But political estrangement would seem to spring from the concrete failure of politics. Disidentification or estrangement from politics (perhaps best called political alienation) is a construct with immediate political relevance—derived from politics and perhaps translatable into politics.

It is appropriate that the effort to unravel the politics of poor neighborhoods emphasizes alienation; of all the perspectives we discuss, it is perhaps the one most consistent with the poor's political marginality. The obvious relationship between marginality and estrangement, however, should not pose a simple conception of alienation or a single-dimensional linkage with political expression. Such narrowness of conception does justice neither to the subtlety of political marginality nor to the varied reactions of the poor. Political alienation, we shall discover, involves not just a positive or negative identification with a political system, but feelings of political ineffectiveness, evaluations of government performance, and attitudes toward the entire political community. The choice between conventional avenues of participation, violence, withdrawal into countercultural systems, or lethargy is very much a consequence of these sentiments; these alternatives are the stuff of political permutations.

We should begin by evolving a conception of political alienation that has conceptual clarity, has a basis in experience, and suggests testable propositions about political expression.

I POLITICAL ALIENATION

In this century, the concept of "alienation" has been used to explain all manner of social and personal malaise—from a search for meaning in lives apparently devoid of substance and value, to loss of sexual gratification, to separation of whole societies from their creative and guiding principles. This seemingly unassuming concept, we are led to believe, is at the root of ghetto riots, student unrest, family breakdown, sexual impotence, high divorce and suicide rates, murder, and rape. In fact, alienation is blamed for (or credited with) almost all behavior of any consequence. The extension of the term to explain almost everything, Keniston has rightly noted, leaves us with a concept that is dangerously rhetorical and emotive, one that is synonymous with a general and often vague feeling that "something is wrong somewhere" (9).

The confusion about alienation is no more apparent than in scholarly thinking about poor neighborhoods, particularly about poor black neighborhoods, where it is commonly assumed that something is certainly wrong and that alienation of some sort is part of their malaise. Ghetto communities have been characterized as suffering from "a profound sense of isolation and alienation," and consequently as more receptive to violence and disorder than other communities (10). But it is not particularly illuminating of either ghetto beliefs or the concept of alienation to state that life is not particularly good in poor neighborhoods, that the poor know it, and that sporadic acts of violence have occurred. This is a mere restatement of what should be apparent to any casual observer of poor neighborhoods and provides only rudimentary theoretical or analytical insights. Such descriptions of ghetto life leave the meaning of alienation vague and its relation to political action inferred from the coincidence of alienation and the eruption of looting and arson. We learn little about how people respond to political institutions or political events, and even less about how the poor evaluate their political alternatives or about the political cost of these options.

A. A Model for the Study of Political Alienation

The study of alienation relies on a generalized sentiment, a feeling that the reality is divorced from an ideal. Both Marx and Hegel, for example, saw man as engaged in a struggle for self-creation necessitated by an alienation of man from his true nature, or more generally, by an alienation of reality from essence (11). Though the general context differs, this is the sense in which Robert Lane treats the problem of political alienation, that is, as a "person's sense of estrangement from the politics and government of his society." He writes: "It may be taken to mean a feeling that these public matters are not 'my affairs,' that the government is not 'my government,' that the Constitution is not 'my Constitution'—in this sense, a disidentification." The alienated man, Lane suggests, is the subject of political institutions; he is not a party to them. Government is run not for him but for others; it is run by rules that "are unfair, loaded, illegitimate . . . " (12). Here alienation is derived not from culture or from personality traits, but from a specific relationship between the individual and his government. The alienated man perceives that the government, or public officials, or the system itself is not what he thinks it should be. Consequently, he disidentifies and feels estranged from politics.

Attitudes of disidentification or feelings of estrangement can be generalized as they are in Lane's analysis ("from the politics and government of his society") or made specific as they are in the works of David Easton, Gabriel Almond, and Sidney Verba. Almond and Verba have outlined some basic questions about the individual's relation to politics that include some major issues in political alienation (13).

1. What knowledge does he have of his nation and of his political system in general terms, its history, size, location, power, "constitutional" characteristics, and the like? What are his feelings toward these systemic characteristics? What are his more or less considered opinions and judgments of them?

2. What knowledge does he have of the structures and roles, the various political elites, and the policy proposals that are involved in the upward flow of policy making? What are his feelings and opinions about these structures, leaders and policy proposals?

3. What knowledge does he have of the downward flow of policy enforcement, the structures, individuals, and decisions involved in these processes? What are his feelings and opinions of them?

4. How does he perceive of himself as a member of his political system? What knowledge does he have of his rights, powers, obligations, and of strategies of access to influence? How does he feel about his capabilities? What norms of participation or of performance does he acknowledge and employ in formulating political judgments, or in arriving at opinions?

These questions comprise what might roughly be called an input-output view of political life. Input processes include the institutions, roles, and individuals that monitor and receive demands for government action and the manner of support (diffuse or specific) provided for the regime, the political community, and political authorities by the general citizenry. Output involves the formulation and implementation of government policy (14). Together these concepts of input (demand and support) and output (policy) form a political system whose social interactions are "oriented toward the authoritative allocation of values for a society" (15).

Within this framework it is possible to differentiate feelings of disidentification and estrangement. People do not relate to government and politics as an amorphous whole to which one is either repelled or attracted; they view government as a complex set of interactions involving a number of important roles and functions (16). They consider the institutions and the authorities who might respond to citizen demands and assess their responsiveness; consequently they are able to estimate their own effectiveness in politics (questions two and four above). Citizens also relate to the institutions and the people that execute the "downward flow of policy enforcement" (or what Easton calls the output of the political system). From observations of policy implementation and from the impact of government policy on their lives, people determine whether government works for their interests or for the interests of others (question three above). Finally, individuals may reject or embrace the entire enterprise: the institutions, authorities, and roles that process demands and receive support; the policy making and enforcement apparatus; and the system formed by the flow of demands and policies and by the community, history, and culture that constitute its *raison d' etre* (question one above).

These three orientations—sense of inefficacy, policy dissatisfaction, and political system rejection—are the elements of political alienation in the following analysis.

B. *Politics, Violence, and Culture*

Sensed inefficacy, policy dissatisfaction, and political system rejection are not simply three analytic facets of a single attitudinal dimension, nor do they comprise a single, uniform response to the political system. Alienation is a complex interaction between people's attitudes and the various aspects of the political order. Concern for government policy and feelings of political effectiveness may or may not be related to each other or to a generalized attitude toward politics. But whatever their interrelation, the impact they have on political involvement is likely to follow a number of logical combinations, as outlined in Figure 5.1.

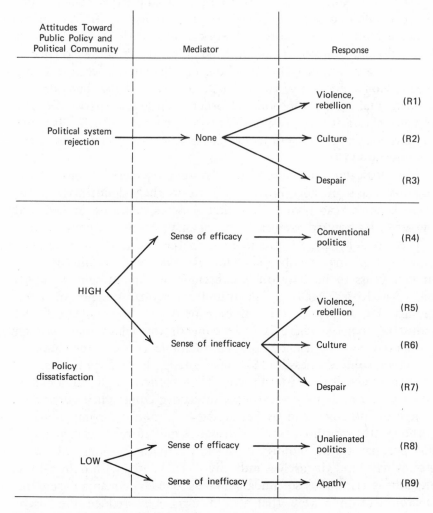

Figure 5.1. Political Alienation and Political Expression.

If a group of citizens were to hold the political system in utter contempt, believing that the system was hopelessly corrupt, committed to interests fundamentally opposed to their own and based on values with which they wholly disagreed, there would be little cause for political participation—at least in those forms sanctioned by the system. It might sink into a near hopeless inactivity, despairing of ever altering oppressive political arrangements (R3); but the group is not without a tenable option. It could seek to reinforce its own values by minimizing exposure to those of the larger society. The group would consequently make no effort to destroy the system but would simply try to ignore and work around it (R2). On the other hand, the group might try to alter the political system by violence or revolutionary action (R1). In choosing this alternative, the group would hope not only to advance its own goals, but also to fundamentally alter the political order. Neither alternative requires the group to assess the responsiveness of government officials, since in neither case are its actions mediated by *conventional* estimates of effectiveness (17).

It is logically unnecessary for "system rejecters" to weigh the responsiveness of government officials in their deliberations. But there is some reason to believe that these calculations, unmediated by attitudes toward conventional channels, may at times operate unperturbed by sensed effectiveness in the broadest meaning. The youth culture in particular, Theodore Roszak argues, is built upon an unwillingness to mediate one's contempt or commitment. It builds on what Roszak calls a "profoundly personalist sense of community," that rejects the values rooted in a technological and industrial society. There is little concern for values such as high productivity or efficiency, but considerable concern for "non-intellective consciousness" (18). The young, Roszak proposes, are disenchanted with the sterility of life in modern capitalist societies and try to avoid it by creating a subjective community outside its sphere of influence and by refraining from political confrontation. Although the youth culture is distinctive and current, its response is not peculiar to the young; it is similar to the response of many groups who find themselves radically disenchanted with political life and whose critique is so fundamental as to exclude manipulating the environment in a way that would marginally reduce the disenchantment. The rejection of manipulation as an option (and hence the criteria of conventional effectiveness) necessitates the sub-ordination of technological, social values to subjectivity and group values.

The contemplation of political rebellion may also be divorced from calculation, particularly where rebellion is unlikely to alter the existing political arrangements. In fact, Camus maintains that suffering moves toward rebellion only when it transcends egotistical action altogether (19). Rebellion draws man away from existential solitude, providing an affirmation of a group value; it is derived from radical discontent and founded on the solidarity of collective understanding. Whereas history is normally moved by expediency and calculation, rebellion is compelled by the values that founded it. Camus cites the Decembrists, among the first Russian revolutionaries, who chose to organize and implement an insurrection. They had almost no support among the general population (they were patricians); their rebellion had no chance whatever of success. On the eve of their rebellion in December, 1825, some of the participants were executed by cannon fire, others by hanging. Their actions were hopelessly inefficacious, but as one of their leaders put it, "it (*was*) a fine death" (20) (editor's note in italic). Rebellion, by Camus's standard, is a movement of the highest values, above history, calculation, and expediency (21).

Dissatisfaction with government policy that is not at the same time tied to a radical estrangement from the political community operates within a completely different milieu. Individuals view government action as detrimental to their interests but not funda-mentally—or at least not hopelessly—opposed to them. Their response, since it is not based on an abandonment of the political system, is likely to be mediated by their assessment of the system's responsiveness. *The clearest route to conventional forms of political involvement in this model is a feeling that government policy inadequately benefits a group or person and that government officials would be responsive to overtures aimed at changing these conditions* (R4). But when feelings about government policy are tied to a belief that government is unresponsive in any event, the choice of political alternatives (R5, R6, R7) is apt to resemble that facing those who reject the political system—violence, culture, or despair. Whatever the response, it should prove qualitatively different from a similar choice based on rejection of the system, for it at least considers the willingness of government officials to respond to pressure. We might expect, consequently, that the alternatives—politics, violence, culture, or despair—are less individuated, with groups at times vacillating between responses or choosing all four.

Although the sense of efficacy (perceived government responsiveness) illuminates alternative responses to dissatisfaction, it provides no basis for understanding the choice between violence, culture, and despair. Both the man who is dissatisfied with government policy and also plagued by a sense of futility and the man who repudiates the system are faced with the choice between violence, subjective group meaning, and withdrawal. But the choice is not dictated by the nature of the alienation. In fact, Parsons suggests, the decision may have nothing to do with politics and everything to do with personality. He maintains that the decisive factor for "alienative dominance" individuals is whether the individual is basically an active or a passive person. When the active personality component is dominant, the individual is inclined to "rebelliousness"; when the passive component prevails, the response is withdrawal (22).

> If the alienative component of ego's motivation is dominant he is by definition less concerned with preserving alter's favorable attitudes than he is with expressing his alienative need-dispositions. Hence in the active case he will tend to act *aggressively* toward alter, to "pick a fight" with him relatively regardless of the risk of alienating alter, to seek a "showdown." If, on the other hand, he is passively inclined, his tendency will be, not aggressively to force a "showdown" but to avoid exposure to uncongenial expectations on alter's part, to be *compulsively independent,* in the extreme case to break the relationship altogether by withdrawing from it.

Although Keniston's analysis is not so simply conceived as Parsons', he too seems to accept a notion of activity-passivity (his "protest-prone personality," for example). Among the psychodynamic attributes that Keniston proposes contribute to protest involvement are a concern "with living out expressed but unimplemented parental values," an "unusual capacity for nurturant identification," and a family background which is "unusually equalitarian, permissive, 'democratic,' and highly individuated" (23). Keniston uses this schema to differentiate the "culturally alienated" from the "activist" (or culture from politics). But might not similar factors explain the decisions made by those who, because of their perception of the political process, have turned away from politics?

The choice between violence and culture might reflect as well an assessment of military strength, indeed a consideration of effectiveness of a different sort. At issue is not whether political authorities are responsive to normal citizen overtures, but whether the violence of an alienated group can alter the direction of public policy or the system itself.

Few alienated groups seek the cataclysm of revolutionary armies confronting the disintegrating forces of the ruling class; many do attempt to alleviate conditions through a moderate application of violence. For example, black people in the United States engaged in acts of violence that the great majority of whites saw as destructive and meaningless, but that many blacks considered effective in ending oppression (24). What is important in confrontation with authorities is not the active-passive mode of the combatants, though that might prove relevant, and not the perception of government officials as unresponsive to normal political pressure, though this may have prompted many to abandon conventional politics, but the belief that looting, rioting, and arson are apt to improve the objective life condition of black people. Opting for violence, then, may reflect a balancing of probable costs and benefits, but it is a calculation that has gone beyond an assessment of conventional political probabilities.

The model suggests another alienation pattern that provides no provocation for political involvement and little ground for faith in the effectiveness of political action (R9). It is difficult to imagine the circumstances under which individuals plagued by this pattern of alienation would engage in politics, violence, or culture. Their perception of government activity suggests a general satisfaction, with little cause for complaint; it is a contentment with a government that operates outside the individual's sphere of influence. This form of alienation promotes inactivity through two basic attitudes: politics is futile and politics adequately serves the needs of the individual. Such beliefs provide no incentive to learn anything about politics and no reason to risk the costs in time, personal energy, or security required for political involvement. This is an alienation that is expressionless, suggesting, perhaps, political apathy (25).

There remains one final response to these beliefs (R8), but it is a residual category, based on the total absence of alienated conceptions of the political order. Individuals in this group are essentially satisfied with government performance and feel conventional political channels are open to their overtures. In no sense do their attitudes toward political life reflect the estrangement or discontent of previous responses, but suggest instead a complete integration of mind and political order. Their attitudes should lead to an unalienated form of political expression, emphasizing conventional political opportunities and minimizing violence, culture, and despair.

It remains for the analysis to demonstrate whether these combinations of alienated belief have currency in poor neighborhoods and whether the predictions of political expression are based on the reality of belief and politics in poor neighborhoods.

II POLITICAL ALIENATION AND POOR NEIGHBORHOODS

If each citizen were to receive the government benefits he expected and thought he deserved, if every citizen were greeted in political chambers with enthusiasm and respect, if each individual were indispensable to the ongoing political community, there would be little reason for considering political alienation. But in no regime are all or even most individuals the preferred company of policy makers; nor do they receive benefits commensurate with their needs. There are groups in every society who see themselves and who are seen by the general population as outsiders or intruders. It is with these groups, the politically impotent and the shunned, that a study of political alienation should begin.

In the United States, that inquiry should begin with blacks and the residents of poor neighborhoods, for they, more than other groups, express the sentiments of alienation (26). In fifteen large cities, blacks indicate greater dissatisfaction than whites with a number of government services, including the public schools, parks and playgrounds, police protection, and garbage collection (27). A national sample shows blacks almost twice as dissatisfied as whites with their children's education, with their income level, with their jobs and working conditions, and with their neighborhoods (28). In riot areas (usually the most impoverished black neighborhoods) the discontent is considerably more pronounced. Fifty-three percent of Watts residents, for example, say they are dissatisfied with the schools, considerably more than among the general black population and four times the national average for whites. Seventy-four percent of black men and 58 percent of black women in Watts believe police rough up people unnecessarily. The discontent with police behavior in Watts is almost seven times the level of dissatisfaction expressed by whites in fifteen cities (29).

It is difficult to establish from earlier survey material whether the poor are more estranged from the political community than the nonpoor. Between 10 and 15 percent of blacks say, in what appears to be an uncompromising rejection of the political system, that the United States is "not worth fighting for" (30). We have no comparable figures for the white population, poor or otherwise, so it is difficult to evaluate these results. In riot areas estrangement approaches and sometimes exceeds this figure; one out of every three rioters say they would refuse to fight (31).

The data present a fairly consistent picture of alienation among the black population, particularly among the black urban poor. The surveys give no evidence that would confirm that the white poor are similarly displeased with government services (like police protection or garbage collection) or feel estranged from the political community. But there can be no question that the poor of all races feel less effective politically than do the nonpoor. National samples in 1966 and 1968 show blacks more likely than whites to feel that "government officials don't care about us." But in 1968 a sample of low income whites indicated more pronounced feelings of political impotence than blacks (32). In fact, the results of a 1968 national election survey show that feelings of political inefficacy are more widespread among the subsistence-level poor of all races (whether they are urban or rural) than among the black population generally (33).

The literature on voting behavior sustains these results, indicating that feelings of political effectiveness are related to a more general status continuum. As Lane suggests, dominant or higher status groups are more apt to feel effective in questions of civic affairs, to believe that government officials will respond to their needs, and to feel that their vote is important in the determination of policy (34).

V.O. Key, Jr., using data from the Survey Research Center surveys of 1952 and 1956, finds that college-educated respondents are much more likely to believe that government is responsive to them (35). Thompson and Horton find alienation (low sense of political efficacy) to be greatest among laborers and farmers and persons with less than a high school education (36). Finally, a path model of political participation in five nations—using a range of independent variables, including status, political information, citizen duty, political efficacy, organizational involvement, and other factors—reveals a clear intervening role for sense of efficacy. It is apparently a primary ingredient for translating social status into active political involvement (37).

Poor neighborhoods, besides exhibiting the sentiments that comprise alienation, also provide the stage on which beliefs are consummated in action. Politics, violence, culture, and despair are not simply theoretical possibilities; they are the regularized political options of the urban poor. Like other members of the larger society, residents of poor neighborhoods may vote or not vote, join a community organization or remain isolated. But whereas many communities (particularly suburban ones) are restricted to these forms of political expression, poor communities provide other alternatives. Political protests, evident in peaceful and disruptive demonstrations, are common and legitimate forms of expression in poor neighborhoods; many black neighborhoods can boast (or lament) the presence of revolutionary organizations (e.g., the Panthers) and more amorphous revolutionary alternatives, such as the riot (38). Between January, 1964, and May, 1968, 215 cities experienced some form of rioting; 49,607 people were arrested, 7942 people were wounded, and 191 people were killed (39). Survey estimates show that approximately 15 percent of riot area residents were actively engaged in the civil disturbances (40). Membership in civil rights organizations (usually the NAACP) exceeds one in five for urban blacks (41), and one might suppose that many of those members have participated in boycotts, demonstrations, sit-ins, and other protest actions.

These general findings, based on national surveys and research in poor neighborhoods across the country, are reflected in the results of Table 5.1 and the more general comments expressed in interviews. Most striking, perhaps, is the consistent strain of cynicism about

Table 5.1. Political Alienation in Five Poor Neighborhoods

Alienation Measures	Neighborhoods				
	Gardner	Belmont	East Side	Summerhill	North Central
1. Sense of inefficacy					
□High	30%	35%	46%	45%	47%
	(144)	(135)	(259)	(213)	(238)
2. Policy dissatisfaction					
□High	33%	15%	58%	26%	41%
	(153)	(178)	(280)	(251)	(250)
3. System Rejection					
□High	52%	29%	51%	21%	42%
	(145)	(155)	(221)	(219)	(226)

politics evident in all five neighborhoods (42). It is a sentiment reflected in the frustration of a black organizer in North Central:

> It's all money. You'll get violations on a house and then the next day the violations aren't there. But they didn't do anything. You see, lots of the judges are landlords. There are only about two judges which are very good.

This cynicism was also apparent in Gardner where perpetual feuding, infighting, and favoritism to family dominate the public images of Model Cities and the Poverty Program, and where public office is viewed as an Anglo domain, secure from Mexican-American influence. The elected political leadership of San Jose is entirely Anglo; the only Mexican-American councilman was appointed to fill a vacancy.

Appalachian whites have almost always proved cynical about government officials—a reputation the officials themselves have done little to dispel. Prohibition brought a form of random law enforcement marked by hypocrisy, payoffs, and personal vendettas, reinforcing a distrust already apparent in the traditionally cozy relationship between governing officials and mining and timber moguls. Caudill writes: "The mountaineer developed the deep-seated conviction that he is governed not by just laws but by corrupt and venal men—men who would betray him when it was to their purpose and reward him when it was to their gain" (43). Their politics is not one of public responsiveness, but of strings and commitments to friends, family, and wealth (44). The Mayor's lament about cynicism and mistrust in the Belmont area suggests that these sentiments have not been confined to eastern Kentucky.

The somewhat shared cynicism about government responsiveness disintegrates, however, in the widely divergent evaluations of concrete public policy. In the two Northern black neighborhoods (North Central and the East Side) residents are extremely critical of government performance and share a more generalized contempt for the political community. It is these sentiments above all else that fit the rhetoric of community leaders, black militants, and the general public's perception of black political belief. Blacks in North Central and the East Side are critical of public education, police practices in the ghetto, and in some respects, the country itself. Rather than the faith and hope evident during migration, these sentiments suggest the concerns of an Eldridge Cleaver: "Behind police brutality there is social brutality, economic brutality, and political brutality" (45). Though the black poor's statement does not achieve the coherence, articulateness, or force of that of an Eldridge Cleaver or a LeRoi Jones, it does speak of the same kind of disenchantment and alienation.

What is striking about these results is not the discontent in Northern black neighborhoods—indeed, there is considerable congruence of belief and condition—but the relative calm of Summerhill and Belmont and the ambivalent feelings in Gardner. Despite public policies that are on the whole highly unfavorable to them, Southern blacks, Appalachian whites, and Mexican-Americans remain relatively uncritical of the schools and the police; excepting Mexican-Americans, they are also fully supportive of the political community.

The Appalachian mountaineers never expected much from government and therefore were rarely critical of its failures in education, highway improvement, or other government services. A long-time resident of Letcher County, Kentucky, told me that "the Appalachian people never see government as for their benefit, but something to be shunned."

> They came from England to get away from government and they didn't want anything to do with it here. Some people moved down into blue grass country where government got started sooner and moved back into the mountains where governments were held off for another sixty years.

It took sixteen years, he explained, before the first mountain county (Floyd) constructed a courthouse. "The very first night that building was opened, someone burned it down."

Expectations for government performance have not been high, rarely anticipating government action that would materially improve or in any way change their lives. In fact, mountaineers had come to expect little from the mining and lumber companies, the unions, or the government. This detachment from institutional life led them to shun an activist or interventionist conception of politics. Ford's survey of the Appalachian region shows no single government service (including road building and upkeep, public welfare and assistance, the keeping of public records and deeds, public health service, police protection, fire protection, sanitary sewage disposal, garbage collection, recreation programs, water supply service, planning, and zoning) "for which a majority of the respondents would hypothetically raise taxes to provide or improve." Only for road building and upkeep are more than a third willing to pay increased taxes (46).

It should come as no surprise, therefore, that few of the residents of Peck's Addition are aware of plans to raze their homes, or that Belmont residents express little interest in a community service center similar to that in the black community of Hamilton, day care, improved education, or anything else. A Belmont organizer laments:

> What you never have, you never miss. We did a survey and never once did anyone mention a need for a center like this one, for recreation, for health services, or day care centers. But they never had them. So they don't know they need them.

This apparent satisfaction of Belmont residents with what their government is doing is less a consequence of what the government has or has not done than a shared expectation that there is little the government should be doing.

Summerhill stands second only to Belmont in contentment with government programs, despite the massive demolition of community housing ("people had to scramble for any hole they could find in the alley"), almost nonexistent housing construction programs, and a general governmental disregard for Summerhill's welfare. Though an Episcopal minister and a number of community organizers believe there is a new community consciousness, one that would in the future deter projects like the Atlanta Stadium, Summerhill blacks are not nearly so critical of government performance or the general political community as their brothers in the North.

The migrants who came to Summerhill with the onset of World War I entered a city that was patently segregated and very much a part of the "Old South." They came mostly from the plantation counties in Georgia, fleeing the boll weevil, hoping to find a job. But there was little reason to expect social justice, freedom, or a serious political role. Blacks were not recruited for Atlanta's burgeoning industry as they were for Northern factories. If they had been, it is probable that Atlanta would have drawn on black populations from throughout the Black Belt, as well as from the most proximate regions (47).

The black community in Summerhill was not built on an expectation for change; indeed, many of the old forms originating in the rural caste structure were maintained in Atlanta until after World War II. As late as the mid-sixties, lunch counters and many public facilities were still legally segregated. Blacks, particularly if middle-aged, were still honoring many of the social customs of the South—including homage and deference. Therefore the ability to evaluate government performance, unfettered by the restraints and socialization patterns of the feudal South, did not come to Summerhill until very late. A new consciousness may have come over the community, as leaders suggest, but it must build on a community that is far from critical of the political system or its work.

The Mexican-American residents of Gardner demonstrate considerably more reserve about the political community, reflecting perhaps a continuing attachment to another political system (see Chapter Six), as well as reflecting the Southern blacks' and Appalachian whites' contentment with specific government policies and institutions (48). This nonalienative tone may reflect what Stan Steiner (49), Cesar Chavez (50), and many others have called a *"patron* syndrome"—a pattern of social relations based upon paternalism, deference, and hierarchy. Whether or not there is such a "syndrome" (and there is considerable dispute on this point), political leaders in Gardner are quick to note the respect usually paid those in official positions. Residents listen to authorities and if they do not heed them, they are reluctant to challenge them. A community worker for the Human Relations Commission, for example, points out the difficulties in showing parents the legitimate grievances of their children:

> The teachers are the "maestro," the knowledgeable people. When a child has a grievance, the parents always blame the child. These demands [made by children at a local school] are very difficult for a parent to believe. They have always been taught to respect the teacher's judgment in these matters.

When a former board chairman of the local poverty program verbally attacked a U.S. Superior Court Judge for racist comments, his words were measured and respectful (51).

> The Mexican-American community will not rest until justice is done, and I feel Judge Chargin will realize this. He is an American, he believes in one God, the man has a conscience and I think he will take it upon himself to resign. Then the Mexican-American people can have faith in the judicial system of California and the United States.

These expressions of deference and respect are stark when compared to the rhetoric of other poor neighborhoods; they underline the relatively uncritical views Gardner residents hold toward the police department, the school system, and other governmental programs (52).

Although political alienation is pronounced in poor neighborhoods, the pattern of response is far from uniform. Belmont residents, for example, are singularly uncritical of public policy and committed to the larger political community, whereas Gardner residents are the least expressive of political futility and the most estranged from the political system. In both Northern black neighborhoods—the East Side and North Central—pronounced estrangement is apparent on all indicators of political alienation. Summerhill shows considerably less discontent with the schools, police, and the political community than other black neighborhoods, but shares with them a sense of political inefficacy.

The alienation model, we shall see, clarifies some of these differences, drawing the essential linkages between these beliefs and the tone and intensity of community politics.

III   POLITICAL ALIENATION AND POLITICAL ACTION

Our analysis is built on the dynamic relationships proposed by the alienation model. The familiar categories of political alienation—sensed inefficacy, policy dissatisfaction, and political system rejection—are the principal ingredients of belief; violence and politics are the elements of response (53). Through a statistical inquiry into these relationships, we attempt to capture the thinking, perhaps the calculation, that dictates the varying political responses of the poor.

Finally, the role of political alienation and its relationship with political expression is examined in light of evidence from these five neighborhoods.

A. *Approach*

The pattern of association between measures of dissatisfaction and measures of political expression are presented diagrammatically in Figure 5.2 using the methods and assumptions of path analysis. The primary determinants of political expression in the model are sensed inefficacy and policy dissatisfaction to one side and system rejection to the other. It provides, consequently, a test of the principal relationships in the alienation model: how do feelings of political futility and public policy evaluations interact to produce violence, politics, or withdrawal? Does disidentification with politics in general foster a receptivity to violence?

The impact of any one factor on another is measured by the path coefficient or standardized regression coefficient. The path coefficient is a measure of impact, with the effect of all other independent variables controlled (54). It is also standardized to enable the reader to make comparisons between two or more independent variables. The coefficient .183 between policy dissatisfaction and receptivity to politics, for example, means that a one

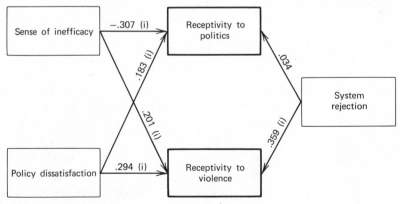

(i) Significant at the .001 level.

Figure 5.2. Alienation as path model.

standard deviation change in policy dissatisfaction produces a .183 standard deviation change in the dependent variable, receptivity to politics. We might also conclude that the impact of political dissatisfaction is less significant than that observed for sensed inefficacy, the latter's coefficient in absolute terms reaching .307. Because path coefficients take into account the impact of other factors in the model, they allow the analyst to compute the combined impact of relevant path coefficients (55).

Path analysis as developed by both Duncan and Boudon and causal modeling in the Simon-Blalock tradition assume that residual terms are uncorrelated and that there are no factors exogenous to the model which produce spurious associations between factors depicted in the model (56). It would be reasonable for us to assume, however, that many of the relations that might be depicted in the alienation model are in fact the spurious result of factors such as age, sex, and education. If women, for example, were more supportive of the political system and disinclined, for any number of reasons, to engage in violence, the resulting association between system rejection and receptivity to violence could prove misleading. But correlation analysis reveals that the zero-order relationship between alienation measures and indicators of politics and violence are not substantially reduced by the introduction of controls for education, age, and sex. We can consider the relationships in the model to be unfettered by these three exogenous factors at least.

B. The Logic of Alienation

The path model presented in Figure 5.2 confirms important aspects of the alienation model: it demonstrates the integral relationship between patterns of estrangement and political options and the mediating role of calculated effectiveness. The combination of paths most likely to produce political involvement includes dissatisfaction with public policy (positive path) and, more important, a feeling that government officials are responsive to citizen overtures (negative path). This seeming paradox of contentment and dissatisfaction represents for poor individuals a provocation—a reason to become involved politically—and an inducement—a reason to believe involvement will not prove futile. But alter the individual's belief that he can affect government policy and the result (evident in the two positive paths from sense of inefficacy and policy dissatisfaction to receptivity to violence) will more likely involve political violence. The calculation of effectiveness in conventional politics, as predicted by the model, mediates an individual's anger with public policy, helping him to choose between conventional forms of political expression and political violence.

The receptivity of poor individuals to violence is a consequence of alienated feelings and convictions, whatever the variety or combination. Sensed inefficacy, policy dissatisfaction, and notably, system rejection each show an independent and statistically significant relationship with the receptivity to violence. These results are consistent with the notion of mediation, as well as with the immediate linkage between generalized dissatisfaction and the resort to violence.

A similar confirmation emerges from the results of Table 5.2. It is obvious that the highest levels of political involvement follow from strong policy dissatisfaction accompanied by a feeling that politics can work (low sense of inefficacy). Participation drops off sharply when discontent with government policy is combined with a belief that politics is futile. Associated with that calculation (as we hypothesized and as, perhaps, logic would have it) is a significant increase in the number of respondents who look to political violence. In this sense, a dislike for what the government is doing will lead to violence or to politics, depending upon the perceived responsiveness of public officials.

The residual group that falls outside the politics of pressure, protest, or violence includes those whom we have called the "politically apathetic." Their general contentment with what the government is doing, accompanied by a sense of political futility, provides neither provocation nor rational basis for political involvement. Willingness to engage in conventional politics is minimal and their contentment with policy outputs ensures little inclination toward violence. Their position, in effect, is one of nonchoice and noncalculation. It is simply a withdrawal. Those who are apathetic see politics as not caring about them and so see no reason to care about it (57).

Table 5.2. Political Alienation and Political Expression

	Percentage "High" Receptivity to Politics	Percentage "High" Receptivity to Violence
System rejection		
High	73%	70%
	(335)	(335)
Low	65%	44%
	(486)	(486)
High policy dissatisfaction—sense of inefficacy		
High	63%	73%
	(177)	(177)
Low	84%	68%
	(174)	(174)
Low policy dissatisfaction—sense of inefficacy		
High	48%	49%
	(196)	(196)
Low	70%	41%
	(320)	(320)

C. Alienation and Mediation in Five Poor Neighborhoods

There can be little doubt that those involved in organizing the politics of poor communities are sensitive to these considerations. Black leaders in the East Side and North Central, some of whom express the most violent, anti-white sentiments and who appear most dissatisfied with government institutions and businessmen, often express feelings of political competence, despite the large degree of unresponsiveness on the part of the institutions with which they deal. A militant black from the East Side, an organizer of radically aliented black youth, states (58):

> I have some hope America can solve its problems. Otherwise, I would give up what I'm doing now and start organizing in another manner.

An aide to Mayor Cavanaugh in Detroit feels that the voice of protest in city politics has dropped off noticeably during the term of a new, more conservative Mayor, not because people in the ghettos are any more satisfied with life in the city but because they see less reason to join protest activity.

> These groups used to come down to City Hall and bang on Cavanaugh's door, because they know he would listen. They'd march on this place and really move it around. But no one comes down to Gribb's office. Why should they? They know he isn't listening.

For many of those active in the politics of poor neighborhoods, the affirmation of effectiveness is an act of faith rather than a perception of reality. They recognize early in their work that the troubles, frustration, and harassment would become unbearable if at the same time they believed politics were futile. An organizer commented on the work of a tenants' organization that included large, well publicized demonstrations and negotiations with city agencies and the utilities companies:

> Sometimes you think you're hitting your head against a brick wall. You look out there and nothing has changed. Then you start seeing the little things and the puzzle comes together. You realize you are doing something. You realize you *can* do something. . . .You have to believe that.

She understood the necessity of sensed effectiveness, regardless of the objective probabilities of the situation. Political estrangement, activists realize, must be tempered, perhaps mediated, by feelings of political effectiveness.

The results in these five poor neighborhoods, confirmed more generally in the preceding section, bear out this logic. Where the poor express dissatisfaction with the schools, the police, or other aspects of government performance, but feel that officials are responsive to their demands, both membership in organizations and receptivity to politics are enhanced. Participation drops off markedly, however, where these attitudes are inverted. Contentment with public policy and feelings of political futility produce limited commitments to conventional politics. Evaluations of government performance and political effectiveness apparently provide the provocations and inducements for participation, helping the individual determine whether he should turn to or away from politics.

These determinant relationships between estrangement and political expression provide a key to personal decision making; they also provide some guidance in explaining the political permutations of poor neighborhoods. The placid, sometimes undetectable politics of Belmont, the intense politics of the two Northern black communities, the seemingly aberrant politics of Southern blacks, and the fractionalized, somewhat confused politics in Gardner do not differ randomly without reference to belief. These community variations follow logically (though not perfectly) from the system of thought that we have called political alienation.

These attitudes are apparent in the extreme reconciliation of Belmont residents, suggesting little provocation for political involvement and a remote basis for political violence. On the other hand, the consistent estrangement of the East Side and North Central residents makes explicable the receptivity to violence that prevails there and, to some extent, the willingness to participate in more conventional politics. What appears in Summerhill as an uncharacteristic passivity, is, in fact, the consequence of an uncritical view of the police, schools, and other services in conjunction with a more generalized contentment with political life. Gardner remains a somewhat confused case, reflecting only mild feelings of political ineffectiveness, a middle-range discontent with public policy, and a high level of detachment from the political community. In fact, the politics of Gardner are equally contradictory—substantial organizational involvement, but low electoral participation and minimal receptivity to politics (59). The aversion to violence in Gardner is obviously unreflective of attitudes toward politics generally, but is consistent with attitudes regarding government responsiveness and public policy (60).

We have established that the politics of poor neighborhoods are divergent; but so too are the patterns of alienative beliefs. In the interweaving of this variability there has emerged some persistent associations between belief and politics and, as a result, important underlying continuities in the political styles of poor neighborhoods.

Chapter Six

The Politics of

Collective Understanding

· · · · · · · · · · · · · · · ·

When Stokely Carmichael injected the phrase "black power" into the Meredith march, he brought the questions of race consciousness and group identity to a new level of prominence. W. E. B. DuBois' earlier pronouncement that the "problem of the twentieth century is the problem of the color-line" (1) was to be elaborated in the mid-sixties by articulate and expansive observations on blackness and racism. A young rebel affirmed the ultimate meaning of "black power" (2):

> We shall beg no more. You shall define our best interests no longer.
> Take your Mississippi hand and your Cicero Christ and may both of
> them be damned.

"Black power," its advocates proclaimed, is a newly awakened comprehension of subordination and the power relationships that underlie it. It means that a black man in America now understands the necessity for a "black panther on his side when he and his family must endure . . . " (3). It means recognizing the realities of political influence and the necessity of group power.

The National Committee of Negro Churchmen declared (4):

> We must not apologize for the existence of this form of group
> power, for we have been oppressed as a group, not as individuals. We
> will not find our way out of that oppression until both we and
> America accept the need for Negro Americans as well as for Jews,
> Italians, Poles and white Anglo-Saxon Protestants, among others, to
> have and to wield group power.

The cries of black spokesmen were demanding of the social order
and destructive of traditional multiracial ties. But the concern with
group power, meaning, and solidarity is in no sense peculiar or
quixotic. The search for group identity draws upon a proud heritage
shared by the Irish, the Jews, the Greeks, and almost every ethnic
group that has struggled for acceptance or respect in this country.
The Irish Catholic Church—an edifice embued with nationalist spirit
and a vehicle for segregated education and social life—was built on
the rock of group solidarity (5). Jews also groped for a distinctive
American identity, struggling with problems of acculturation, group
purpose, and "Zionism" (6). Indeed, preoccupation with separatist
development or concern for a lost identity are inherent in the
struggle for self-preservation and advancement. No minority or
oppressed group can escape or has escaped the questions of who
"we" are and who "they" are.

The feelings a group develops about itself and about other groups
are significant for politics; they may prove more important to
political mobilization than attitudes toward politics themselves.
Discovering oneself and one's relation to dominant or competing
groups is not simply an adventure in identity devoid of practical
consequences. Identity and politics are inseparable. From group
identity emerges group purpose, modes of expression, objects of
contempt, and reasons for rejoicing; in politics groups find the
vehicles for expression (as the Irish, the Italians, and now the blacks
have discovered).

We find in this chapter that group consciousness is important to
the life of all poor neighborhoods, helping to ensure the distinctive
aspects of their politics, even in the face of common modernizing
circumstances. Blacks, Appalachian whites, and Mexican-Americans
all struggle to understand their group and others; each group has
evolved a sense of self and society and of the relation of one to the

other. Out of these group identities—oppositional in one case, traditional in another, taciturn in the last—have emerged the group responses that have been reflected in community politics: the violence of the East Side, the pacifism of Gardner, the nonpolitics of Belmont.

I DIMENSIONS OF GROUP CONSCIOUSNESS

Group consciousness cannot be understood as a simple dichotomy between "us" and "them," our group and their group, the good guys and the bad guys. Few groups see life that simply; the lines in conflict situations are rarely that clearly drawn. We cannot assume that the consciousness of blacks, Appalachian whites, or Mexican-Americans is unidimensional, encompassing all they feel for their brothers and all their reactions to dominant groups or authority. Group consciousness is a complex phenomenon, involving an assessment of group values and purpose, personal interests, and the values and opportunities of the larger society. Establishing an identity of interest, though evident to the public as polarization or separatism, emerges from a more subtle questioning of one's goals, the reality of group experience, and the nature of dominant groups and institutions.

To say that blacks are committed to blacks, or Mexican-Americans to Mexican-Americans, is an observation without serious content. Little is known about the nature of the commitment—the meaning it provides members of the group or its importance in evaluating those who are not black or Mexican-American. An analysis of group consciousness must go beyond the counting of "black power" adherents and consider consciousness as a guide to group life. We must ask of consciousness what the poor of all races must ask themselves: what is it we share? What do we want out of public life? What groups or factors are responsible for our condition?

A. Factor Analyzing Group Consciousness

The civil rights struggle of the early sixties, the riots of the late sixties, and the aftermath have brought to public attention certain key words including "black capitalism," "green power," "voting power," "black power," "separatism," "racism," "militancy," and many others. The respondents in the Mexican-American and three black communities were asked to respond to a number of questions posing the issues raised by these terms.

1. Do you agree or disagree? Stores in a black (Mexican-American) neighborhood should be owned and run by black people (Mexican-Americans).
2. Do you agree or disagree? Black people (Mexican-Americans) would do better if they only voted for blacks (Mexican-Americans).
3. Do you agree or disagree? Black people (Mexican-Americans) will have very little say in the government unless they all decide to vote for the same candidates.
4. Do you agree or disagree? Blacks (Mexican-Americans) blame too many of their problems on whites.
5. Do you agree or disagree? Black people (Mexican-Americans) who want to work hard can get ahead just as easily as anyone else.
6. Do you think black (Mexican-American) elected officials generally can be trusted?
7. Do you believe schools with mostly black (Mexican-American) children should have mostly black (Mexican-American) teachers?
8. Do you agree or disagree? In deciding how to vote, you should pay more attention to a man's stand on the race issue than to what party he belongs to.
9. Do you think the idea of "Black Power" is a good idea or a bad idea?
10. Some black leaders have suggested setting up a separate nation inside America run by black people only. Do you think this is a good idea?

Factor analysis enables us to draw out of these items the underlying factors (or themes) that dominate the responses to "race issues." We are searching, in effect, for the "real questions" that the poor ask themselves when contemplating their identity of interests and their feelings about those who are not poor. The concern with ownership of commercial enterprises, electoral solidarity, and the efficacy of hard work may prove interesting in themselves, but common patterns of response may reveal yet more important observations about group solidarity or group polarization. By searching for these factors, the analysis of group commitments can proceed beyond the headlines "community control" and "racial hostilities," and begin to capture the feelings that structure group commitments (7).

B.   Factors in Black Identity

The factor analysis of these items (Table 6.1) demonstrates at the outset that although the term "black power" and the proposal for a separate black nation raise the public ire and provoke numerous studies (like this one), ghetto residents' evaluations of them do not relate to each other nor to the responses to other items employed in the analysis. There is no underlying dimension of race consciousness that is captured by the straightforward reaction of ghetto residents to the terms "black power" and "separate nation." They apparently represent the response of blacks to a public controversy, divorced from underlying dimensions of group consciousness.

Other factors, however, account for considerable variance in response and make substantive sense. In black communities, three items cohere to a factor we might label "black unity" or "black autonomy." These items explain twice the amount of variance of either "black power" or "separate nation" evaluations, and they are central to the themes underlying traditional ethnic politics in America—economic control of commercial establishments in the neighborhood, bloc voting, and casting ballots for "your own kind." Together these questions suggest a picture of political action not very different from that advocated by Stokely Carmichael and Charles Hamilton. They write (8):

> The concept of Black Power rests on a fundamental premise: *Before a group can enter the open society, it must first close ranks.* By this we mean that group solidarity is necessary before a group can operate effectively from a bargaining position of strength in a pluralistic society. Traditionally, each new ethnic group in this society has found the route to social and political viability through the organization of its own institutions with which to represent its needs within the larger society. Studies in voting behavior specifically, and political behavior generally, have made it clear that politically the American pot has not melted. Italians vote for Rubino over O'Brien, Irish for Murphy over Goldberg, etc.

The first factor in black communities poses this issue: to what extent should black people come together and form an effective political bloc? It concerns the willingness of people to seek common cause at the ballot box and in the market place.

The second factor includes two closely related items—whether

Table 6.1. *Factor Analysis of Black and Mexican-American Items*

| | Factors | | | | | |
Black Items	1	2	3	4	5	Communality
Stores in black areas should be black owned.	.731	.178	-.205	.171	-.054	.640
Black people should vote only for black candidates.	.710	-.211	-.024	.033	.259	.617
Blacks should vote for the same candidate.	.735	-.016	.196	-.065	.042	.585
Blacks blame too many of their problems on whites.	.096	.788	-.062	.056	.085	.644
Black people can succeed as well as anyone else.	-.108	.826	-.086	-.040	-.057	.706
Black officials can be trusted.	.209	-.060	.758	.167	.118	.664
Black schools should have black teachers.	.219	.107	-.712	.135	.207	.627
Black power is a good idea.	.370	.145	.019	.720	.016	.676
Support separate nation for black people.	.108	.037	.049	.029	.960	.938

Table 6.1. Factor Analysis of Black and Mexican-American Items (continued)

	Factors					Communality
	1	2	3	4	5	
Black Items (continued)						
Blacks should vote according to stand on race issue, not party.	.468	.170	-.032	-.661	-.040	.687
Sums of squares	2.052	1.445	1.178	1.040	1.063	6.784

	Factors					Communality
	1	2	3	4	5	
Mexican-American Items						
Mexican-Americans can succeed as well as anyone else.	.848	-.000	.143	-.091	-.132	.766
Mexican-Americans should vote for the same candidate.	.674	-.012	-.033	-.022	.435	.645
Mexican-Americans should vote only for Mexican-American candidates.	.408	-.648	-.338	.111	-.016	.714
Stores in Mexican-American areas should be Mexican owned.	-.202	-.849	.168	-.004	-.040	.792

Table 6.1. *Factor Analysis of Black and Mexican-American Items (continued)*

	Factors					Communality
	1	2	3	4	5	
Mexican-American Items (continued)						
Mexican-American schools should have Mexican-American teachers.	.214	-.477	.209	-.483	.105	.561
Mexican-Americans blame too many of their problems on whites (Anglos).	.097	-.072	.917	.037	.064	.861
Mexican-American officials can be trusted.	.015	.068	-.085	-.912	.050	.847
Mexican-Americans should vote according to stand on race issue, not party.	.020	.016	.074	-.079	.936	.889
Sums of squares	1.437	1.379	1.062	1.094	1.103	6.075

blacks have equal opportunity in society and whether whites are unduly faulted by critical blacks. These items pose a provocative question for the black community: who is to be held accountable for the social and economic conditions of black people in America—the social order that establishes a context for black failure or the pathologies of black people themselves? The question raises a fundamental moral choice between introspection, self-appraisal, and personal improvement on the one hand, and social responsibility and social change on the other.

These two dimensions enable us to grapple seriously with the meaning of black consciousness outside the glare of debate that rages in the public media. We are not speaking of power—at least not in a simple sense—or of the separation of black people from the remainder of the white population. Black consciousness is (1) a belief that black people should act in concert to gain economic and political benefits, and (2) a sense that the root causes for collective black disadvantage can be found in the larger white society (9).

C. Factors in Mexican-American Identity

The results of the factor analysis on Mexican-American items indicate some continuity between the two types of racial communities, but they also indicate an important divergence of response. Factor two is not identical in composition to factor one in the black communities, but is apparently tapping the same notion—Mexican-Americans should be together and autonomous. They should own the stores in their neighborhoods, should vote together, and should face teachers of their own race in the classrooms. In a more ambiguous way, factor one in the Mexican-American community reveals a similar dimension, including attitudes toward bloc voting and, in weaker terms, voting for "your own kind." But factor one is confused by an issue that is part of a fundamentally different dimension in the black communities. Whether Mexican-Americans can attain success goals in the larger society is part of factor one in this analysis; whether Mexican-Americans blame too many of their problems on whites forms an entirely independent factor, divorced from any conception of group unity.

An extremely important pattern of response is emerging that we take note of here and elaborate on later. Conceptions of togetherness and common group interests, are important in the Mexican-American community as they are in black communities. Both factors one and two raise this issue. But what does not emerge in the Mexican-American community is an unambiguous notion of societal or race responsibility. Group consciousness in the Mexican-American community includes many of the beliefs that make up traditional ethnic politics, but it does *not* incorporate the choice facing black residents between self-appraisal and social responsibility. The absence of such a dimension, we shall discover, is integrally involved with the effects group consciousness has on political mobilization and with broader issues in group identity.

II   THREE MEANINGS OF CONSCIOUSNESS.

> One day he was reading the book, and it suddenly came to him, and he said to himself, if I'm proud of me, I don't need to hate Mr. Charlie's people. I don't want to. I don't need to. If I love me, I can also love the whole damn human race. Black, brown, yellow, white (10).

We have singled out two important aspects of group consciousness that are only vaguely captured by the data used in this analysis: one is assertive, the other oppositional. A group can search out its traditional values, its frequently overlooked and "disreputable" leaders, its history, and its intrinsic worth. The basis of group consciousness in this case is a turning inward on the reality of group experience and a confrontation with the larger society based on it. But group consciousness may also be oppositional—primarily a response to society's intrusions, a critique of its presumed "racist" practices and institutions. This response is antipathetic, dwelling only secondarily on aspects of the culture and history that, although indeed real, are often removed from the present experience of the group. A third form of consciousness—in fact a residual of the other two—asks few questions of history or culture, and rarely contemplates questions of guilt or responsibility. Although it recognizes distinct qualities of the group, it turns inward and becomes aloof from activism, assertion, or pride. Feelings of group distinctiveness are tinged with a sense of inferiority and resignation. Solidarity provides an escape from, rather than a vehicle for, confrontation.

A.   Black Consciousness: An Oppositional Response

Group identity in the black communities stresses two essential themes: the political autonomy of black Americans and the role of white society in the "black condition." Although both are important to black consciousness, the evidence that is considered in this chapter suggests the latter is preeminent. Black consciousness is in large measure derived from feelings of political alienation, and together with notions of estrangement, fosters a broadened receptivity to violence. In addition, the oppositional aspects of black identity distinguish consciousness in the black community from that in Mexican-American neighborhoods. By emphasizing black consciousness as an oppositional response, then, we reflect the importance of the theme among the black poor and also highlight that aspect of black consciousness that makes black identity a special case of group consciousness.

These themes are posed by Malcolm X, for he, more than any recent black leader, has portrayed the plight and worth in blackness. Even his search, however, dwelt on a critique of white society. He understood what it is to be black, but, as Floyd Barbour noted, "he preached who the enemy was" (11).

> What you and I need to do is learn to forget our differences. When we come together, we don't come together as Baptists or Methodists. You don't catch hell because you're a Baptist, and you don't catch hell because you're a Methodist. . .you don't catch hell because you're a Democrat or a Republican, you don't catch hell because you're a Mason or an Elk, and you sure don't catch hell because you're an American; because if you were an American, you wouldn't catch hell. You catch hell because you're a black man, you catch hell, all of us catch hell, for the same reason.
>
> We have a common enemy. We have this in common. We have a common oppressor, a common exploiter, and a common discriminator (12).

The assertion of race values in this case is not a simple rediscovery of one's worth; it is a response to another group's assertion of its race goals. Malcolm X himself said that the black man's racism is produced by white racism. "My reaction is the reaction of a human being, reacting to defend himself and protect himself" (13).

Other black nationalist movements that rely on black symbols, African culture, and nationalism also emphasize oppositional themes in their appeal. A Black Muslim prosecutor in a mock trial of the white man offered the following summation (14).

> I charge the white man with being the greatest liar on earth! I charge the white man with being the greatest drunkard on earth. . . . I charge the white man with being the greatest gambler on earth. I charge the white man, ladies and gentlemen of the jury, with being the greatest peace-breaker on earth. . . . I charge the white man with being the greatest deceiver on earth. I charge the white man with being the greatest trouble-maker on earth. So, therefore, ladies and gentlemen of the jury, I ask you, bring back a verdict of guilty as charged.

The guilty verdict took only a few seconds.

The oppositional theme is even clearer in the cry, "black power," since it dwells only peripherally on African culture and black history. Its meaning is found in an appreciation of control and coercion, in the centrality of power in racial oppression. Power in America, Carmichael says, is "white power," even if few people consider it in these terms (15). If the existing position of the races is to be reconstructed, that effort must concern itself with power. Black people will have "to consolidate behind their own, so that they can bargain from a position of strength" (16). This unity of purpose, coupled with a cultural consciousness, enables black people to alter the pattern of oppression. LeRoi Jones writes (17):

> Black Power as an actuality, will only exist in a Black-oriented, Black-controlled space. It is White Culture that rules with White Guns. Our only freedom will be in bringing a Black Culture to Power. We Cannot Do This Unless We Are Cultured. That is, Consciously Black.

Black consciousness and black culture, however, are necessitated by white guns.

In building an oppositional consciousness, many black movements have sought to recapture a sense of being black, of having roots in another land, in other religions, and in another history. Through such symbols leaders have sought to create black movements that are not wholly oppositional in their formulation. Frequently it has not mattered where the land or the history was found as long as it was not white. C. Eric Lincoln writes (18):

> It matters little whether the homeland of the dispersed Black Nation is said to be Asia or Africa. For the black nationalist, Afro-Asia is a single continent, and the Black Man's Zion is where the white man is not.

E. U. Essien-Udom maintains that Black Muslims perceive a separate nation in dual terms—as a "Negro homeland" and as an image of a "post-Apocalypse Black Nation" (19).

Though black Americans have taken pride in the emergence of nation-states throughout Africa, it is unclear how much the symbolic emphasis on African history and Middle-Eastern religions means to the mass of black people (20). Although blacks trace their ancestral past to the African continent, they have been severed from that history by the radical imposition of the slave traffic and slave institutions. Blacks were brought to America under the most brutal conditions (ten of fifteen million dying in transit) (21) and incorporated into a system that sought to divorce them from almost all previous experience and culture. Stanley Elkins writes (22):

> Actually, a great deal had happened to him already. Much of his past had been annihilated; nearly every prior connection had been severed. Not that he had really "forgotten" all these things—his family and kinship arrangements, his language, the tribal religion, the taboos, the name he had once borne, and so on—but none of it any longer carried much meaning. The old values, the sanctions, the standards, already unreal, could no longer furnish him guides for conduct, for adjusting to the expectations of a complete new life.

The continuity with the African past was further disrupted by the mixing together in the process of sale of different African tribes (though mostly West African) (23) and later by mixed African and European parentage (with which blacks were not permitted to identify).

Even if we accede to the view of some historians that important elements of West African culture have been preserved in slavery and post-slavery black communities, it does not follow that blacks are cognizant of this continuity or that they find it salient. The image of the black "mammy," with kerchief-wrapped head, has been traced to practices common among West African women (24). Though important to anthropologists (and increasingly, to vanguard black leaders), this linkage does not, by itself, create the sort of cultural meaning that shapes group identity. It has not been established that black people are aware that the spectacle of "possession" common to the black church is also prevalent in West African tribal religions (25). The continuity between the Damascus Baptist Church in Macon County and the tribal religions of West Africa may prove important in creating a cultural bond and commitment, but it is a bond that must be created in the minds of the people. The consistency of idioms and grammatical forms in West Africa and the American South is very likely hidden from black people by the more immediate and more profound influence of English and European cultural forms.

Because of this separation from tradition, some recent black revolutionary spokesmen have questioned whether the African experience can be useful to American blacks. Claude Lightfoot, a black Marxist, has faulted Carmichael and Hamilton for leaning "toward the error of rigidly equating the condition of black America with that of Africa" (27). He indicates that the liberation struggle in the United States must instead come to terms with a uniquely American experience. Frantz Fanon, perhaps the best known of the black revolutionaries, also concludes that American blacks must recognize their essential separation from African tradition and experience. He writes (28):

> But little by little the American Negroes realized that the essential problems confronting them were not the same as those that confronted the African Negroes. The Negroes of Chicago only resemble the Nigerians or the Tanganyikans in so far as they were all defined in relation to the whites. But once the first comparisons had been made and subjective feelings were assuaged, the American Negroes realized that the objective problems were fundamentally heterogeneous.

Except for short-term interest in African events or pangs of pride, black Americans have not demonstrated a strong identification with African history and culture. Throughout the growth of the Black Star Lines under Garvey's tutelage, the *Chicago Defender* incessantly posed the question: "It might be interesting to count noses and see just how many there are among us who hail from Africa. . ." (29). Malcolm X himself recalled (30):

> I have never understood why, after hearing as much as I did of these kinds of things, I somehow never thought, then, of the black people in Africa. [Malcolm X's father was a Garveyite.] My image of Africa, at that time, was of naked savages, cannibals, monkeys and tigers and steaming jungles.

W. E. B. DuBois expressed his own frustration when in the early twentieth century he tried to stress the black man's unity with blacks in other parts of the world (31).

> . . .I had emerged with a program of Pan-Africanism, as organized protection of the Negro world led by American Negroes. But American Negroes were not interested.

This section stresses the oppositional theme in black consciousness and consequently minimizes those elements of group identity predicated on tradition or a cultural integration. It does not question the existence of a group tradition, but emphasizes those aspects of consciousness that make black identity distinctive and that are likely to explain unique aspects of black politics. The formulation is unidimensional and overstated, of course, but it does not preclude a cultural integration or the increasing relevance of the African experience. All black neighborhoods, for example, display the cultural apparatus identified with soul—"preachers, disc jockeys, soul singers, emcees, and comedians." From this apparatus a group sense emerges—a feeling that black people understand each other, that all have something in common (32). "The soul ideology," one author maintains, "ministers to the needs for identity and solidarity" (33). The diffusion of soul through the black community brings home to everyone the burden black people have borne, their stoic resolve, the need to "keep on pushing" or the assurance "you can make it if you try." It accentuates their language, their walk, their feelings, and the honesty in being black (34). But although soul identity provides a cultural tradition, it is rooted in plight and the effort to cope with poverty and oppression. It is a witness to personal struggle and contempt for white people. The solidarity that emerges from soul, therefore, reflects both themes in black identity—opposition and solidarity.

The black struggle in recent years has begun to bridge the chasm that existed between the black historical experience and the immediate situation; the movement is increasingly spearheaded by cultural and political activists and the young. The wearing of a dashiki or other African garb, the learning of African languages, and the heralding of tribal heroes help lay a foundation for solidarity that transcends the oppositional thrust in current forms of consciousness. Although it is difficult to tell how far black consciousness has been transformed by a growing awareness of transcontinental roots, there can be little doubt that the process of self-examination and identity formation is going on.

Black people in America may be going through a process of discovery similar to the quest of Ralph Ellison's invisible man (35).

> I was pulled this way and that for longer than I can remember. And my problem was that I always tried to go in everyone's way but my own. I have also been called one thing and then another while no one really wished to hear what I called myself. So after years of trying to adopt the opinions of others I finally rebelled.

For years, black Americans have been called one thing, then another, and their consciousness, this discussion suggests, has reflected their opposition. But black leaders are seeking to name themselves (Stokely Carmichael proclaimed, "For once, black people are going to use the words they want to use") (36) and build a group consciousness that is predicated on a sense of history as well as oppression. The future of black consciousness very likely lies in continued self-examination and the efforts to make distinctive African traditions part of a larger group consciousness.

B. La Raza: Traditional Response

Oppositional themes are not central aspects of Mexican-American identity; indeed, the absense of an underlying concern with Anglo responsibility is what distinguishes group consciousness in the Mexican-American and black neighborhoods. If our data are accurate, la Raza is not, as some have suggested, "an anti-gringo thing" (37). It dwells only marginally on the misdeeds of Anglo institutions and practices. Its concern is not oppression but the shared history, values, and language that give meaning to group identity.

La Raza reflects a tradition in Mexico and the Southwest that is very much with the people of Gardner, East Los Angeles, and other urban centers throughout the region. When a young chicano in East Los Angeles called for a Mexican-American version of black power, his comments were challenged by an assertion of traditional values (38).

> I think we have to go farther than that! Brown power has to be our cultural heritage. So we can get those values that were inherent in the Indians of ancient Mexico. And we can take those same values and same culture and use it in our lives and our movement.

La Raza may involve power—by definition, a response to Anglo power—but it is more than that, for la Raza insists that power be grounded in a living tradition. La Raza is a turning inward to preserve and assert values that are still part of the beliefs and behavior of many older Mexican-Americans, particularly among the lower class. Chicanos, Eliu Carranza writes, "are seeking the meaning of their predicament not within the Anglo-white set of values, but within *la raza,* i.e., their people who have been and remain buried alive in spicville, in greaser town, in Mexitown, or, if you prefer, in *'el barrio'. . .*" (39). La Raza is a return to a history that is immediate and real, to the "Eagle and Serpent of the Aztec civilization," to "Don Benito Juarez Guardian of the Constitution," to "Emiliano Zapata" (40). It is part of a tradition that is not being rekindled so much as reassessed and reasserted. La Raza is a reliance on a history, a tradition, a civilization that people know and live. The history need not be written and learned, only affirmed (41).

The concern with tradition and history in Mexican-American communities is distinct from the emphasis on reaction in black neighborhoods. The marked segregation of blacks and chicanos (42), and the considerable antipathy of Mexican-Americans for blacks (43) is reinforced by alternate conceptions of their own racial group and the dominant white (Anglo) society. Mexican-Americans spend less time considering Anglo responsibility and devote more attention to the congruence of race pride and American citizenship. The constitution of the League of United Latin American Citizens declares their aim is "to develop within the membership of our race the best, purest and most perfect type of a true and loyal citizen of the United States of America" (44)—a sentiment echoed by many benefit societies, civil rights, and veterans organizations. Until recently few Mexican-American organizations (including the Community Service Organization, G.I. Forum, and the Mexican-American Political Association) provided a sustained attack on Anglo racial domination. Racial discrimination and disrespect were denounced, but these denunciations did not form a more general concern with racial domination.

Mexican-American solidarity is rooted in centuries of Mexican history. Its concern is for the values of their parents, the "motherland," the symbols of Mexican independence—the Aztec eagle, Mexican national holidays (May 5 and September 16) (45); its preoccupation, the security of land and spiritual guidance.

Land plays a large part in the history of rural Mexico and the southwestern United States. Americans of Mexican descent have always maintained an attachment to the land, even when their migrations led them to the cities of California. Tijerina based much of his appeal in New Mexico on the necessity of self-protection, "so that the thieves will not inherit the earth" (46). He claimed the Anglos had stolen the Mexican-American land and that action had to be taken; indeed, Tijerina and some followers seized national park land. A major effort of the Delano grape strike was the purchase of forty acres of land to act as the hub of the strike and the foundation of a cooperative movement. On a photograph of the barren plot were inscribed the words of Emiliano Zapata, "To have a piece of ground is to have roots in the community" (47). Even today, Mexican-Americans in Gardner live on small plots of land. The lawns are conscientiously cared for, the bushes and trees pruned; some plots are farmed. The tenements and row houses characteristic of Northern slums are alien to the life style and traditions of San Jose's Mexican-American population.

The immediacy of that tradition is reflected in the conventional and radical politics of Mexican-American communities. In organizing grape and lettuce workers in California, Cesar Chavez did not hesitate to wrap his movement in the traditional values and symbols. He used what one author calls "a combination of religious pageantry, evocation of the heroes of the Mexican Revolution, and nonviolent civil rights techniques. . ." (48). Chavez used a "lenten fast for peace and nonviolence" as a vehicle for uniting farm workers and garnering support from a larger public. Religious symbols reminiscent of the Latin-American Catholic Church are evident at all festivals, political gatherings, and strikes. When Chavez began his "lenten fast" a makeshift church was set up in the back of a truck and "The Forty Acres" was blessed by a priest of the Lady of Guadalupe Church in Delano.

Ties to the past have been reinforced by the continued migration from Mexico, the opportunities for visitation, and for some, the prospect of repatriation (49). Consequently the average immigrant has continuous contact with his native culture. The traditional Spanish language remains an integral part of his community life (50), and events in the "homeland" become part of the migrant's political reality, almost as much as they have for the Mexicans who never left the farm. Zapata, for example, is a folk hero for Mexicans here in the United States, even for those who have lived here all their lives. They respond to the contours of Mexican political life as the Irish followed and supported events during the Irish Civil War (51).

The Mexican-American culture has flourished because, in one sense, adherents to the dominant culture did not want to see it flourish. The Spanish-speaking population has always faced discrimination in the Southwest and as a consequence has been isolated. *The Arizona Guide* (WPA) describes the process for migrants to Arizona (though a similar pattern emerges elsewhere) (52).

> In general the Arizona-Mexicans have been segregated from the more fortunate Arizonians, both as strangers belonging to an alien race of conquered Indians, and as persons whose enforced status in the lowest economic levels make them seem less admirable than other people. They have consequently retained a firmer hold on their native customs and folklore than have other groups of foreigners less discriminated against.

In small Mexican communities in the borderlands of Texas, New

Mexico, and Arizona, and the barrios of Texas and California, pockets of Mexican culture persist and, in some senses, thrive. Spanish is the primary language, Catholicism the dominant religion; Mexico provides the principal symbols, tradition, and history. The feebleness of assimilation has ensured the feebleness of acculturation.

Finally, the culture has been preserved through what Cary McWilliams describes as the Anglo's annual "genuflect. . .before the relics of the Spanish past" (53). Almost every community in the Southwest pays homage to Mexican traditions, though the emphasis is on the "old Spanish families" (54) or the "rancheros," a more "respectable element" than the Mexican or Indian. Tucson has its *La Fiesta de los Vaqueros,* Santa Barbara its *La Fiesta* with the ride of the *Rancheros Visitadores,* and San Jose its *Fiesta de las Rosas* parade. Though there can be little doubt that the heritage portrayed is fantasy and perhaps an insult to those who live by it, the exercise cannot help but reinforce the continual presence of cultural symbols.

The concern of "la Raza," though in some ways sustained by these distortions, is not with the "pure" Spanish descent or the claims of the best families (55). It centers, rather, on the traditions of the *mestizo*—the Spanish language, the lower class family patterns, the insular ways of the *colonia,* the struggle for land and liberation (56). Some in the vanguard of "chicano nationalism" have expressed their solidarity with Puerto Rican Liberation and Black Liberation (57), perhaps even emulating their indictment of Anglo society. The thrust of la Raza, however, is more toward self-examination and the past than against the "gringos." La Raza, though fueled by a heightening struggle between Anglos and Mexican-Americans, is grounded not in alienation but in a living tradition, a culture people know and breathe.

C. "Hillbillies": A Taciturn Response

> Black children know they're black, but mountain children ain't got nothin' to relate to but coal dust.
>
> Community organizer
> Eastern Kentucky

The solidarity of Appalachian whites is not expressed in protest marches, sit-ins, cultural organizations, or civil disorders. Their commitment to one another does not emerge in confrontation with the dominant authority. They have not indicted that authority; they do not question its right to rule. Whereas blacks express solidarity in their opposition to oppression and Mexican-Americans in their knowledge and identification with the Mexican heritage, Appalachian whites find meaning in neither thread of consciousness. Their consciousness is an identification without commitment, without search, and without confrontation. Their solace is in a shared plight and a shared resignation.

The failure of Appalachian whites to recognize a community of interests that transcends family is apparent to political leaders in Belmont as it has been in Appalachia itself for some time. Ford's survey of the southern Appalachian region noted that "the bonds of loyalty to group or community are often so tenuous as to appear lacking altogether" (58). Little sense of collective interest emerges in the church, the PTA, or any social institution that transcends the family (59). Nor is there any interest in group destiny or group history. A long-time resident of Letcher County observed, "Mountain people don't know anything about their origins and don't care either."

Appalachian migrants have had to deal with substantial discrimination and harassment. Though they have not organized in civil rights organizations to confront these abuses, they have not stood by idly. A white migrant in Chicago commented (60):

> Then they'd start throwin off on the hillbillies, which they call us the hillbillies. As far as that, we knew we was hillbillies but to be called that, the way they put it, they just made a nasty word out of it. They just kept shovin the Southern people around till finally the Southern people showed em that they wasn't gonna be shoved around no more by em. Well, they just started fightin back with em.

A young woman involved in community work in the Appalachian hills recalls the struggle between blacks and whites in Cincinnati:

> When I lived in Cincinnati, somebody calling one of us a hillbilly would bring on quite a fight. That's how Randy got those scars. Knife wounds. There was always fights between the hillbillies and the niggers.

But willingness to avenge a personal insult, cloaked in the terminology of intergroup conflict, does not represent an advanced form of consciousness. Appalachian whites do not generalize specific affronts to reach an understanding of discrimination, nor do they consider the difficult problem of responsibility. Despite a difficult work situation—one that many Appalachian whites would gladly abandon—and marked discrimination in social services, very few migrants are willing to admit that discrimination plays a role in their plight. The Beech Creek study found that 90 percent of the male migrants and 70 percent of the women insist their job opportunities are no different from those of the average Ohioan. Schwartzweller and his associates write, "Beech Creekers are reluctant to talk about such things; the thought of social discrimination runs against their equalitarian grain, and a good mountaineer would never allow himself to admit to having been 'victimized' in any shape, form, or manner by others" (61). Their assessment of personal circumstances is removed from considerations of system or social responsibility. Discrimination and prejudice are personal responses, unfettered by broader patterns of oppression.

The two essential strains of consciousness—so important to the group solidarity of black and Mexican-American communities—command almost no attention from Appalachian whites. They are not concerned with patterns of oppression, nor are they preoccupied with the cultural forms that emerged on the frontier. They do, however, express a strong desire to return "home" (62). Appalachian whites long for the familiarity of the Kentucky hills. In the face of tedious production lines in Detroit, Akron, and the Ohio Valley and the fast pace of urban life, many of the migrants look back on a day when "the mountaineer sleeps back in the hollow, eating his beans and cornbread," joins in a little square dancing, and hears some "down home" music (63).

The group consciousness of Appalachian whites does not evolve out of questioning as it does with other oppressed groups. They ask nothing of their ancestors and nothing of dominant groups. Their solidarity emerges out of a common dislike (at least among the men) for their living conditions and from a willingness and an opportunity to return to the more placid life of the Kentucky hills. Consciousness for them is nostalgic and, in some senses, an escape. Whereas other groups assess similar economic and political circumstances and work to develop a community of interests or a common enemy, Appalachian whites shun these questions, choosing instead a shared longing. Their consciousness is a retreat into a period and a way of life destroyed by mining and lumber companies. It is devoid of confrontation, self-examination, or struggle.

III GROUP CONSCIOUSNESS IN POOR COMMUNITIES

The themes of autonomy and responsibility give meaning to generalized feelings of group solidarity, but they do not dictate the *level* of commitment in either black or Mexican-American neighborhoods. The poor certainly ask questions of their heritage and of dominant groups, but their answers are not dictated by the existence of the questions. We would not predict, for example, simply because "black power" is an issue, that large numbers of residents advocate it. In this section we find that, despite the importance of group consciousness and the prominence of certain themes, poor communities vary markedly in the extent to which they offer solidary responses. These differences exist both between Mexican-American and black neighborhoods and between Northern and Southern black communities.

Mexican-American identity emerges directly from a living tradition, a common language, isolation from mainstream society, and renewed relations with the homeland. Gardner and San Jose, no less than Mexican-American communities throughout the Southwest, provide these ingredients. Spanish is the primary language in the barrio; its prominence is assured by Spanish radio programming, Spanish newspapers, and visits to Mexico. A Mexican-American in the Mayfair District of San Jose recalls her mother's efforts to instill in her a feeling for the Mexican heritage (64):

> My mother never stopped telling us about the old days in Mexico. . . . She never tired of telling us stories of her native village in Guanajuato; she never let us children forget the things that her village was noted for, its handicrafts and arts; its songs and its stories about the "big men" in the village and their accomplishments. She made it all sound so beautiful with her descriptions of the mountains and the lakes, the old traditions, the happy people, and the dances

and weddings and fiestas. From the time I was a small child I always wanted to go back to Mexico and see the village where my mother was born.

But despite the strong influence of the Mexican heritage, the number of adherents to a strong Mexican identity is limited. Though the question of group identity is salient for Mexican-Americans, few Gardner residents show solidarity in their responses (see Table 6.2). Moreover, conflicting views on this issue—the desirability of assimilation versus acculturation—have produced identifiable social groups with differing commitments to cultural autonomy. Some Gardner residents call themselves "Mexicans." They are virtually unconcerned with "la Raza" or other political slogans; their stay in the United

Table 6.2a. Group Autonomy (i)

	Neighborhoods			
Identification	Gardner (ii)	East Side	Summerhill	North Central
Low				
Zero	21%	24%	16%	30%
One	41%	31%	34%	37%
Two	27%	28%	22%	22%
Three	12%	17%	28%	10%
High	(153)	(280)	(251)	(250)

(i) Group autonomy is formed by counting affirmative responses to the following questions:
1. Stores in a black (Mexican-American) neighborhood should be owned and run by black people (Mexican-Americans).
2. Black people (Mexican-Americans) would do better if they only voted for blacks (Mexican-Americans).
3. Black people (Mexican-Americans) will have very little say in the government unless they all decide to vote for the same candidate.
(ii) This count only approximates the true dimension in Gardner, but it was used to assure consistency in the measure across communities. Consequently comparisons between black and Mexican-American communities should be made with caution.

Table 6.2b. Group Blame

		Neighborhoods		
		East Side	Summerhill	North Central
Inner-directed hostility (i)	Zero	24%	49%	49%
Ambivalence (ii)	One	34%	42%	33%
Outer-directed hostility (iii)	Two	43%	8%	18%
		(280)	(251)	(250)

(i) Believe both statements, that is, that blacks blame too many of their problems on whites and that blacks can get ahead as easily as anyone else.
(ii) Believe either statement but not both, that is, that blacks blame too many of their problems on whites *or* that blacks can get ahead as easily as anyone else.
(iii) Affirm neither of these statements.

States is temporary. One organizer said, "They are here to make their bread and get out." Others, who prefer to be called "Mexican-Americans," are better adjusted to their new roles and more concerned with economic success and mobility. A younger group that has become prominent in recent years calls itself "chicano"—phraseology that many other Mexican-Americans find insulting. This group is more assertive about particular group interests. These alternative conceptions of group identity have added fuel to the group trauma that is reflected in the fractionalized politics of Gardner.

The struggle that has so often divided the community has also produced a strong desire for reconciliation. A Gardner organizer commented on these problems:

> We need to get ourselves together. We have to love one another. We've been trying to ease the conflict on the ESO board so we can work together better. This conflict has to be stopped.
>
> I sometimes think that federal money is put here to hassle us, to make us fight among ourselves. Before we can get money like this,

we have to get ourselves together first. Otherwise, we can't
differentiate friend from foe. We don't know who our brother is.
These piddly pennies force brother against brother.

Another organizer believed the division over group identity will soon
be superseded by a growing singularity of understanding and a new
unity of purpose:

There was a time when being called "Mexican" was a negative thing.
Only the Mexicans identified with Mexico. Now we are all concerned
with the 5th of May, the 16th of September.

In this view, chicanos, Mexicans, and Mexican-Americans are joined
by their ties to the Mexican past.

Anti-Anglo sentiments only infrequently achieve public expression, though there is growing evidence of hostility among the young
and college students. Anglos are involved in most organizations
serving the community, from the Congressional District Office, the
Human Relations Commission, the War on Poverty, to the United
Farm Workers Organizing Committee. Residents often emphasize
that their feelings and actions are not "anti-gringo" as such and show
overt hostility toward only one Anglo institution—the police (and
even here the response is highly inconsistent). Leaders and organizations on the whole are more concerned with finding a common basis
for political action than with questions of guilt or responsibility (65).

What proves of marginal interest in Gardner—the responsibility of
Anglos (or whites) in the social system—is a preeminent concern in
the East Side. The solidarity of East Side residents is not, by and
large, predicated on African traditions or the culture of the South,
but self-protection and an indictment of white social institutions.
This strong group identity infects the community response to politics
and to itself. Congressman Diggs, who holds a safe seat because of
strong and consistent East Side support, derives his strength from
both a thriving funeral business and a history of unjust treatment by
white authorities. A candidate for local office describes the history
surrounding the Congressman and the reaction of East Side residents
to it.

His father was an important politician on the East Side back in the
thirties. He was railroaded into jail for a year on an offense white

men committed every day. Everybody knows about it. And those
not old enough to know were sure to be told by their parents.

That is the difference between the white and black communities in
Detroit. The black community is tight-knit. It has to be. He knows
that he can be cut down for things the white man will never be hit
with. Look at Adam Powell. The community knows this. The only
place a black has to go is back to the black community.

Coleman Young, perhaps the best known statewide black politician,
is also from the East Side and has depended on its unity and support
in times of trouble. Young withstood the assault of the House
Un-American Activities Committee, knowing full well that the black
community was beside him in the struggle; as a resident put it,
"Through struggle we have learned who our enemies are."

The themes of autonomy and blame are not necessarily contradictory, as indicated by the factor analysis; both contribute to the
identity of black Americans. A recent mayoral race between a black
and a white candidate, however, produced a conflict of themes that
was perhaps concealed in the past. Richard Austin was the first black
candidate in Detroit history to actively seek the mayor's office. But
what must have seemed assured—the support of the East Side black
community—was placed in jeopardy by the candidate's foothold in
both the black and white communities. An aide to Congressman
Diggs stated:

It didn't happen with Austin. . . . Perhaps had he been a different
kind of black person. The nature of his work, his being a CPA, has
always kept him socially with whites. He's had white accounts and
so on. Austin didn't work with these poor blacks up and down the
street like Diggs does. Austin wasn't known by the important black
families.

When faced with supporting a candidate who was black but did not
understand the protection and security of the black community,
many East Side residents proved reticent. Voting turnout on the East
Side was less than that for whites in Detroit and substantially below
the East Side turnout for the preceding Presidential election.

A remarkable 43 percent of East Side residents proved critical of
white society on both "group blame" items. This level of response is
twice that of North Central and five times the level of "outer-

directed hostility" in Summerhill. In the words of the Congressman's aide, East Side residents "have learned well the lessons of Reconstruction."

For the past two decades, Summerhill residents have played a vital role in the electoral politics of Atlanta, forming what Edward Banfield calls one leg in a three-legged stool. Their bloc vote, along with the votes of middle class whites and the support of progressive business interests and the press, have assured the tenure of "liberal" Mayors Hartsfield and Allen. In 1969 they and other black residents elected black candidates to the office of Vice Mayor, as well as five aldermen, three members of the Board of Education, and fourteen state representatives. In the early sixties, Summerhill residents in impressive numbers supported the boycotts that helped force the integration of lunch counters in Rich's Department Store and other food establishments throughout downtown Atlanta. Summerhill blacks, consequently, have learned well the power accruing to strategic unity. This is reflected in the substantial support they gave to propositions to ensure black control at the ballot box and in the marketplace.

Unity of purpose, however, has not altered the economic conditions that leave many Summerhill residents without work or sufficient food, nor has it prevented the city from isolating the neighborhood through extensive highway construction. Yet the residents of Summerhill do not want to view their plight as a consequence of outside forces; they choose instead to examine their own responsibility. One community organizer has suggested, "The black in the South hasn't had the opportunity to feel about white people and his situation like the black man in the North." He has yet to learn what East Side residents already know about Reconstruction.

Although the blacks of North Central Philadelphia ask the same sorts of questions about themselves and whites, a much smaller percentage are willing to commit themselves to race goals. They demonstrate neither Summerhill's belief in race unity nor the East Side's sensitivity to the external environment. Almost one-third of the residents affirm none of the items that make up the "black unity" theme and almost half are uncritical of the social order on both "responsibility" items. The search for identity or group purpose (which achieves some form of expression in Summerhill and the East

Side) provides no basis for solidarity in North Central. The "brotherhood" of black people, seemingly uniform and universal to the public eye, has different meanings and varying salience in poor neighborhoods.

The absence of strong racial bonds in North Central is interesting in light of the community's intense political involvement. Residents are highly communicative about politics and well informed; they vote in substantial numbers; they demonstrate high levels of organizational participation; and their involvement with protest activity is second only to that in Summerhill. But unlike Summerhill, the East Side, and Gardner, their involvement is not tempered by a sensitivity to race issues, the need for unity of purpose, or the social responsibility of the larger society. In the next section we shall begin to understand how an attenuated race consciousness and sustained political participation can, at the same time, foster and detract from political mobilization.

The only cultural organization that has tried to capitalize on the rich folk background of Belmont whites is O'Tuck—Ohio Kentuckians. It offers folklore and folk music, often providing big name entertainment from the Grand Ole Oprey. But the organization was not begun nor is it sustained by the interest of poor whites. A principal organizer commented, "We just couldn't make it with this class of people." They relied instead on a leading realtor and an insurance man, "men who had money and who could help me raise money." Belmont residents will attend an O'Tuck Festival at the Butler County Fairgrounds, listen to the music, and recall the good times back in Harlan or Breathitt County. The music reminds them of common origins and nurtures nostalgia, but fails to weave a strong bond of community.

The major expression of their group identity is the stream of cars fleeing Hamilton on weekends and holidays, returning to Kentucky for a glimpse of the hills and a reunion with relatives.

These five neighborhoods are grappling with questions of identity and solidarity, providing group commitments of differing meaning and differing intensity. Out of these alternative conceptions of self and others emerges one of the keys to the politics of poor neighborhoods.

IV   THE POLITICAL RELEVANCE OF GROUP CONSCIOUS-NESS

The forging of a group identity is a difficult, introspective process that forces people to turn in on themselves to search for what they share and feel in common. It is an examination that sometimes appears exclusive of "outsiders," drawing boundaries between people and building a solidarity among group members. Whether the meaning is traditional (relying on a history and a living culture), oppositional (concerned primarily with questions of responsibility or blame), or taciturn (an identification of condition with little reference to community or culprit), group consciousness tends to particularism and self-examination.

But separate identities, no matter how difficult or introspective the search, cannot be separated from politics. Identity and politics feed on one another. Oppression and contempt cannot be assessed without reference to political authority. A community of interests and purpose cannot be evolved without reference to its political opportunities. Without politics, group identity becomes limited in meaning and potentiality.

It becomes apparent in this section that the search for group meaning is influenced by political experience and that feelings of solidarity themselves are in important respects determinant of political expression. The group identity in black neighborhoods—particularly sensitive to issues of responsibility and oppression—responds to feelings of estrangement. It is intimately bound up with the resort to violence, but has little significance for more conventional forms of involvement. Black consciousness is oppositional, highly alienative in tone, and violent in its consequences. The traditional tone of Mexican-American identity (though also related to feelings of estrangement) is less dependent on these feelings and wholly different in its political consequences. Group commitment in the Mexican-American community fosters a range of political expression, short of violence.

A.   Political Estrangement and Group Consciousness

As a result of forced internment executed by the War Department and the War Relocation Authority during World War II, 6000

Japanese-Americans expressed disloyalty to the United States and another 3000 refused a categorical affirmation of their loyalty. Many of these men and women turned instead to their Japanese ancestry (66):

> These are the scars I have, keepsakes of my army service for this country [There are scars on his chest acquired during World War I]. It is no longer my country. I am now a hundred percent Japanese. I spit on these scars of the United States.

For many of the evacuees, the internments produced or heightened emotional ties to the Japanese homeland and many "had come to the wishful conclusion that Japan would win the war" (67).

The expression of "disloyalty" was most pronounced in the camps operating under the worst conditions. At the Manzanar camp in California, over half of the evacuees refused loyalty to the United States. The camp was physically substandard, near a hostile settlement, spied upon by the FBI, and administered haphazardly (68). In Minidoka, a camp with much more tolerable living accommodations, "disloyalty" reached only 8 percent. Grodzins concludes (69):

> Above all, the experience of Japanese Americans demonstrates how loyalty is influenced by life-situation. Declarations of loyalty and disloyalty were concrete responses to concrete situations. Disloyalty grew from estimates of past experience, current plight, and what the future might hold.

Arnold Rose has suggested that the development of group identification is one possible response to the vulnerability of an identifiable minority and its forced dependency on the majority population. Group identification under these circumstances is a "defensive device"; it provides certain compensations and molds the minority into a fighting force. The group seeks out past leaders who are labeled great statesmen and artists, and accentuates certain aspects of the culture, viewing them as "outstanding manifestations of folk genius" (70). Group identification permits the building of "group self-confidence, pride, bonds of loyalty," and internal communication in the face of degrading assaults from the majority forces (71); in other words, it fosters group morale.

Group consciousness in the black neighborhoods is largely a consequence of dissatisfaction with institutional life and the general political community; to a lesser extent, this association is apparent in the Mexican-American community as well. The association between group identity and alienation measures prevails whether we examine dissatisfaction with the schools, police, and electoral politics, or sense of political effectiveness, or general disaffection with the political community. But although the relationships are strong and consistent in both groups, the gammas in Table 6.3 suggest the associations are more pronounced in the black communities. Only for sense of political efficacy is the relationship in the Mexican-American community more striking. A multiple correlation analysis between race identification and all three disaffection measures reveals a .39 coefficient (multiple r) for the black communities, but only a .26 coefficient for the Mexican-American community.

The earlier examination of the factor analysis showed that black residents are apt to order their responses around a dimension of consciousness concerned with accountability. They are likely to ask, "Are the root causes of our plight to be found in the larger society, its racism and oppressive acts, or among ourselves?" East Side residents are inclined to offer the former response, North Central and Summerhill residents the latter. Since this dimension is salient to the development of black consciousness, it is not surprising that it relates strongly to the extent of expressed dissatisfaction with institutions outside the black community. Conversely, the question of accountability was not salient in the Mexican-American community, suggesting a weaker association with political alienation.

B. Group Consciousness and Political Expression

Group consciousness has an important, independent effect on political expression (although the consequences for black and Mexican-American neighborhoods are radically different). The path model discussed below and the tables presented later in the chapter confirm the strong alienative character of black consciousness and its relationship with political violence. The group consciousness of the Mexican-American community is less bound by feelings of alienation; it has little to do with expressions of violence. Its impact is confined

Table 6.3. Group Consciousness and Political Alienation

	System Rejection		Sense of Inefficacy		Policy Dissatisfaction	
	High	Low	High	Low	High	Low
Black Neighborhoods						
Percentage "high" group consciousness (i)	56%	28%	48%	34%	51%	31%
	(260)	(416)	(330)	(393)	(316)	(465)
Gammas	.532		.274		.411	
Probability	.001		.001		.001	
Mexican-American Neighborhood						
Percentage "high" group consciousness	49%	34%	56%	36%	45%	41%
	(75)	(70)	(43)	(101)	(51)	(102)
Gammas	.302		.390		.080	
Probability	.052		.014		Not significant	

163

(i) Group autonomy and group blame were combined in this analysis for both consistency and simplicity of presentation. There can be little doubt, however, that the combined measure taps different attitudes in the black and Mexican-American communities. This raises few difficulties for black respondents, since each of the items falls on a distinctive and important factor. For Mexican-American respondents, however, the items included in the measure do not emerge directly out of the factor analysis. There is little difficulty with the items comprising group autonomy (two of these fall on the second factor), but the items that form group blame do not follow a sensible pattern. One item is important in defining the first factor, along with a race autonomy item; the other forms an entirely separate factor. Factor one explains 18 percent of the variance of all race questions. Together these three factors, encompassing all the items in "group consciousness," explain almost half the variance.

This combination of items does not distort the results of the analysis, as long as we keep in mind the factors that have intellectual coherence in these communities. Group consciousness among black respondents is comprised of two sets of attitudes—group autonomy and group blame. Most important, however, these two aspects of consciousness relate to the measures of alienation and political expression in nearly identical fashion (the gammas are of the same sign and approximately the same magnitude). Hence their combination in no way distorts the relationships that are discussed in the text.

Group consciousness among Mexican-American respondents is comprised of one coherent attitude set—group autonomy—and three other items that have a statistical affinity only in the black neighborhoods. But once again, the combination of these items does not distort the data analysis. The two separate indicators of group consciousness are similarly related to political alienation measures (gammas are of the same sign and approximately the same magnitude). In addition, group blame bears no relation to measures of political expression, so the inclusion of these items in the group consciousness measure in no way affects the direction of relationships (the sign) and only marginally reduces the magnitude. But it is important to keep in mind that the results that include group consciousness in the Mexican-American community are a consequence of group autonomy items. Group blame items are included in the computations but do not appreciably affect the results.

164

to the more conventional forms of political action.

These dual conceptions of consciousness emerge in the path model. All relevant factors have been included in the model except organizational membership (its position is approximated by the relationships with receptivity to politics); path coefficients have been computed for each causal assumption. The path coefficient is no more than a standardized regression coefficient, that is, *"how much change* in the dependent variable is produced by a standardized change in one of the independent variables when the others are controlled" (72). Thus it is possible to determine which variable has the greatest impact on receptivity to politics or receptivity to violence, independent of other factors in the model (73).

It is obvious that disaffection measures have a marked impact on group consciousness in both the Mexican-American and black communities (though, as noted earlier, the impact is greater in black neighborhoods). More interesting from the perspective of this chapter are the coefficients between the two independent variables (estrangement and race consciousness) and measures of political behavior (receptivity to politics and receptivity to violence). In the black communities there is no determinant relationship between either estrangement or race consciousness and receptivity to politics, but both factors have a strong, *independent* effect on receptivity to violence (Figure 6.1a) (74). Together, these concepts explain 26 percent of the variance in receptivity to violence and 11 percent of the variance in receptivity to politics (most of which can be accounted for by estrangement). In Table 6.4, this overall pattern is confirmed: group consciousness appears in a contradictory relationship with conventional political expression, but in a pronounced and consistent association with receptivity to violence. Only in Summerhill, where commitment to group autonomy is widespread, is there also a cogent relationship with nonviolent political expression.

Black consciousness emerges as an internally consistent phenomenon—stressing oppositional themes, related to alienation and conducive to violence. Consciousness in the Mexican-American community is a distinctive phenomenon, consistent in its concern with autonomy and important to community politics. It does not encompass an overriding concern with Anglo responsibility; it is assertive of traditional group interests and unconcerned with violence. The strong positive path coefficient between group

Table 6.4. *Group Consciousness and Political Expression*

| | Mexican-American | | | | Black Neighborhoods | | | |
| | Neighborhood—Gardner | | East Side | | Summerhill | | North Central | |
Group Consciousness	Low	High	Low	High	Low	High	Low	High
1. Percentage organizational membership	15% (88)	25% (64)	17% (152)	17% (126)	7% (152)	19% (97)	27% (170)	14% (80)
Gamma	.316		.008		.582		-.386	
Probability	.09		Not significant		.001		.014	
2. Percentage "high" receptivity to politics	48% (88)	66% (65)	55% (154)	67% (126)	73% (152)	64% (98)	75% (170)	73% (80)
Gamma	.363		.250		.201		.072	
Probability	.014		.033		.133		Not significant	
3. Percentage "high" receptivity to violence	33% (88)	37% (65)	64% (154)	79% (126)	41% (153)	56% (98)	37% (170)	83% (80)
Gamma	.087		.362		.293		.778	
Probability	Not significant		.003		.015		.001	

consciousness and receptivity to politics as well as the unimpressive path to violence confirm this identity (Figure 6.1b). So do the results of Table 6.4.

These relationships are not functions of demographic factors such as age and education. The correlation between black consciousness and receptivity to violence is unaffected by the introduction of first an age, then an education control; nor is it affected by the introduction of both items. The associations of organizational membership and receptivity to politics with Mexican-American consciousness are also unaffected by these items (Table 6.5). It is possible, of

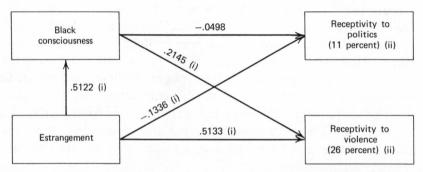

Figure 6.1a. Determinants of receptivity to politics and violence: black neighborhoods. (i) Significant at .01 level; (ii) percentage of variance explained.

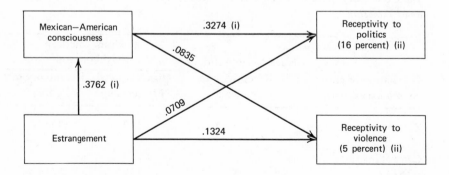

Figure 6.1b. Determinants of receptivity to politics and violence: Mexican-American neighborhood. (i) Significant at .01 level; (ii) percentage of variance explained.

course, that these correlations obscure the impact of race consciousness on some subgroup of the poor population, but careful
examination of the data reveals no such pattern. The same findings
prevail for all age and educational subgroups, including those under
twenty-six years of age, high school graduates, or otherwise.

Belmont is a community that, though bound by a group
identification, has asked few questions of itself or the surrounding
institutions. It dwells neither on the responsibility of non-South-
erners for their condition, nor on the rich cultural heritage in
Appalachia. Consequently the pressure of identification that moves
blacks toward violence and Mexican-Americans to conventional
political expression plays a small role in Belmont. Their identification is an escape from the urban condition, a return to "cornbread
and beans," a resignation to their plight. Without the search for
meaning or the provocation of difficult questions, their group
identity leads them away from Belmont and away from politics. The
politics and violence that emerge from the group identity in poor
black and Mexican-American communities pale in the face of a
taciturn consciousness.

*Table 6.5. Group Consciousness and Political Expression Controlling for Age
and Education*

Correlation of group consciousness with	Black Neighborhoods Receptivity to Violence	Mexican-American Neighborhood	
		Organizational Membership	Receptivity to Politics
Zero order correlation	.251 (i)	.129	.254 (i)
Controlling for			
Age	.321 (i)	.139	.251 (i)
Education	.341 (i)	.133	.254 (i)
Both	.314 (i)	.145	.251 (i)

(i) Significant at the .01 level.

C. Group Consciousness and Vertical Intrusion

We have considered the question of group consciousness primarily as a vehicle for fostering political participation and increasing the receptivity of ghetto residents to political violence. Feelings of solidarity may, however, have important consequences for the political mood outside the question of involvement. In this section, we consider how group consciousness encourages indigenous leadership, responsive to the poor themselves.

A central fiber of ghetto life is dependency. Roland Warren has listed five essential functions of a social system (including production-consumption, socialization, social control, social participation, and mutual support—health and welfare, etc.) and finds that "they are performed in the ghetto in a manner that virtually assures dependency" (75). Welfare services, schools, political organizations, and police are all under the dominant influence of institutions that are run on a citywide basis and are usually guided by the values and preferences of this larger community. Groups in poor neighborhoods, if they are to survive, must relate to institutions that are intrusive to their communities. At the same time, their dependence on outside forces makes them independent of groups or institutions in their own neighborhoods, thus fragmenting the organizational base of poor communities (76). To some extent this type of dependence fragments any community, rich or poor, but the problem is magnified in poor communities by the range of social functions performed by the government, by the poor's relative powerlessness with reference to governmental institutions, and by "value" differences between neighborhood and government that, on the whole, are more marked for poorer neighborhoods.

The "vertical" intrusion of outside institutions into poor communities not only increases the extent of fragmentation but also encourages individuals and groups to relate to the values of the larger society rather than those of the community. James Q. Wilson and Carmichael and Hamilton point out that Congressman Dawson in Chicago was a forthright spokesman for the black community before he became a member of the city Democratic organization. After joining the organization, he spoke out on race issues only with the greatest reluctance (77). For similar reasons, Saul Alinsky considered the poverty program a piece of "political pornography." He observes that "Good potential (negative) leadership is seduced by payoffs, rentals of premises, jobs and specialized pressure such as money grants or projects to 'company union' rivals" (78). Organizations in poor communities (except the most nonpolitical) tend to rely on outside agents for their political and financial support. Support from institutions and groups outside poor communities pervades revolutionary organizations, protest groups, and conventional organizations. This dependency (or "vertical" intrusion) makes mutual interdependence in poor communities at best fragile and at worst impossible.

There are degrees to which poor communities are able to "use" this dependency. Some neighborhoods are insensitive to the existence of dependency or do not find it objectionable. Others are aware of its necessity but wary of its effects, and they may act to create independence within a context of dependence. Group consciousness, we shall see, may play a vital role in the ability of a community to deal with dependency.

North Central Philadelphia represents a model of attenuated group consciousness. The residents are not particularly open to political strategies requiring racial unity and are likely to seek out the root causes of poverty in their own communities rather than in the larger society. But North Central demonstrates an intense political involvement. This combination of factors has produced a highly disjointed form of political mobilization—considerable activity, but little unity of purpose and few identifiable or persistent community leaders. Individuals who have emerged through the civil rights movement or other aspects of the black struggle have entered the party organization (which is extensive in North Central), the Poverty Program, or Model Cities—all of which are under the firm control of the Mayor. An architect of a community development corporation observed that his colleagues have been "bought off into government agencies." What the community has left is a variety of "institutionalized black middlemen."

The East Side of Detroit is a model of a different sort. Residents are distrustful to the extreme of outside institutions and politicians and hold the larger society responsible for conditions in the ghetto. But like North Central, the East Side depends on the politics of outside actors. Funds are made available to tenants' organizations, community action groups, housing groups, and various poverty programs. Political support is lent by liberal city politicians, the Federal Government, and the United Automobile Workers. But the political tone differs from that of North Central. From the most conservative black politicians to the most militant residents of the community (all of whom operate within the framework of dependency) there is a sensitivity to the duplicity and undependability of the white world, and a belief that life itself can be protected only within the "womb" of the black community. Even local politicians whose livelihoods are most intricately bound up with the white world espouse unfailing loyalty to the "black folk" of Detroit. Unlike North Central, there is a broad range of leadership active on a daily basis which keeps race issues before the public.

How do we account for the divergence between these two neighborhoods? One plausible explanation is a difference in the success of the intrusions. In North Central there are many effective vertical intrusions into the community (the party, the Poverty Program, and Model Cities) whereas in Detroit there is no serious party organization and a less centralized Poverty Program. But differences in group consciousness also distinguish these neighborhoods. The residents of the East Side are sensitive to the question of accountability and are distrustful of "outsiders," whereas North Central residents are not. Accordingly, the East Side has granted a cloak of protection to leaders who remain true to the race; leaders in turn have responded with public loyalty to the "color line" and sensitivity to race concerns. North Central leaders have no comparable base on which to stake their survival. They seek whatever security is possible in the opportunities provided by intrusive institutions.

V   CONCLUSION

Gardner's Mexican-American community is barely interested in questions of accountability or blame; it is concerned instead with questions of group unity and autonomy. It is a community bound by traditional values and a continuous, relevant history that provides the substance of group assertion. Consciousness of race issues and concern for autonomy manifest themselves in a number of political forms, but bear little relation to violence.

The consciousness and history of black communities are very

different. Group autonomy is a central concern in black consciousness but so are the issues of accountability and responsibility. Blacks
who are sensitive to the "color line" are interested not simply in
their own solidarity but also in the role and guilt of the larger white
society, its governmental policies, and the racism of its public
officials. These attitudes are reflected in the strong association
between disaffection measures and black consciousness, as well as in
the rhetoric of black literary and political spokesmen. Black
consciousness incorporates oppositional themes and consequently
grapples with "white power," white values, and white history; it does
not draw solely on the black experience in Africa, the Mideast, or
Asia for its meaning. The political manifestation of black consciousness occurs more as a broadened receptivity to violence than as
conventional politics.

From these streams of consciousness emerge the politics of five
poor neighborhoods. The nonviolent activism of Gardner is apparent
in "la Raza." The resignation and placid style of Belmont politics are
reflected in the limited solidarity of its residents. Even the
vicissitudes of black politics, so apparently paradoxical in past
discussions, achieve sensibility in light of black consciousness.
Without an understanding of oppositional themes and the varying
commitments to it, it is difficult to explain the defensive and violent
aspects of East Side politics or the leaderless and diffuse quality of
politics in North Central. The unalienated and nonviolent tone of
politics in Summerhill emerges directly from its limited indictment
of white society.

The sense of group identity draws on history and collective
experience and provides a guide to group meaning and purpose; it
offers an interpretation of reality and opportunities, helping to
translate feelings into a distinctive political style. But group
consciousness is a highly particularized phenomenon, setting people
apart, creating multiple perspectives on politics. In the next chapter
we consider a system of belief that tries to transcend the particularism of group consciousness and the peculiarity of its politics.

Chapter Seven

The Politics of Class

. . . .

The story of the American worker (many of whom reside in poor neighborhoods) is the failure of the American Dream—a failure of opportunity and mobility. Few Horatio Algers are to be found on the automobile production line at River Rouge. Domestics and day laborers rarely make the leap from low-paid, menial work to ownership and affluence. Though American business still affirms the efficacy of the Alger fantasy—"Your opportunities will be limited only by your vision of what your future may become, your abilities and how you use them, your character and your determination" (1)—workers deal on a daily basis with a different reality. Mass production industries do not offer an escalator of job opportunities: the most unskilled and lowest-paid workers at the bottom and management positions at the top (2). Inheritance and advanced education, not diligence, hard work, and enthusiasm, are at the root of occupational advancement. For the poor who have failed to acquire even the better-paying industrial jobs, the prospects of "success" are even more remote. "The busboy or dishwasher who works hard becomes," Elliot Liebow observes, "simply, a hard-working busboy or dishwasher" (3).

That the worker in the United States has not wholly rejected this fantasy or formulated a radical class ideology is a phenomenon often observed, and remains one of the great paradoxes of American political life (4). The old ideologies—ones that rejected individual mobility and challenged the existing pattern of income and power distribution—play little part in industrial life, prodding few workers to revolution or radical obstruction. Instead, the American worker carries on. Though perhaps unhappy with the work routine and the debasing of his abilities (5), the worker creates a niche of personal responsibility and position that is in some sense protected. Some workers, despite the lack of upward mobility, find satisfaction and personal worth in their jobs. Coal mining, for example, provides the lure of a work group, a mining community, a confrontation with the natural environment relatively free of supervision and repetitive enterprise (an environment foreign to urban factories) (6). For many other workers, a radical paring down of expectations reduces the American Dream to irrelevance. These workers do not dream of owning steel mills or wearing white collars, but look instead to other more tangible goals. They play down the importance of their work, asking little more of it than job security and income adequate to support a car (7). Others simply avoid questions of mobility or equality by insulating themselves from invidious comparisons. People are considered morally equal (before the Lord), dwarfing in importance material comparisons; inequalities in status or social rewards are minimized by compensatory considerations—"the majority of them that are rich have got more worries" (8).

No matter what mechanism workers employ to mitigate the unreality of the Dream, they still must cope with the pervasive normative framework affirming it (9). Consequently most workers continue to pay allegiance to individual mobility despite the surreal quality of such a pursuit. Though workers frequently guard against personal commitments to mobility and success, their affirmation of the norm mitigates the pressure toward a distinctive working class perspective. It creates, instead, a feeling of *embourgeoisement*. A new working class is created, one that shuns the violence of class conflict and emulates the norms and values of the dominant classes. Its concerns are limited and derivative—"occupation, mobility, short-term coalitions, and consumption" (10).

Most of the reasons used to explain the attenuated consciousness of the working class are not adequate to explain the limited consciousness of the poor. The working class of poor neighborhoods is not radically differentiated into skilled, semiskilled, and unskilled workers, not kept apart by different colored collars, and not segregated by technical training or advanced education (11). Only 5 percent of the five neighborhood sample have gone beyond high school and fewer than one in five have progressed into white collar jobs (even these are congregated primarily in clerical and sales positions). If there is a "new middle class"—"this group that is no group, class that is no class, and stratum that is no stratum" (12)—it is not important to the demography of poor neighborhoods. Indeed, the poor resemble Apter's "functionally superfluous"—marginal groupings that play a limited role in the occupational structure and have few prospects for upward mobility (13). Their superfluity finds different outlets (e.g., women on ADC, unemployment insurance, and marginal construction jobs), but they share a position at the lowest end of the social order. They are in some sense abandoned by the occupational structure, as their neighborhoods have been abandoned by the city and the upwardly mobile.

Like workers in general, the poor have not formulated a radical class ideology, despite the extent of their plight and the uniformity of their position. Indeed, Table 7.1 confirms that the poor are well aware of limited economic opportunities and fully cognizant of the differing perspectives on public policy held by the poor and the wealthy. Despite this consciousness of economic circumstances, however, the poor do not consistently express a belief in income inequality or income supports. The poor in five neighborhoods overwhelmingly reject the notion of an equal income for everyone regardless of job category and vary in the extent to which they support a guaranteed subsistence income. Though the poor are fully cognizant of their condition, they are not resolved to affect changes that would alter these conditions.

These results raise serious questions about traditional formulations of class, principally their primary underlying assumption that a class perspective emerges from plight (14). It has been presumed, quite logically, that a common misery would breed a common resolve to end it. But the apparent *embourgeoisement* and co-optation of many

Table 7.1. Class Position and Class Ideology

Items	Neighborhoods				
	Gardner	Belmont	East Side	Summerhill	North Central
A. Class Position					
1. "It's been said that in the United States no matter how hard some people work they will never be rich."					
True	71% (153)	78% (178)	77% (280)	83% (250)	82% (250)
2. "For the most part, do you think that poor people and rich people agree about what things the government ought to do?"					
No	77% (153)	64% (178)	76% (280)	73% (250)	81% (250)

B. Class Ideology

1. "Do you think all people have the right to have enough money to live on, whether they are working or not?"

Yes	23% (153)	32% (177)	44% (280)	78% (250)	72% (250)

2. "How would you feel if everyone got paid the same amount of money, no matter what his job was?"

Good idea	10% (153)	13% (178)	11% (275)	27% (247)	10% (250)

workers and the listless ideology of the poor cast doubt on this assumption. Neither the evident oppression of the poor nor their own recognition of it is sufficient to kindle a marked class ideology among the poor. To understand the development of class among the poor, we must go beyond the simple one-step model of plight and ideology to consider other aspects of marginality and other aspects of consciousness.

We shall find that the plight of the poor has not been defined uniformly in terms of capital and labor or in terms of working class and bourgeois values. In fact, many poor people—black, brown, and white—have looked to the large industrialist or the large farmer (agribusiness) as guardians of their interests, and many have faced large-scale industry from a vantage point of such dependency and marginality that oppositional roles proved impracticable or were crushed. The lure of the cities was, after all, the lure of developing capital. Factories provided jobs; bosses viewed their work places as a "happy family." Labor organizations threatened the prerogatives of management, challenged its good will, and indeed, threatened the peace that brought the poor to the cities. Business provided jobs where trade unions restricted employment, setting up barriers to the employment of these new unskilled and low-paid workers. In their struggle for survival, blacks, Mexican-Americans, and Appalachian whites struck an alliance with business associations and large manufacturing concerns, guaranteeing themselves jobs and helping to limit the effectiveness of unions. They found that a predominant, often ruthless, business class and a working class unsympathetic to the new migrants formed a volatile combination, unconducive to sustained class action on their own part. An understanding of plight, therefore, must take into account those traditionally viewed as enemies. In none of these communities is there a simple or consistent script where the poor hate the rich and labor challenges capital.

We shall find that even when an oppositional ideology develops along class lines, it does not emerge simply out of plight, class hostility, or alienation. Class ideology among the urban poor is primarily a consequence of group solidarity and self-knowledge; it is intimately involved with group or race consciousness. Alienation is realized as a class understanding only when transformed by an immediate group experience and understanding. From this focused and inner-directed concern emerges the more global perspective on wealth, poverty, and redistributive justice.

The varied politics of poor neighborhoods, we shall see, can be attributed in some measure to the understanding the poor have about themselves and an evolving oppositional or class ideology.

I CLASS ORGANIZATION AND THE POOR: THE BLACK EXAMPLE

It would be a mistake to assume that because the poor are the most oppressed of all working class groups, they are therefore the most sensitive to class ideology. The urban poor do not emerge from class struggle. Their history does not bring to mind a string of confrontations with the values of capitalism or the American Dream, with the managers or owners of American industrial enterprise, or with those few individuals who dominate the country's wealth. As incongruous as it must seem, the black poor, Appalachian whites, and Mexican-Americans have at times established friendly, working relationships with those groups whom others have dubbed the "enemy," and have only within brief periods posed a serious challenge to the prerogatives of business. An uneasy but substantial alliance of the wealthy and the poorest of the black workers was forged in the post-Reconstruction South (15), black ministers and company executives in the urban North, and bosses and Appalachian families in the factories of the Midwest; and after early attempts at labor organization were brutally crushed, an apparent calm settled over the relations between Mexican field hands and cannery workers and agribusiness in the fertile valleys of California.

The instruments of the working class—trade unions, socialist groups, and the Communist party—were often at odds with or indifferent to the new urban workers. These conflicts were particularly sharp in their dealings with the mass of unskilled black workers. Trade unions restricted access to employment and excluded non-white workers from their membership; the socialists ignored these newer forces in the working class, concentrating their attention on the German and Jewish working classes who dominated their ranks. Only the Communists committed themselves to organizing nonwhite workers as "the vanguard of the proletarian forces at home" (16), but even they forsook the new poor when convenience or the

International required otherwise. Twentieth century migrants found the spokesmen of the working classes and the instruments of class action arrayed against them, indifferent to their concerns, or inconsistent in the advocacy of their cause.

The American Federation of Labor was particularly insensitive to the new poor, viewing their migration to the North and West with considerable "anxiety." Their Thirty-sixth Annual Convention resolved "to inaugurate a movement looking toward the organization of these men in the Southern states, to the end that they may be instructed and educated along the lines of the trade union movement, and thereby eliminate this menace to the workers of the Northern states" (17). However, their efforts to include poor black workers in the South were nearly imperceptible, while their discriminatory practices in the North continued unchecked. Gompers, and after him, Green, permitted affiliated unions to exclude black workers, provided there was no specific constitutional prohibition. The International Association of Machinists exploited the organization's ritual to exclude blacks; the Glass Workers, Granite Cutters, and Plumbers used tacit consent; and a large number of unions, including the Boilermakers, Iron Shipbuilders, and Maintenance-of-Way-Employees, used segregated auxiliary unions. The AFL sanctioned these arrangements, effectively precluding black participation in collective bargaining arrangements and hiring halls (18). A. Phillip Randolph labeled the auxiliary unions "colonies of colored people to the empire systems," and black workers "economic, political, and social serfs" who possess "none of the rights that the white population in the mother country enjoy, except the right to be taxed" (19). Even after World War II, the AFL convention refused to disband the auxiliary unions (20).

Having been effectively excluded from the trades (21), black workers first confronted the labor movement in the mass production industries. The AFL made only a half-hearted attempt to organize these low-skilled workers. It feared that the sheer size of this industrial proletariat and its undifferentiated employment circumstances would destroy the traditional basis of the Federation (22). The Machinists created nonexistent locals and the Federation imaginary internationals that left the mass of poor workers, white and black, unorganized and unrepresented. The Congress of Industrial Organizations, however, beginning in the late thirties made serious

efforts to organize steel, automobile, rubber, and textiles, invariably confronting the problem of black participation. Unlike their
counterpart in the crafts, the CIO determined to fight racism in its
own ranks, reflecting the early "open door" policies of John L.
Lewis and the United Mine Workers. Although the CIO persuaded
some of the black press and a few black leaders of its sincerity, the
great mass of unskilled black laborers remained dubious and
uncommitted. Black workers, who had come into the steel mills as
strikebreakers in 1919, feared that a strike in the late thirties would
endanger their already precarious positions. The director of the Steel
Workers Organizing Committee noted with regret in 1936, "The
organization of the Negro steel workers will follow, rather than
precede, the organization of the white mill workers" (23). Blacks
played a marginal role in the 1941 strike at Ford; only the
intervention of black leaders who opposed a "back-to-work"
campaign in their neighborhoods averted a serious race riot (24).
Although the CIO organizing campaigns brought many blacks into
the union movement, much of the poignancy of the campaigns had
been lost by the middle fifties. The merger agreement of the CIO and
AFL gave little salience to racial discrimination, leaving most
exclusionary union practices unaffected (25).

The black masses did not respond to the call of the CIO. No blacks
joined the Detroit sit-in movement and few were active in the Steel
Workers Organizing Committee, though many were to join these unions
after their recognition and later to become active in their governance.
Their reluctance was born in the post-Reconstruction South, where
progress was seen not in struggle but in "alliance with the 'better
class' of whites—that is, with liberal capitalists, do-good philanthro-
pists, and occasional Southern bourbons who maintained an attitude
of benevolence toward their former slaves" (26). Their faith was
maintained through the populist struggles, even shunning populist
flirtings with interracial solidarity. They voted instead with those
"liberal industrialists" who warned of "Negro Rule" (27), though it
is not entirely clear the black vote was freely cast. Woodward
writes (28),

> Negro plantation hands and laborers were hauled to town in wagon
> loads, marched to the polls in squads, and voted repeatedly. Negroes
> were hauled across the Savannah River from South Carolina in

four-horse wagon loads and voted in Augusta. Whiskey was
dispensed by the barrel in Augusta wagon yards, and cash payments
made to voters.

When lower class whites learned the lesson of this unholy alliance,
the affinity of poor blacks and Bourbons was cemented: "The white
people dare not revolt so long as they can be intimidated by the fear
of the negro vote" (29). A coalition of poor whites, former populists,
and racists legislated the disenfranchisement of black voters across
the South.

The vision black leaders held for their people rarely included a
workers' struggle to displace capital; rather, they foresaw black men
as "captains of industry" and a large pool of black clerks and petty
merchants. In the business world, racial prejudice would be set aside.
Booker T. Washington declared at a meeting of the National Negro
Business League that wherever he had "seen a black man who was
succeeding in business, who was a taxpayer, and who possessed
intelligence and high character, that individual was treated with the
highest respect by the members of the white race" (30). Following
Washington's lead, leagues of black businessmen were established
throughout the country, cementing fragile coalitions of financially
inconsequential and unstable black enterprises. The Colored Merchants Association (CMA) grocery stores spread across the United
States, catering to black patronage and seeking general stock
ownership by poor blacks. So that blacks might take advantage of
these opportunities in business, black universities in the South
shifted their emphasis to business education and imbued these
courses with the fervor appropriate to "economic salvation." The
poor blacks who remained in the rural South or in the inner city,
unmoved by the "myth" of black enterprise, could read in the black
press of the petty exploits of black businessmen and wealthy blacks,
blown out of all proportion to reality (31).

It is little wonder that labor unions were hardly mentioned in this
vision. What was required was not collective action to restrain
business practices, but perseverance in personal enterprise, job
training, neatness, thrift, and industry (32). An editorial in Booker T.
Washington's *Colored American* declared (33),

> There is seldom a time when a strike is justifiable. . . . To attempt to
> break up another man's business because he employs labor unsatis-

factory to you, or because he grants equal privileges to all respectable citizens, is revolutionary and anarchistic. The use of force to keep another man from working wherever he can secure employment is a crime against society.

Leaders encouraged strikebreakers as a means of opening up employment formerly denied to blacks; they considered organizing "colored artisans" into separate unions that would serve primarily as strikebreakers rather than as collective bargaining agents. Black trade unionists who defended the right of workers to strike emphasized that there was no serious dispute between labor and capital and that the appropriate goal of their organizations was to encourage economy and temperance, industry, and education (34).

Unlike the trade unions before the CIO and the Socialist party (35), the Communist party took special notice of the "color problem." Rather than view the mass of unskilled, nonwhite workers as a hindrance to organization or a threat to the "established" working class, the Communist Left turned to blacks as a central organizing force in the workers' movement. Since blacks were the most downtrodden of the working class and the most exploited, they figured prominently in the party program, and were even considered at one point to be the vanguard element among the proletarian forces. This understanding of color and the special concern with the role of the black proletariat prompted party efforts that rebounded to the advantage of blacks. Black political leadership was recruited (36); black labor federations were created. Because John L. Lewis was willing to rely on Communist organizers, the party gave special attention to black workers in meat packing, rubber, steel, and automobile industries (37).

Despite the party's preoccupation with the black condition, few blacks ever rallied to its banner. Black leaders in the arts, in civil rights organizations, and the labor movement flirted from time to time with the party or its affiliates—the National Negro Congress (38) and the Committee for the Negro in the Arts (39), among others—but nearly all remained dubious of the party's intentions and motivations. The very logic underlying Communist interest in the black masses belied, in their view, genuine concern for the race; it betrayed an intention to exploit black alienation for the overriding interest of the party. The black man, Wilson Record writes, "not only would be in the vanguard of the proletarian forces at home; but he would also be instrumental in awakening and leading the colored races of the rest of the world in the struggle to overthrow capitalism" (40).

This impression of Communist intentions was reinforced by a lack of direction in party affairs that seemed to redefine the role of the black proletariat depending upon the interests and wishes of the International. During the three decades following World War I, the party evolved a variety of strategies for dealing with American blacks, some that were insensitive to sentiments in the black community, some that brought the party into direct conflict with established black institutions (such as the Church), and yet others that attempted to limit civil rights activity. After blacks failed to rally behind the Russian Revolution and its programs, the Sixth World Congress in 1928 helped evolve an approach that included an independent black nation (41). The program of self-determination was wholly inappropriate to the Southern context where many blacks sought to flee the area or seek some integrated resolution of race problems. For many black leaders, including those of the NAACP, this new Communist approach seemed little more than "ideological red-winged Jim Crow" (42). During this period, consequently, the party opposed nearly all the established black organizations—betterment groups, interracial, and nationalist organizations (43). When, in the middle thirties, the party reverted to a United Front approach, it was forced to ease these earlier hostilities and establish new directions that were palatable to black groups. The churches and the NAACP, previously the lackeys of capitalists, were now "very close to the daily needs of their poor parishioners" (44). But when, during World War II, A. Phillip Randolph sought to lead blacks in a march on Washington for jobs, an end to discrimination, and basic political rights, the party bitterly opposed the disruption of the war effort. Randolph was described by the party as a "Fascist helping defeatism," threatening the vitality of the Russo-American alliance (45).

The spokesmen for class politics—those groups that might be expected to formulate a class ideology—maintained an ambivalent attitude toward the poor. The Communist party, the socialists, and the labor movement at best failed to identify black concerns and interests and at worst proved openly hostile. The trade unions viewed the movement of blacks into the cities as a threat to their hegemony and sought to exclude them or segregate them in auxiliary unions. Although the CIO brought large numbers of blacks into labor organizations, blacks were not involved centrally in the organization of large-scale industry and were given little attention in the AFL-CIO merger in the mid-fifties. The Communist party, though concerned with the "color problem," vacillated on policy toward blacks and appeared to subordinate black interests to the interests of the party.

Few blacks joined the Communist party or voted Socialist, but large numbers of blacks have joined labor unions. In 1971 well over three million blacks belonged to labor unions, comprising over 16 percent of the total union membership in this country. Black membership is concentrated in the Longshoremen, Steelworkers, Autoworkers, Meatcutters, Packinghouse Workers, International Ladies Garment Workers, Building Service Employees, State, County and Municipal Workers, Letter Carriers, Postal Clerks, and the American Federation of Teachers (46). However, increasing black involvement in labor organizations has not been accompanied by an evolving class ideology or class affinity. Blacks have not traditionally identified with working class movements, were not instrumental (except as scabs) in the struggles that created the unions, and now find themselves involved primarily because they increasingly fill the unskilled industrial jobs once occupied by the Germans, Italians, Poles, and other ethnic groups.

If blacks are to develop a class ideology, it will emerge not from their participation in a workers' struggle but from some other source. We see in the next section that the poor of these five communities share a similar experience with capital and labor and face similar problems in formulating a class ideology.

II   LABOR AND CAPITAL IN FIVE POOR NEIGHBORHOODS

The striving for justice, security, and affluence in five neighborhoods has not been couched in class terms. The poor have not drawn a line between themselves and their employers, not identified the factories or bosses as their oppressors. Ford Motor Company, the Growers Association, and Champion Papers, the obvious heavies in a class analysis, traditionally have not been set off in the minds of the poor. The poor have not found an identity of interests with other working class groups residing in the city. The impoverished blacks on the East Side have rarely sensed a compatibility with their Polish neighbors in Hamtramck; nor have the blacks in North Central looked to the working class Jews and Italians of Northeast Philadelphia. The Mexican-Americans of Gardner have expressed solidarity with neither the blacks who live in San Jose nor the Italians and Portuguese who work in the same canneries and who once picked the same crops. No black man, no matter how committed to workers' solidarity, would dare move into Fairfield Township or many sections of Gardner.

The absence of working class solidarity or a class ideology is particularly striking in the East Side where a generalized alienation is pronounced and where a strong labor movement has opened up opportunities for blacks in all branches of the auto industry. The blacks of the East Side, however, approach questions of working class concern from a history far removed from class struggle. When blacks first came to Detroit in large numbers, their primary means of employment was the auto industry, particularly the Ford Motor Company. Almost 10 percent of the workers at River Rouge were black, though they were concentrated in the heavy jobs in the foundry and on the loading platforms (47). These extraordinary job opportunities were achieved through a strong cooperative relationship between Ford and black church and civic leaders. Don Marshall, sometimes referred to as the black "mayor" of "Paradise Valley," distributed jobs for Ford, as did a number of local ministers. Jobs at Ford were frequently the reward for good works in the church; and the good works of the corporation were often extolled from the pulpit itself (48).

When the unions began their bitter struggle for recognition, the black community was unsupportive. The Urban League, financed almost entirely by the Employer's Association of Detroit (49), advised "colored workers, as to the necessity for cultivating qualities highly prized by employers, viz., punctuality, reliability, dependability, loyalty" (50), and not unexpectedly opposed the sit-down strikes. The Colored Elks declared: "Unionism is calculated to do our people all sorts of harm and injure them with the employing class of America. . ." (51). The Interdenominational Ministers' Alliance, comprising most of the conservative black preachers, urged black workers not to join the UAW but, if forced to join a union, rather the more palatable AFL affiliate (52). When Ford was struck, blacks played a very ambiguous role. Somewhere between 800 and 2500 black workers failed to walk out of the plant and bands of blacks on two occasions attacked and broke union lines. A "back to work" campaign, variously active in the black neighborhoods of Detroit, failed because a number of black leaders feared race riots if blacks were to play a prominent "strikebreaking" role (53).

Though the UAW is established in Detroit and blacks are established in important union offices, a marked tension remains. Black workers comprise an increasingly large portion of the work force, most noticeably in the inner city Chrysler facilities. Sixty to 70 percent of the union members in Chrysler Local 7, at Chrysler Eldon Gear and Axle, and at Dodge Main are black (54). DRUM (Dodge Revolutionary Union Movement) originated at Dodge Main; other black separatist factions developed at other plants—FRUM (Ford Revolutionary Union Movement), ELRUM (Eldon), JARUM (Jefferson Avenue), MARUM (Mack Avenue), and CRUM (Chrysler Revolutionary Union Movement) (55). Although these groups have not succeeded in displacing established UAW leadership, including blacks, they highlight the tension that exists between younger black workers and older white, ethnic workers.

The on and off alliance of the UAW and black political leaders has also worked tensions into a black-white, working class movement in Detroit. The Trade Union Leadership Conference, comprised of black trade unionists, has battled with the UAW over important party positions and helped elect Jerome Cavanaugh over the opposition of the UAW. Incompatibilities between the black and union agendas are frequently played out in the District Democratic Organizations where the UAW puts its money and staff. The Thirteenth District, incorporating much of the East Side, has long been a stronghold of UAW influence, an example, one black leader has suggested, of "plantation politics."

Unions and blacks are no longer warring parties, the former confronting management and the latter allied with it. Black leaders and union officials have made their peace, despite the tensions that we have mentioned. The District Democratic Organization endorsements, the ministerial alliances, and the UAW endorsements are usually compatible, reflecting a common desire for moderately liberal and often black public officials. But it is an alliance blacks fell into, one they did not seek and formerly did not desire. Their coalition is one of convenience. It was not forged in common struggle, guided by a common perspective on ownership, the malfeasance of management, and the inequity of income distribution.

In neither North Central nor Summerhill are the forces that alienate poor blacks from working class movements as pronounced and dramatic as in Detroit. Neither was blessed with a Henry Ford. The sit-in movements that so convulsed the auto industry and the city of Detroit were never to forge a militant labor movement in Atlanta or Philadelphia. Their labor organizations would rarely set the agenda of electoral politics in their respective cities; their endorsements would never pose the central electoral choices, as they did in Detroit. But the problem of solidarity reared its head in these cities, raising similar questions for the black leadership and labor organizers. Summerhill highlights the affinity of poor blacks and wealthy whites, even in the absence of protracted and violent labor turmoil.

Rioting broke out in central Atlanta on September 22, 1906, on the fringes of the "Old Fourth Ward" and Summerhill. For four days, "destruction, looting, robbery, murder, and unspeakable brutality" (56) raged in the streets that formed the core of black commercial life. Gangs of poor whites chased blacks through the streets of Atlanta, often shooting them down in the streets. As his counterpart would do some six decades later, the Mayor of Atlanta mounted a box and beseeched the crowd (57):

> For God's sake men, go to your homes quietly, and leave this matter
> in the hands of the law. I promise you that every negro will receive
> justice, and the guilty shall not escape.

The violent disturbances in 1906 immediately followed the gubernatorial election pitting Clark Howell against Hoke Smith. The former sought "justice for the railroads" and ran with the backing of the traditional Democratic party and the controlled black vote; the latter demanded stringent regulation of the railroad and, above all else, the end of "negro domination" and the disenfranchisement of the black voters (58). Smith received the active support of the

Populists (always strong in Georgia), Tom Watson, and the growing urban working class. C. Vann Woodward described the record of bigotry that culminated in rioting and the termination of black political involvement (59):

> During the campaign the papers of Atlanta were almost daily filled with sensational stories of Negro atrocities. Lynching was openly advocated and frequently practiced. A concerted crusade of race bigotry and hatred was preached.

The *Atlanta Journal* wrote in an editorial, "It is time for those who know the perils of the negro problem to stand together with deep resolve that political power shall never give the negro encouragement in his foul dreams of a mixture of the races" (60).

When the courts in the middle forties ruled the white primary unconstitutional, blacks once again became active in Atlanta politics, striking alliances not very different from those that preceded disenfranchisement (61). The Atlanta Negro Voters League, directed by a cadre of ministers, officers of the Urban League, a newspaper editor, the president of Atlanta University, an executive secretary of the YMCA, and a businessman, sought to create a black voting bloc that could prove pivotal in a balance of power and that, in fact, served to enhance the moderate, liberal business-oriented leadership of the city. Mayor Hartsfield was the first to rely on Voters League endorsements and was followed in later years by Ivan Allen (62). Along with the press and the business power structure, the blacks helped form the ruling coalition in Atlanta, to the exclusion of poorer whites, presumably natural allies in the working class (63). When in 1961 the black leadership split over the sit-in movement, the Negro Voters League persisted in their support of the President of the Chamber of Commerce and garnered 73 percent of the black vote for his candidacy (64). Not until the mid-sixties did the coalition seriously begin to falter and by the 1969 mayoral race, the coalition had crumbled altogether. Rodney Cook, the candidate of business, the press, and normally, the substantial black vote, lost out to a more liberal Jewish candidate who won with the black vote.

The history of Mexican farm workers in the southwestern United States is pockmarked with examples of incipient labor organizations. During the early Depression years the rich agricultural areas of

California were swept by agricultural strikes. In 1933 50,000 workers joined work stoppages affecting almost 65 percent of the state's crop (65), and in 1936 25,000 Mexican workers struck, tying up the citrus crop in Orange County (66). Unions were active even before the Depression: in 1903 Mexican and Japanese sugar beet workers struck in Ventura; in 1922 there was an effort to unionize grape pickers in Fresno; and in the late twenties, 3000 workers joined the *Confederacion de Uniones Obreras Mexicanas,* a union formed along ethnic lines.

Virtually all the strikes, except those settled quickly, were crushed by the violence of growers, vigilantes, and police. The growers' bitter denunciation of any long-term collective bargaining arrangements made industrial unions precarious (the rancor was especially marked when farm workers were organized by industrial or Communist unions). The Agricultural Workers Industrial Union (IWW) was able to recruit about 20,000 members in 1916; by 1917 its leaders had been driven out of the fields or placed in jail; the union disintegrated (67). The Cannery and Agricultural Workers Union (C&AW), whose headquarters was in San Jose, also courted a membership of 20,000 agricultural workers. In April of 1933 the union's Communist leadership called out Mexican, Filipino, Puerto Rican, and Caucasian pea pickers in Santa Clara County and later in the year led a walkout of cherry pickers (68). But like their wobbly predecessors, the union was crushed by official intimidation and police violence. In addition, many farm workers (about half of whom were not citizens) were reluctant to join any labor organization, particularly one led by Communists. The C&AW was troubled at the outset not simply by official opposition, but also by the vulnerability of migrant workers and the anti-Communist appeals of the Mexican consul (69).

With the defeat of agricultural unionization in the early thirties, a calm settled over the relations between labor and capital, creating what Carey McWilliams calls "the present-day tendency of the immigrants to retire within the confines of the Mexican *colonia* and to seek . . . a bicultural accommodation" (70). Mexican workers were no longer centrally involved in the labor struggle. Their employment on farms, in railroad construction, and in mining shielded many Mexican workers from the new industrial unions. The tendency of migratory labor to travel and work in family units and with ethnically homogeneous groups further reinforced their sense of distinctiveness and isolation (71). Only with Cesar Chavez' United Farm Workers Organizing Committee have substantial inroads been made in the unionization of Mexican farm laborers. But at the zenith of its success, many workers did not join the union and numerous local Mexican-American organizations remained anti-union, including local chapters of the Community Service Organization, Latin American Citizens Association, and the *Sociedad Progresita Mexicana* (72).

The California AFL greeted the influx of Mexican laborers into migratory occupations and urban employment with hostility and discrimination. At the national convention in 1926, the California delegation fought for an "exclusionist plank regarding Mexican immigration," and an official of the state organization declared in 1928, "If we do not remain on guard it is not going to be our country," and government institutions will be dominated by "a mongrel population consisting largely of Mexicans" (75). The craft unions excluded Mexican labor as their counterparts on the East Coast did blacks; and though the canneries were successfully organized in San Jose in the late thirties and early forties, Italians and Portuguese dominated the work force. Now that Mexican labor is predominant in the plants, few Mexicans have been able to gain leadership positions in the union. For the mass of Mexican labor working in the canneries and packinghouses, the unions are considered part of the job, controlled by hierarchies in which Mexican-Americans play little part (74).

The identification of Mexican-Americans with the working class is confounded by the problem of color in Mexican-American communities. Although those outside the Southwest are likely to look upon Filipinos, blacks, and Mexicans as "third world" peoples united by oppression and racism, it is an image not necessarily congruent with the image Mexican-Americans have of themselves. Mexican-Americans in San Jose, for example, are as segregated from black residents of the city as they are from the Anglo population; in Los Angeles the separation between blacks and Mexican-Americans is even more pronounced (75). A survey in Los Angeles found that few Mexican-Americans objected to marriage with Anglos, but they were nearly unanimous in objecting to marriage with blacks (76). If an identity of interests is to be established across the working class, it is apparent that such a relationship will be shaped by the Mexican-American's sensitivity to color.

The success of the United Mine Workers in the Cumberland Plateau should not obscure the distrust highlanders have of unions and the extraordinary faith they have expressed in management, even in the face of some of the most exploitative management practices conceivable. Field workers for the UMW in the twenties were viewed with almost as much hostility by the miners as by management, both groups fearing that a union would impose collective bargaining and infringe upon the personal relationship between the miner and his boss (the owners certainly feared other consequences as well). "Trust and affection," Harry Caudill writes, "died with remarkable slowness, and only after they had been dealt many blows—blows impelled more often by desperation and a blind urge to survive than by malice or ill-will" (77).

Though many mountaineers in the plateau and some in Hamilton have "beenraised to back the union" (78), support for the union has declined. A long-time resident of the Plateau and a supporter of the union commented,

> The only people who cared about the union were the mine workers who were starving in the thirties. In the twenties, they hated the union. But their sons don't feel much for the union. In fact, many a father and son won't talk to one another because the son is working for an independent operator.

Another native of the hills and organizer lamented the abandonment by the union of its former activists.

> The union didn't do anything for these people. Bill McPeak lost a leg and had all sorts of things done to his house and his girls. He really gave his life for that union. But when the mine mechanized and dropped from 300 miners to 30, they couldn't be bothered with it. Some of the older miners aren't getting pensions or their medi-cards. They contracted to some other union and they don't give a damn about these people. The union really has done some bad things around here.

Unions came of age in Hamilton, Ohio, when Champion Papers settled in 1967. A paternalistic management had established a strong bond of loyalty with Appalachian workers. It provided paid vacations a decade before most union plants; it offered workers life insurance packages, time-service features (to provide retirement savings), and a formal retirement plan. Union organizers were received with hostility by the Appalachian workers as well as by management. "Of course, the company had the best public relations job going," a recent Mayor remembered.

> It was unbelievable. Champion cleared a baseball diamond, let their employees use it. Gave supplies to the schools. Provided pensions. Also, low wages. But the public relations was first rate. If you worked for Champion, you were set. The word union was a dirty name around here.

After World War II, the atmosphere began to change. Industries began the exodus from Hamilton, causing a retrenchment of employment opportunities for Appalachian migrants. More important, however, was that management began to shift to more professional personnel, to men less concerned with the family image or with loyalty. At Champion Papers, the Mayor recalls, "A strong Army man, a captain I think, really cleaned house. Chopped jobs right and left." In the mid-sixties Southwestern Ohio Steel was organized. Beckett fell in 1966, a year before Champion. The union won recognition at Champion Papers by a few votes ("7 or 9," an employee recalled). At Mosler Safe, an independent union ("company union," if you will) defeated both the United Automobile Workers and the Steelworkers in a recognition election and the former in a two-way runoff.

The association of the poor with working class organizations is ambiguous in all these neighborhoods, sometimes reflected in open hostility, sometimes in indifference, and increasingly in an uneasy participation. The established labor movement has not proved receptive to black and Mexican-American workers; in most cases this hostility was reciprocated by a cozy relationship between the poor and management. The alliance of poor blacks with business was particularly important to the pre-World War II politics of Detroit and the post-World War II politics of Atlanta. Though CIO unions have brought blacks and Mexican-Americans into the labor movement, blacks were rarely active in the formative stages of the unions and are now involved with them primarily as a condition of their employment. The Mexican workers' early attempts at unionization were rebuffed by established unions; Communist unions died in some cases for lack of support and in others because of violent repression. Poor whites in Belmont, though not excluded from union activities, proved loyal to management beyond the period when most workers had ceased to believe in business benevolence, company unions, and the company family. The struggle to engage them in unions is not yet won.

The poor of these five neighborhoods face the issues of working class solidarity, redistributive justice, and equality, not from a history of class struggle, but from a relationship with the ruling classes, sometimes marked by trust and cooperation, often by ambivalence, and only infrequently by group conflict. It is not apparent that the poor desire a redistribution of the wealth or hold beliefs that contradict the "ruling ideas." It is not apparent that they feel a natural affinity for other workers; in fact, the poor of these neighborhoods have had to struggle against other working class groups to gain jobs and a fair wage. The class position of the poor, consequently, is ambiguous, vacillating between both sides of what is perhaps an illusory class division.

III   BASES OF CONSCIOUSNESS

Union organizers and social scientists alike have assumed that class consciousness emerges from economic conditions, from desperation, and from hostility for management or the rich. It is this under-standing that leads John Leggett to his analysis of working class consciousness and economic insecurity (agrarian-industrial mobility, tenuous occupational position, and membership in a marginal racial or ethnic group) (79). Southern-born blacks and European-born Poles, therefore, form the vanguard of class conscious workers (80). Similarly, E. P. Thompson proposes that the craftsmen and artisans of early nineteenth century England, threatened by the "freedom" of capitalist enterprise ("whether by new machinery, by the factory-system, or by unrestricted competition, beating-down wages, undercutting his rivals, and undermining standards of craftsman-ship") turned to some form of class action (81). Out of the Luddite and other struggles, workers gained a sense of conflict in history (82) as well as a "consciousness of the identity of the interests of the working class, or 'productive classes,' as *against* those of other classes" (83). Though there are marked differences in these two analyses—Leggett anticipates a strong consciousness among the uprooted whereas Thompson looks to those who are threatened by the uprooted (84)—both men rely on marginality and desperation as bases for expanded consciousness and a theory of conflict.

These conclusions are bewildering in light of our description of these five poor neighborhoods. The inner city urban poor are the product of marginality, both in the rural setting to which they trace their origins and in the urban setting where they presently face their plight. They hold marginal positions in the occupational structure, live in threatened neighborhoods, and have few economic or political resources. Yet our data and descriptive material suggest little sense of class conflict, an inchoate feeling for the dichotomy between the "productive classes" and the poor, and a fragmentary view of the working class. These impressions prevail despite occasional flights into oppositional roles (85). Despite extreme marginality and flirtations with opposition strategies more suited to class conflict, few among the poor have formulated a class ideology; certainly, few are committed to income redistribution or income guarantees.

The emphasis on marginality and economic condition derives, perhaps, from a too limited view of class consciousness and a distortion of Marx. Though Marx offers a forceful picture of a developing class, broadened through increasing exploitation and coalesced through conflict with the ruling classes (86), he provides for a more complex view of consciousness. It is not based simply on condition and desperation, or opposition and conflict, but depends as well on awareness and self-understanding (87). Marx's understanding of group activity is not limited entirely by the failure of polarization or alterations in the functional bases of social conflict (88).

The advancement of the class struggle, Marx believed, required that the preoccupation of the working class be raised beyond the "level of economic necessity to the level of conscious aim and effective class consciousness" (89). Marginality and plight are not sufficient for class struggle; they represent an immature condition for effective class action. What is required, instead, is an objective process of transcendence that enables individuals to rise above the "mere immediacy of the empirical world" (90), and aspire toward a sense of totality. The proletariat, Marx believed, stood at the center of a total system and held a unique perspective for comprehending society in its entirety (91). The insufferable quality of life and the heinous practices of employers become sensible in this totality? they no longer move the proletariat to blind rage or senseless reaction. Consciousness as transcendence, as an aspiration for totality, therefore, brings the worker to an understanding that is beyond simple dissatisfaction with condition. His consciousness is on a "path leading from the 'class opposed to capitalism' to the class 'for itself' " (92).

The distinction between a group consciousness based on opposition or on self-understanding is important to Marx's analysis and central to our discussion of class ideology. Marginality, insecurity, and oppositional perspectives inadequately explain the class commitments in poor neighborhoods, failing to lay an adequate basis for consciousness or to explain the restrained class ideology of the poor. By adopting a view of marginality that also takes into account the mechanisms of self-understanding and self-assertion, however, we are able to view class ideology within a context more suited to the empirical realities. Both the attenuated consciousness of the poor and the variety of their politics become more sensible as a result.

IV   CLASS IDEOLOGY: ESTRANGEMENT OR SOLIDARITY?

Harold Cruse understood a fundamental fact about American Communism—and the American brand of socialism. Its vitality was predicated not on an emergent solidarity that transcended all working class groups, but on the affinity and understanding of national groups. Finnish and Russian groups (particularly the Jews) dominated the party and dominated in nationalist terms. Cruse notes that the "Jews were also able to play a three-way game inside the Communist leftwing: as 'Americanized' Jews, a la Gold; as Jewish Jews; and as pro-zionist, nationalistic Jews" (93). They moved in and out of these identities without threatening their solidarity with the working class or jeopardizing their legitimacy in the party. But the party expected very different things of blacks. As the most oppressed and exploited working class group, the blacks were to forge the vanguard of the proletarian struggle. On their shoulders rested the responsibility for working class solidarity; they alone were to rise above the pettiness of nationalist squabble, particularism, and revisionist distractions. Unlike other groups who were to mold the party, blacks were to submerge the distractions of color and forge a mythical unity of peoples. Theirs was to be a party where "black and white, native and foreign-born, Gentile and Jew all joined together in heavenly discourse without ethnic frictions" (94). To that mythical end, the blacks were obligated to submerge the desire for "Negro Zionism"—repudiating Garvey and the U.N.I.A.—and cultural nationalism (95). They were not to achieve the imprint of national identity but to realize themselves on behalf of all workers.

What the Communist party asked of blacks is not very different from what is being asked of the poor generally—a submergence of group identity for the interest of workers everywhere. Before grasping the particularism of their own group experience, poor blacks, Mexican-Americans, and Appalachian whites are being asked to ignore their distinctiveness and grant the overriding importance of class struggle. But as with the role expected of blacks at an earlier time by the Communist party, the demand may be unreasonable in terms of group importance and ill-advised even in terms of class struggle. It may well be, as Claude Lightfoot suggests, that "the principal trend of black nationalism does not deny the necessity of unity of black and white" (96), and as Legget's empirical material indicates, that the development of race and class symbolism are highly intercorrelated (97). Class ideology, in short, may emerge out of group solidarity, not itself a party to class conflict.

Intimately bound up with national identity and class solidarity are the questions of consciousness raised by Marx in our previous discussion. On the one hand is a view of consciousness that emerges directly from marginality. The poor experience insecurity in the employment market, in their separation from the land, and in the humiliation of racial prejudice. Their marginality is immediately tied to expressions of discontent and an understanding of class divisions. The other view supposes that economic necessity alone is not sufficient to mold consciousness, that beliefs emerging from it alone are immature in an important sense—providing few impressions of totality and little ability to transcend immediacy. Objective consciousness arises from group identity and understanding, where consciousness transcends a "class opposed to capitalism" and formulates a class "for itself."

Whether class ideology is bound by either of these two conceptions of consciousness can indeed be ascertained by reference to our previous analysis. If class ideology were primarily a response to social discontent and negative feelings about "unproductive classes," we would expect a strong correlation with political alienation and, in black and Mexican-American communities, with hostility toward white or Anglo institutions. If on the other hand, class ideology emerges from a group autonomy and understanding, its correlation with dissatisfaction measures should prove less significant than that with feelings of group autonomy. The choice is then between an alienative-oppositional form of consciousness and one derived from group autonomy.

The pattern of association in Figure 7.1 is consistent for both black and Mexican-American communities: group autonomy is the primary correlate or determinate of class ideology. The path coefficients (beta weights), exceeding .300 in both cases, reduce to almost insignificance the results for any single measure and even overshadow the combined impact of all the estrangement measures.

These results underline our initial expectation that class ideology in poor neighborhoods is not solely an alienative system of belief. Above all else, it is based on a group understanding and a group assertion that is itself predicated on marginality but also on a particular cultural and historical experience that is not class-based. Through the examination of this experience, the poor develop a sense of self, enabling them to translate alienative feelings into a more transcendent perspective on group relations.

These distinctions between alienation, understanding, and class ideology emerge in the acrimony and violence that characterized the riots (civil disturbances or rebellions) of the 1960s. Ben Gilbert of the *Washington Post* described the anger of a middle-aged black man as he faced a shattered drugstore window (98).

> There were tears in his eyes, and he was angry. He began shouting about the white man's evil. He picked up a city trash can off the sidewalk and threw it through the drugstore window. Still screaming, he went across the street and threw a bottle from the street gutter through the window of the National Liquor Store.

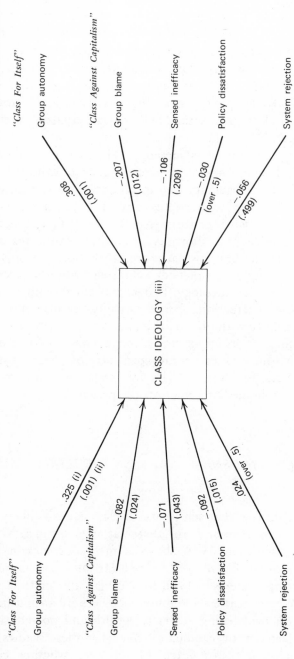

Figure 7.1. Determinants of class ideology. (i) Beta weight; (ii) significance; (iii) see Appendix B.

199

Expressions of hostility, like this one, became more frequent in the mid-sixties, but also more legitimate. People expressed pride in what they had done, displaying their loot as trophies (99). What had emerged, Tomlinson speculated, was a "riot ideology." Segments of the black community have come to view their actions as appropriate and effective, as a response to "the conditions of Negro life that had always existed" (100). They express strong dissatisfaction with the white community and its institutions and indicate a strong preference for violent means.

But riot ideology is not class ideology. There may well be a pattern of belief that is anti-white, deeply alienated—hostile to politicians, the police, bureaucrats, and merchants—and at the same time, integrally bound up with expressions of political violence. Indeed, the data in this work confirm that the resort to violence is very much a consequence of hostility to white institutions and generalized estrangement. But this pattern of alienation and opposition (which often concludes in violence) is different from the pattern we have observed for class ideology. It does not emerge out of the barrel of a gun, from disaffection, or from hostility toward whites. A concern with redistribution and basic life guarantees emanates from a shared understanding of group interests and a concern for group autonomy. It is in some senses an advanced form of consciousness similar in many ways to Marx's "class for itself," maturer in its formulation than an immediate reaction to marginality or a "riot ideology."

V   GROUP CONSCIOUSNESS, CLASS IDEOLOGY, AND POLITICS

Previous research confirms that sensitivity to class issues is likely to create a working class vote and, for that matter, a business vote. Richard Centers' sample in 1944 shows a marked coalescing of "radical" voters around Franklin Roosevelt (101); other samples show a similar voting pattern in 1948 for Truman and in 1952 for Stevenson (102). Where workers and union members are antibusiness and concerned with broadening access to wealth and power, they tend to vote for Democratic candidates. But what these studies do not show, and have not attempted to test, are whether class consciousness increases the likelihood of political involvement and whether it guides workers in the choice of appropriate political strategies.

Class ideology, Table 7.2 shows, does not have an important effect on politics in poor communities, *outside of its symbiotic relationship with group consciousness.* Concern with redistributive justice or income supports bears no relation whatever with the resort to violence and is only weakly associated with more conventional political action. Coefficients in both black and Mexican-American communities are small and for the most part insignificant, although the tabular analysis shows some impact on political involvement. In Gardner and the East Side, strong class sentiments—an affirmation of both class items—produce a marked increase in the receptivity to politics, though in neither community do more than 8 percent of the respondents hold such beliefs (Table 7.3). The impact in Summerhill is pronounced where class sentiments are relatively widespread and an association with receptivity to politics is evident. Only in North Central are the results ambiguous.

The political importance of class ideology, however, is not to be found in its independent impact on political involvement, but in its profound analytic and empirical complicity with group consciousness. Class ideology, as the data suggest, can not be weighed by itself; there is only a scant, barely perceptible pattern of association with political expression measures. As the data indicate, however, class ideology is caught up in a thought process dependent upon the formulation of group consciousness. Class ideology emerges not from distress but from a group understanding that places its particular interpretation on social conditions. The two sets of beliefs are likely to work on one another, helping the poor to decide on appropriate political options and their relation to dominant classes and other working class groups (see Figure 7.2).

VI CONCLUSIONS

By reexamining the question of class consciousness, posing the issue in terms of self-understanding and assertion rather than as a reaction to marginality, we have begun to unravel some fundamental paradoxes. The poor, it seems, share circumstances characterized by

Table 7.2. Class Ideology and Political Expression

Independent Variables	Black Neighborhoods		Mexican-American Neighborhood	
	Beta Weights	Significance	Beta Weights	Significance
A. Association with receptivity to violence				
-System rejection	.213	.001	-.126	.145
-Sensed inefficacy	.099	.002	.175	.046
- Policy dissatisfaction	.167	.001	.054	over .500
-Group identification	.307	.001	.105	.228
-Class ideology	-.091	.004	.066	.415
Multiple correlation (r^2)	30%		6%	

B. Association with
receptivity to politics

-System rejection	.004	over .500	.111	.179
-Sensed inefficacy	-.372	.001	-.232	.007
-Policy dissatisfaction	.172	.001	.123	.127
-Group identification	.056	.125	.296	.001
-Class ideology	.082	.015	.028	over .500
Multiple correlation (r^2)	17%		13%	

Table 7.3. Class Ideology and Political Expression: Percentage "High"
Receptivity to Politics

Class Ideology (i)	Poor Neighborhoods			
	Gardner	East Side	Summerhill	North Central
Low	55%	55%	41%	71%
	(114)	(151)	(46)	(66)
Medium	44%	64%	86%	77%
	(27)	(106)	(145)	(163)
High	83%	74%	51%	62%
	(12)	(23)	(59)	(21)
Gamma	.075	.226	.025	.000
Probability	Not significant	.038	Not significant	Not significant

(i) See Appendix B.

low income, instability, and neighborhood abandonment. Despite their marginality, however, the poor remain uncommitted to reordering the country's wealth. On the East Side, where residents are extremely distrustful of whites, noticeably estranged from the political community and critical of political institutions, commitment to a class ideology is hopelessly low—well below that of other poor black neighborhoods. But as we have seen, class ideology does not emerge from discontent and alienation, but from group understanding and solidarity. The race consciousness of the East Side, however, is highly oppositional and only weakly developed as a solidary sentiment. Class ideology is most pronounced in Summerhill, a community that watched a stadium and superhighways displace thousands of its residents, yet showed few indications of discontent.

Riot ideology has proved not to be a class ideology. Alienation and hostility do not translate into a commitment for reordering basic economic relations. The extreme marginality of these neighborhoods and the discontent expressed (most noticeably in the black communities) do not of themselves bring about an understanding at

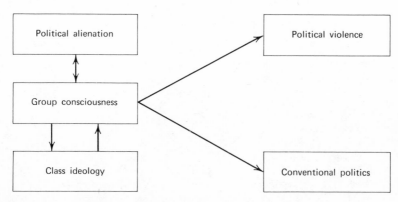

Figure 7.2. Class consciousness and politics.

the social level. Class ideology assumes importance in the thinking of the poor when they turn in upon themselves, establish their own interests, and assert themselves in politics based on their own solidarity.

The translation of these sentiments into political expression, however, is made difficult by the peculiarities of group consciousness. In Gardner, the Mexican-American community, group solidarity is preeminently a concern with group autonomy; these group commitments foster conventional political expression. But adherence to this notion of *"la Raza"* is not widespread, thus limiting its impact on politics and limiting as well the role of class ideology. Black consciousness, dependent more on oppositional themes and alienated beliefs, heightens receptivity to violence. Because class ideology relies on the nonoppositional aspects of group consciousness, however, its impact is muted in the black communities.

Class ideology is not realized in the politics of poor neighborhoods; it will achieve political expression, perhaps, only when there is a basic shift in thinking about group and self. "Class politics" will emerge not from a heightened sensitivity to oppression or increased alienation, but from a broader acceptance of *la Raza* in the Mexican-American community and the emergence of a black identity that is rooted, above all else, in history, cultural integration, and self-examination.

Chapter Eight

Conclusion:
Radical and Liberal
Political Man

. . . .

The First Scenario: From the South's Black Belt, the Cumberland Plateau, and Mexico's Central Mesa, the poor came. They abandoned peasantry to take up the work of America's cities and factories. In the heart of the cities the poor found crowded, deteriorating housing; in the River Rouge plant, the canneries, and paper mills, they found the lowest-paid, least desirable jobs. These were not their cities nor their companies. The production line, the cities' highways, and buildings moved on inexorably, indifferent to the concerns of the poor; history and politics, growth and conflict continued to unfold with only a glimpse to the impoverished populations who gnawed at the cities' cores. In their powerlessness, their superfluousness, the poor turned in on themselves and their own problems. They viewed politics as might a foreign people: it was not their concern. The poor developed few organizations and few political contacts. While elections and civic issues occupied the cities' attention, the poor remained indifferent and uninvolved. For the poor were the object of, not a force in, history.

The Second Scenario: Here, too, the poor fled the hinterlands of North America. They came to the cities, to production lines, crowded housing, and poverty. Here, too, the poor were isolated and manipulated by history and politics. But in their isolation, their crowding and numbers, the poor discovered a basis for change. Like the ethnic populations of a previous era, they began to view themselves as a cohesive group and to act, indeed demand, collectively. They formed their own organizations—churches, social clubs, and betterment groups; they played and voted together. The poor became power brokers in history, struggling, tinkering, and bargaining for their share. History did not belong to them alone, but responded to the bargains and pluralism of which they were a part.

The Third Scenario: They fled; they migrated; they, too, found an inner city resplendent with poverty and despair, lacking in political opportunities. They considered the route of their ethnic predecessors—pluralism—and the temptations of resignation. But distorting their contemplation of strategy and change was a need to confront authorities and challenge their control over the poor. The poor joined organizations and voted, but failing to gain control of their lives, they forged an amorphous protest movement. They walked picket lines, blocked lunchcounters and welfare offices, boycotted merchants, chanted, and screamed. The younger and more militant abandoned the conventional instruments of outrage and turned to sporadic looting, arson, and catharsis. Abandoned by the city, confined to the worst housing and worst jobs, the poor were not satisfied to resign or tinker; their struggle was a confrontation with history.

The twentieth century urban poor might have enacted any one of these scenarios. They emerged from an historical epoch characterized by diminishing economic and political opportunities in the country-side, the lure of industrial employment in the cities, and the concentration and isolation of impoverished urban populations. But the singular process that uprooted the peasant populations of Mexico's Central Mesa, the South's Black Belt, and the Appalachian coal counties, that molded a population movement, and that created the deteriorating inner cities failed to dictate a political response. Only the barest respect for the facts could suppose that poor neighborhoods across the country share one of these scenarios. Instead the poor have adopted a multiple response to conditions. The scenarios of resignation, pluralism, and confrontation are all prevalent forms of political action.

The diversity of politics in these poor neighborhoods is evident in the contrasting approaches to violence (three of every four East Side residents score "high" on receptivity to violence compared to only one of three in Gardner); in the varying commitments to political expression (three of four scoring "high" in North Central but only one of two in Gardner); in the differing levels of organizational membership (twice as high in North Central as in either Belmont or Summerhill); and in the capacity of these communities to marshal their strength at the polls (nearly twice as many residents voting in the East Side as in Summerhill). The world of intense organizational involvement, community conflict, and nonviolence that characterizes Gardner bears little resemblance to the violent but protective mood of the East Side. The passivity of Summerhill and Belmont contrasts with the intense but diffuse political life of North Central. From these impressions emerge not the logic and story line of a single scenario, but a picture of political movements worlds apart.

To create a design out of disorder, a scenario from apparent anecdotes, we introduced a number of concepts—lower class culture, political alienation, group consciousness, and class ideology. With these tools, we hoped to isolate some of the central determinants of politics in poor neighborhoods and to show how intercommunity differences might be explained. Only then could we hope to understand the multiple images of poor neighborhoods and the failure of modernization and urbanization to forge a singular political style.

It is time to take account of our successes and failures.

I BELIEF AND POLITICS IN POOR NEIGHBORHOODS

At the outset, we noted that the focus of our research would not encompass the full range of political determinants (thus deemphasizing historical and immediate structural factors) but would center instead on beliefs about community, interests, and opportunities. We included in this analysis feelings about fate and control, political institutions and political community, group identity, and generalized class commitments. Using these categories, we sought to trace the linkages between belief and action, and to suggest some of the broader environmental considerations that might structure the climate of opinion.

We found the emphasis in the sociological literature upon "lower class" culture not without merit and statistical support, but evidently limited in its political consequences. Cultural themes—particularly present orientation and interpersonal distrust—assume prominence in the street corner environment, where a focus on immediacy, spontaneity, fantasy, and powerlessness consume larger concerns, including politics. But the prominence of cultural themes on the street corner fails to demonstrate a larger community effect on political expression. The predominant elements of the poor population—including women, many adolescents, and most men of middle age—are unreceptive to street corner values and therefore removed from a broader "lower class" cultural influence. Only in Belmont, the Appalachian community, is there a broad-based cultural orientation and a consistent depressing effect on political involvement.

By employing three specific relational concepts, political alienation was transformed from an amorphous feeling about political life into a concrete assessment of political opportunities. Policy dissatisfaction, sensed inefficacy, and system rejection (the ingredients of alienation) are salient to the poor, making sense of political experience and suggesting political possibilities. Specifically with these three concepts we were able to demonstrate the profound relationship between patterns of estrangement and political options, highlighting the mediating role of calculated effectiveness. Political involvement is most pronounced where individuals see a reason for their commitment (pronounced policy dissatisfaction) and calculate that their efforts will not prove futile (diminished sense of inefficacy). But where discontent (including policy dissatisfaction and system rejection) is pronounced and individuals feel public officials are unapproachable, political involvement turns toward violence. Political withdrawal or apathy is evident when alienated beliefs provide neither a provocation (little policy discontent) nor inducement (strong feelings of futility) for political involvement. These patterns of response reflect the poor's political experience both before and after migration and provide realistic guides to political opportunities.

Group identity is evident in three forms, each relating in one way or another to group cultural history and group experience with dominant elements in society. The first is oppositional, evident in the black neighborhoods and concerned primarily with the responsibility of white society for conditions in the ghetto. The second is traditional and typified by the Mexican-American community. Its preoccupation is not so much with Anglo groups as with a cultural tradition and strong, continually reinforced ties to Mexican social and political life. The third form of identity represents more a residual concept than a distinctive form of consciousness. In the Appalachian white community there is little consideration of discrimination, culture, or history. Its consciousness is a recognition of similarity without an assessment of responsibility or identification of group history. The data analysis and observation demonstrate a strong association between an oppositional consciousness and receptivity to violence, traditional consciousness and receptivity to conventional politics, and taciturn consciousness and political inactivity.

Although commitments to highly particularistic racial or ethnic identities are important to the politics of poor neighborhoods, broader categories of consciousness (class ideology, for example) have almost no direct impact whatever. The poor have not traditionally viewed their interests as common or as opposed to those of capital and wealth. Whatever class commitments do emerge stem not directly from plight but from a strong group or racial consciousness. Class ideology and group consciousness work on one another in a symbiotic way, building self-understanding, a devotion to group autonomy, and in the end, a commitment to politics. Class ideology is translated into political expression not through an abstract identity of class interests (or the instruments of class action), but through a more focused understanding of racial or group identity (or the instruments of race goals).

By raising and developing these four concepts—lower class culture, political alienation, group consciousness, and class ideology—we have traced a central path to politics in poor neighborhoods. These issues are not abstract constructs, removed from the realities of conflict and struggle. They are fundamental to an individual's grappling with life choices and to a community's capacity to live and grow; they are above all the questions the poor must and do ask of themselves. Without resolving basic notions of fate and interpersonal trust, of collective and individual interest, and of particular and generalized values; without examining the contours of group history and culture or the predominant influence of outside groups and institutions; and without formulating some conception of the political system (what it does, what it represents, and how it responds), it is difficult to imagine how the poor might begin to forge some satisfactory accommodation to circumstances or some strategy for change. No matter how amorphous a group's sense of these issues, their consideration is at the root of their political style, whether liberal or radical.

In Tables 8.1 and 8.2, the determinant relationships between the six attitudinal constructs and differing political styles are presented graphically. Regression equations were computed for receptivity to politics and receptivity to violence in each of these poor neighborhoods, employing all the independent variables important to our earlier analysis. Presented in the tables are the standardized regression coefficients for each independent variable and the total amount of variance explained by the equations. From this data we can ascertain which factors are most important to the political style of each city and the degree to which, in the aggregate, they can account for the variance of political response *within* each city. This analysis permits us to translate the generalized association between belief and politics (e.g., an oppositional consciousness is conducive to political violence) into a specific prediction for each neighborhood. In the process we lend greater validity to the generalized association and give reality to the causal processes molding alternative political styles.

The conflict-ridden politics of Gardner are not made sensible in these equations; we had no measure of factionalism. However, the orientation toward conventional forms of political expression in preference to violence is readily apparent. Alienated beliefs (with one minor exception) maintain the pattern of association evident in the black and Appalachian white communities. But developing group identity is the most important consideration in a heightened political involvement, by itself accounting for 8 percent of the variance in receptivity to politics (1). Group identity in Gardner, however,

Table 8.1. Receptivity to Politics: Attitudinal Determinants

Independent Variables	Neighborhoods					
	Gardner	Belmont (i)	East Side	Summerhill	North Central
Policy dissatisfaction	.127 (ii)	-.063	.226**	.192**	.089
Sensed inefficacy	-.212* (iii)	-.178*	-.441**	-.387**	-.173*
System rejection	.111	.298**	-.074	.044	.045
Group consciousness	.299**	—	.088	.077	.062
Present orientation	.006	-.224**	.193**	-.056	.001
Distrust	-.079	.039	-.262**	-.193**	-.081
Class ideology	.029	.009	-.065	.056	.016
Percentage of variance explained (R^2)	14%	11%	38%	22%	5%

(i) In Belmont the dependent variable is membership in a community organization.
(ii) Beta weight.
(iii) One asterisk is significant at the .05 level; two asterisks are significant at the .01 level.

Table 8.2. Receptivity to Violence: Attitudinal Determinants

	Neighborhoods				
Independent Variables	Gardner	Belmont	East Side	Summerhill	North Central
Policy dissatisfaction	.057	—	.227**	.107	.167**
Sensed inefficacy	.149	—	.140**	.112	.006
System rejection	-.109	—	.223**	.125*	.342**
Group consciousness	.106	—	.272**	.248**	.331**
Present orientation	-.092	—	-.067	-.054	.071
Distrust	.031	—	.046	.022	-.079
Class ideology	.089	—	-.085	.027	-.101*
Percentage of variance explained (R^2)	7%	—	31%	14%	43%

unlike its counterpart in black neighborhoods, contributes only marginally to the creation of a violent political style. The measures of belief together account for only 7 percent of the variance in receptivity to violence; group consciousness by itself contributes almost nothing at all (1 percent). These patterns of association reaffirm the general thrust of alienation and the particular role of group consciousness in the Mexican-American community.

The politics of Belmont, at first glance, appears aberrational, distinct from the dynamics that created the nonviolent pattern in Gardner and the varieties of black politics. But although the regression analysis reveals certain distinctive aspects of belief and politics in Belmont, other patterns are more suggestive of uniformity than irregularity. Measures of class ideology and distrust are unimportant to Belmont, as they are to the other neighborhoods; patterns of estrangement conform to the general relationship with political involvement. Belmont is unique, however, in the strong association between present orientation on the one hand and reduced organizational participation on the other. The impact of this cultural theme, ambiguous in other neighborhoods, is central to the explanation of its political indifference.

Beliefs provide a stronger guide to politics in the East Side than in any other poor neighborhood studied. They account for 38 percent of the variance in receptivity to politics and 31 percent of the variance in receptivity to violence. Particularly important to conventional political involvement is the calculation of effectiveness, since it alone accounts (uniquely) for 18 percent of the variance. Other measures of belief are important to politics, notably cultural themes and policy dissatisfaction, but sensed ineffectiveness prevails over all other indicators. Receptivity to violence, however, is more the result of alienation and group consciousness measures. The strength of these associations and the high levels of estrangement and oppositional consciousness in the East Side are largely responsible for the violent mood of ghetto politics in Detroit.

The politics of Summerhill is often at variance with the political tone of the East Side. There is a weaker commitment to violence and a more conventional orientation toward political expression. The patterns of association between variables, however, are almost identical to those in the East Side. Sensed inefficacy remains the most important determinant of politics (unique variance explained,

13 percent) and other measures (alienation, group consciousness, and lower class culture) nearly reproduce the East Side configuration. Except for the less pronounced explanatory power of these variables, their determinant relation with receptivity to violence follows the path pioneered earlier by the East Side. There can be little question that although the politics of the East Side and Summerhill are at odds, the same processes of mind are involved in their creation.

Conventional political expression is not well explained in North Central. The combination of the alienation measures, group consciousness, cultural themes, and class ideology together explain only 5 percent of the variance in commitment to politics. The only attitudinal measure of any consequence (not surprising given the results of other communities) is the consideration of political effectiveness, but alone it can account (uniquely) for only 3 percent of the variance. The story of political violence is remarkably different. Nearly all the indicators show an exaggerated relationship with violence, particularly dissatisfaction with the political community and race consciousness, each accounting (uniquely) for 7 percent of the variance. The association of these two measures with violence is more pronounced than in any of the other communities; combined with the other indicators of belief, they account for 43 percent of the variance.

The role of belief in community politics is an interesting blend of uniformity and variety. Distinctive patterns emerge, as just described; group consciousness in Gardner, cultural themes in Belmont, sensed inefficacy in the East Side and Summerhill, and group identity and system rejection in North Central. Despite these unique combinations of belief and their obvious relationship to the permutations of political styles in poor neighborhoods, however, there emerge some strong causal connections reflecting the basic dynamics of these neighborhoods that transcend their idiosyncracies. The calculation of political effectiveness is involved in the politics of every community, no matter what political form it eventually takes. The mediation of rationality, the calculation of costs and benefits, cannot be removed from the politics of poor communities, no more than it can be ignored in politics generally (2). Political alienation in any form or combination makes a unique and significant contribution to the use of political violence, reducing nearly all other factors if not to insignificance, then to comparative unimportance. Group consciousness is also capable of transcending community peculiarities to structure a range of political responses. In black communities, it provides a strong stimulus to violence; in the Mexican-American community it makes a substantial contribution to politics short of violence.

What remains unanswered, however, is whether these indicators of belief, important to the politics of individual communities, can make sensible the apparently paradoxical political differences that exist between them.

II   EXPLAINING POLITICAL PERMUTATIONS

It does not follow that, because a complex of attitudes and beliefs helps mold the politics and violence of specific neighborhoods, it can explain the differences that set these communities apart. Indeed, the feeling of political impotence or futility may mediate personal decision-making in Gardner as well as the East Side. This shared dynamic, however, might as easily exacerbate as reduce political differences, depending upon the importance of other beliefs and other nonattitudinal determinants of political expression. Our central question consequently remains unanswered. We have yet to determine whether the dynamics of belief and politics as we have described them can account for the contrasting political styles of poor neighborhoods.

To focus on this issue we have constructed a game. At the beginning of this chapter we introduced regression equations for each city as the best available estimate of its political dynamics. We are assuming, in effect, that whatever the currency of certain beliefs in a neighborhood (whether dissatisfied or contented with public policy, for example) their determinant relationships with alternative forms of political expression are captured in the regression coefficients. If the level of policy dissatisfaction were increased from a value of 2.0 to 3.0, we would expect the respective regression coefficients to translate this change into a new order of receptivity to politics and violence. Therefore the regression equations for particular neighborhoods allow us to assess, under the prevailing patterns of association described in the previous section, how changes in belief would alter the political expression.

The play in our game emerges from this query: what manner of political expression should we expect if the *distribution* of opinion in neighborhood A were the same as in neighborhood B? We are asking, in effect, if the residents of neighborhood A were just as alienated, group conscious, and present-oriented as those in neighborhood B, would the politics of A and B look similar? What if the distribution of attitudes in neighborhood B were altered to approximate those in neighborhood A? In fact, we are toying with the emotions of poor neighborhoods, molding them to conform to other poor neighborhoods (though leaving the general association of belief and politics in neighborhoods A and B unaltered), then sitting back to watch the results. If after this exercise we find that the initial disparity in their politics is minimized, we can infer that beliefs help account for the contrasting political styles of poor neighborhoods. This methodology enables us to preserve the essential relationships within each community while making interneighborhood comparisons that take into account all relevant beliefs simultaneously. The result is a simple hypothetical convergence or divergence of politics, dependent solely upon the capacity of beliefs to explain interneighborhood differences.

We can illustrate this game using selected results from Table 8.3. The actual difference in receptivity to politics between the East Side and North Central is 47 points (real difference). If we take the regression equation that explains the receptivity to politics in the East Side but change the attitudinal values to conform to North Central (i.e., using the mean values for group consciousness, sensed inefficacy, policy dissatisfaction, etc., from North Central) the difference would be reduced to 27 points (imaginary difference). The alteration produces a convergence (47 minus 27) of 20 points. A reversal of the procedure, preserving the regression equation for North Central but altering the means to conform to sentiment in the East Side, yields a convergence of 4 points (47 minus 43). There can be little question in this pairing that a consideration of beliefs helps make sensible the observed differences in political expression.

An examination of Tables 8.3 through 8.5 confirms, with one important exception, that the patterns of political belief in poor neighborhoods play a substantial role in the variety of their politics. The substitution of means in the three black neighborhoods (producing six imaginary differences for receptivity to politics and

Table 8.3. Pairing of Neighborhoods on Receptivity to Politics

Substituting Means Of	Using Regression Equations From			
	Gardner	East Side	Summerhill	North Central
Gardner		R. D. = 22 I. D. = 52 Convergence = -30	R. D. = 57 I. D. = 89 Convergence = -32	R. D. = 69 I. D. = 79 Convergence = -10
East Side	R. D. (i) = 22 I. D. (ii) = 11 Convergence (iii) = 11		R. D. = 35 I. D. = 37 Convergence = -2	R. D. = 47 I. D. = 43 Convergence = 4
Summerhill	R. D. = 57 I. D. = 83 Convergence = -26	R. D. = 35 I. D. = 22 Convergence = 13		R. D. = 12 I. D. = 9 Convergence = 3
North Central	R. D. = 69 I. D. = 89 Convergence = -20	R. D. = 47 I. D. = 27 Convergence = 20	R. D. = 12 I. D. = 7 Convergence = 5	

Pairing Between

	Gardner and Black Neighborhoods (iv)	Black Neighborhoods
Average real difference	49	31
Average imaginary difference	67	24
Percentage reduction	-37%	23%

(i) The actual (real) difference of means (receptivity to politics) between Gardner and the East Side, abbreviated R.D. It is attained by multiplying the dependent variable mean by 100. Example: receptivity to politics (mean) = 2.67; adjusted mean = 2.67 x 100 = 267.

(ii) The imaginary difference (I. D.) of means (receptivity to politics) between Gardner and the East Side, using the regression equation for Gardner but the appropriate independent variable means from the East Side. Substitution was made only for important independent variables (standardized regression coefficient greater than .100).

(iii) Convergence is the difference between the real difference and the imaginary difference. A positive value means the substitution of means brought the two neighborhoods closer together in their politics. A negative value means they have moved further apart.

(iv) Results for only those pairings that include Gardner and one of the black neighborhoods. We can tell as a result of these calculations whether the politics of Mexican-American and black communities converge.

Table 8.4. *Pairing of Neighborhoods on Membership in Community Organization*

Substituting Means Of	Using Regression Equations From				
	Belmont	Gardner	East Side	Summerhill	North Central
Belmont		R.D. = 7 I.D. = 2 Conver-gence = 5	R.D. = 5 I.D. = 7 Conver-gence = -2	R.D. = 1 I.D. = 0 Conver-gence = 1	R.D. = 10 I.D. = 6 Conver-gence = 4
Gardner	R.D. = 7 I.D. = 2 Conver-gence = 5				
East Side	R.D. = 5 I.D. = 3 Conver-gence = 2				

Summerhill   R. D. = 1
          I. D. = 2

          Conver-
          gence = -1

North Central   R. D. = 10
          I. D. = 2

          Conver-
          gence = 8

Pairing Between Belmont and Other Neighborhoods

Average real difference	6
Average imaginary difference	3
Percentage reduction	50%

Table 8.5. Pairing of Neighborhoods on Receptivity to Violence

Substituting Means Of	Using Regression Equations From			
	Gardner	East Side	Summerhill	North Central
Gardner		R. D. = 88 I. D. = 53 Convergence = 35	R. D. = 36 I. D. = 42 Convergence = - 6	R. D. = 34 I. D. = 46 Convergence = -12
East Side	R. D. = 88 I. D. = 85 Convergence = 3		R. D. = 52 I. D. = 24 Convergence = 28	R. D. = 54 I. D. = 25 Convergence = 29
Summerhill	R. D. = 36 I. D. = 14 Convergence = 22	R. D. = 52 I. D. = 17 Convergence = 35		R. D. = 2 I. D. = 14 Convergence = -12
North Central	R. D. = 34 I. D. = 34 Convergence = 0	R. D. = 54 I. D. = 25 Convergence = 29	R. D. = 2 I. D. = 7 Convergence = - 5	

Pairing Between

	Gardner and Black Neighborhoods	Black Neighborhoods
Average real difference	53	36
Average imaginary difference	46	19
Percentage reduction	13%	47%

six for receptivity to violence) produces a general convergence of political expression or political style. Initial (or real) differences in response were marked, particularly between the East Side and the other black neighborhoods. Because of these substantial disparities, we noted the paradoxical failure of poor neighborhoods to forge a singular political approach or political movement. The simple substitution of beliefs alters that pattern. The initial average difference of 31 points for receptivity to politics is reduced to 24 points—in effect, an explanatory power of 23 percent. The average real difference for receptivity to violence was 36 points; the average imaginary difference was 19 points. This simulation of beliefs in black neighborhoods dramatically reduces the observed differences by almost half.

The East Side is a particularly violent community—the scene of the most destructive and widespread civil disturbance, the area where expressed support for violent political options is most pronounced. The violence of its political image contrasts markedly with Summerhill and North Central where violence is a less important theme. The more conventional orientation of North Central and Summerhill is evident in the willingness of these communities to support a variety of pressures and protest strategies that preclude political disorder and physical violence. The East Side poor, on the other hand, are less open to the more routine acts of pressure and persuasion, less willing to expend their energies on political means that depend on the persuadability or good will of public officials, merchants, or landlords. These differences are the stuff of contrasting political styles and the statistical indicators that led us to the failure of design in poor neighborhoods

At the root of this divergence, however, are concrete differences in belief. Although the East Side is more supportive of violence and less supportive of more conventional forms of expression, it is also uniformly more alienated and more conscious of racial distinctions. Its residents feel less effective politically, and are more critical of the police and the schools, more estranged from the general political community, and more sensitive to the responsibility of whites and their political instrumentalities. These differences, however, can be translated into a concrete convergence of political styles. Once the alienative tone of the East Side is pared down to the more optimistic mood of North Central and Summerhill, particularly the sense of political futility, the perspective on conventional politics begins to look more uniform; once the reactive consciousness of the East Side is made more insipid (in addition to lessening its alienation), political violence begins to look less attractive. The result is a convergence of political styles. The mechanism is the variety of political belief in poor neighborhoods.

In Table 8.4 there is limited evidence that the resigned and peaceful politics of Belmont—seemingly outside the range of styles in other neighborhoods—approximates them once the disparities of belief are taken into account. The reconstruction of mind in Belmont to conform to the Gardner, East Side, Summerhill, and North Central patterns produces a decided shift toward their levels of expression. A heightened estrangement from the political community and the shifting of time horizons to take into account more distant goals increase the level of organizational membership, bringing it more in line with the other neighborhoods, including North Central where the initial differences were most marked. The average real difference was 6 points and the average imaginary difference only 3 points. As a result of variation in political belief, the average difference is reduced by 50 percent (3).

Beliefs are important in Gardner, but they provide an ambiguous guide to the peculiarities of its political style. The orientation toward violence in this Mexican-American community can be made, using belief, to converge on the record of black neighborhoods; a 13 percent reduction of variation is evident in Table 8.5. Heightened feelings of futility and greater group solidarity produce this effect. But similar changes in belief (see Table 8.3) produce no convergence whatever in receptivity to politics and in fact lead to a substantial exacerbation of interneighborhood differences. The substantial contribution of belief in explaining the apparent anomalies of black politics, or Appalachian apolitics, falters in the face of selective "third-world" incompatibilities. It is apparent that the roots of explanation lie elsewhere.

We have played a game where feelings and emotions and perspectives on life and politics were manipulated in order to assess their explanatory power. Through the machinations of the game, we were able to examine every conceivable two-way comparison, taking into account the effect of differing levels of belief. The play of the game provided for a convergence of political styles in black communities, between the Appalachian white and other neighborhoods, and in a very selective way, between the Mexican-American and remaining neighborhoods. The political permutations of poor neighborhoods that dominated our attention in this work became more sensible as a result. Through the understanding of beliefs and their variation, we have reduced the salience of conflicting political styles and provided a clue to their origins.

It is now time to examine the limits of our explanation.

III   THE LIMITS OF EXPLANATION

Our work has not been trivial, our results not without possible consequence. First we described the mutuality of historical experience that molded twentieth century urban poor neighborhoods and highlighted the peculiarities of politics that keep them apart. In subsequent chapters we formulated important conceptions of belief that capture the poor's sense of time, self, and interests, and traced the complex interaction between these beliefs and political expression. Finally, we sought to exploit these relationships to bring clarity to what formerly lacked design. But by no means have we provided an explanation that is adequate to the variety of politics in poor neighborhoods.

At the simplest level, our analysis leaves considerable variance unexplained. Within each neighborhood, the complex of measures that purport to measure belief are only partially determinant of receptivity to politics and violence. Merely 7 percent of the variance in receptivity to violence is explained in Gardner and only 5 percent of the variance in receptivity to politics in North Central. But even in the regression equations of best fit—particularly the East Side—more than half the variation in the dependent variables is unaccounted for. Beliefs are undoubtedly important to the political styles of each of these neighborhoods, but they provide an incomplete elucidation of the variation.

A similar limitation is apparent in the explanation of interneighborhood disparities. The simulated manipulation of attitudes shows that variation in beliefs can produce a convergence of political expression in a number of important comparative settings—within

black neighborhoods, between Appalachian white and other neighborhoods, and (for receptivity to violence) between the Mexican-
American and the three black communities. Once again, however,
most of the differences between neighborhoods persist, despite the
simultaneous consideration of all beliefs. In one case, the introduction of beliefs only further compounds the confusion of political
design.

In another, more important sense, these results allow only
circumscribed inferences about the politics of poor neighborhoods.
The conceptual design linking a range of beliefs with political
expression provides, in this view, a further delineation of interneighborhood differences rather than their explanation. Beliefs may be as
integrally involved with the effect as they are with the cause.
Whereas our analysis posited feelings of estrangement and oppositional
consciousness as determinants of political violence, a more comprehensive causal scheme might presume that they are part of the
phenomenon of violence itself. Beliefs and politics in this larger
network of cause and effect are the phenomena that vary by
community. The origins of beliefs and politics are found not in one
another, but in more basic historical or experiential factors.

This ambiguity stems from a conflict of perspectives that cannot
be resolved in an objective sense. It poses fundamental dilemmas in
assessing ultimate causes, boundaries and distance. When the authors
of the *American Voter* (4) examined the conceptual model underlying their analysis of the voting act, they chose to picture the causal
process as a funnel—the vote itself at the tip, partisan attachments at
the bottommost and narrowest portion of the funnel, and basic
demographic factors at the expansive areas toward the top. Although
each of these factors might provide a causal explanation of voting,
they fall at different points in a chainlike cumulative process and
consequently offer differing perspectives on explanation. Each point
on the funnel provides valid areas of inquiry; each taps legitimate
causes of political behavior, but one area comes closer to yielding an
ultimate explanation. Partisan attachment is very close in a conceptual sense to the act of voting itself. An elucidation of voting in
its terms provides an immediate, limited, and perhaps inconclusive
result.

Our emphasis upon belief provides (as did the approach of the
American Voter) an explanation of political expression in terms that

are immediate and limited. The presentation of ultimate causes, though hinted at, are removed from this text. A fuller explanation requires a model that is more demanding of history, that seeks to trace politics from acts of violence and confrontation, to associated beliefs, and to the varieties of political experience. The limits of explanation can be transcended only by breaking down the limitations of conception.

A more broadly historical and crosscultural perspective on politics reveals yet another limitation of explanation, a problem common to other works on political participation. In examining the political mobilization of poor neighborhoods, concentrating on political apathy, organizational membership, political involvement, protest, and receptivity to violence, we have outlined a range of political options conforming to the reality of political alternatives in a given political context. We have described community politics in these terms and assessed neighborhood differences within the confines of their range. But contrasts, differences, and permutations are definitive only within this reality; and the reality is bound by time (mid-twentieth century) and place (urban America).

Of course, the range of political opportunities could be expanded substantially if we were not bound by the limitations of this experience. Excluded from our purview has been the formation of cabals, correspondence societies, and conspiracies. We have not discussed the receptivity of the poor to revolutionary maneuvers. Are they willing to seize factories and the institutions of domination? Are Appalachian whites receptive to a seizure of Champion Papers, the blacks of River Rouge or Mexican-Americans to the seizure of the canneries or agribusiness? We have not observed or contemplated the willingness of the poor to join revolutionary armies or their commitment to radically new political arrangements. In limiting our comparisons to conventional politics and random violence, we excluded a range of comparisons mandated by a more expansive consideration of politics.

The failure to contemplate the full range of political opportunities raises questions about the reality of our observed differences. A difference between one and three is considerable if the full range of values is one to three. But its significance seems less important where the full range extends from one to ten. Perhaps the heat we generated over the fractionalized, nonviolent political style of

Gardner and the violent mood of the East Side would have seemed less noteworthy if our conception of the problem encompassed the failure of revolutionary politics. In this view, all the poor neighborhoods would have appeared similar in their presentation, offering trivial variants of conventional politics but uniformly removed from the full range of political possibilities.

These limitations are real, not the work of statistical nit-pickers, historians and institutionalists, and revolutionaries. This work has thrived on the limited variation it has explained, a narrow causal process involving belief and politics, and a limited range of political opportunities reflected in the reality of American politics. Its answers are important within the terms of the questions asked; its results useful to understanding belief, politics, and the struggle of poor people for recognition and public benefits. A more complete portrayal of politics in poor neighborhoods awaits a more advanced statistical presentation, a causal model that incorporates the subtleties of historical and institutional experience, and finally, a view of political life that is more expansive in its view of political options.

This work recognized its limitations and settled for them, but limitations provide an opportunity as well as a focus. From them, we find direction and reasons to look further.

NOTES

. . . . . .

Chapter One: Introduction

1. Karl Marx, *Capital,* Vol. I (New York: International Publishers, 1967, pp. 713–716).

2. *Ibid.,* pp. 630–632. Although this view of political man relies heavily on a Marxist analysis of "primitive accumulation," the conception of political style is not drawn from Marx, nor does it follow necessarily from his works.

3. C. Wright Mills, *The Sociological Imagination* (New York: Oxford University Press, 1959).

4. *Ibid.,* p. 4.

5. See Appendix A.

6. The five poor neighborhoods are in no sense representative of the low income population in general. In 1971 almost 70 percent of low income people were white, less than a third were black, and fewer than a tenth were Spanish-speaking. Though these neighborhoods are unrepresentative in the broadest sense, they do reflect ecological developments in poor neighborhoods. Increasingly, the poor are black or Spanish-speaking rather than white (Anglo), and urban rather than rural. Within the central cities the numbers of black poor more closely approximate the numbers of white poor; the black poor are also, on the average, more than eleven years younger. Consequently the urban poor white population is increasingly comprised of elderly "ethnics" and Appalachian and South-

ern migrants [Department of Commerce, Bureau of the Census, *Char-acteristics of the Low Income Population, 1971* (Washington, D.C.: Current Population Reports, Series P-60, No. 86, December, 1972, pp. 1, 57, 64)].

In Chapter Two we see that these neighborhoods, though not broadly representative, are strategically placed in relation to basic twentieth century population movements. In this sense they are representative of the communities that house the first native American urban poor.

The American Indian and Puerto Rican poor are neglected in this study. The former constitute a miniscule fraction of the urban poor and the latter only one-fifth of the Spanish-speaking poor (*ibid.*, pp. 1, 70).

Chapter Two: The Etiology of Poor Neighborhoods

1. Edward C. Banfield, *The Unheavenly City* (Boston: Little, Brown and Co., 1970, p.12).

2. The great bulk of mail orders sent from the United States to Mexico have traditionally designated the *Mesa Central* as their destination (nearly 55 percent in 1926). A substantial number have also been sent to the *Mesa del Norte*, but only 15 percent of the total. The importance of central Mexico in this traffic is even more pronounced for California [Manuel Gamio, *Mexican Immigration to the United States* (Chicago: The University of Chicago Press, 1930, pp. 13—18)].

3. Department of Commerce, Bureau of the Census, *Negro Population in the United States 1790—1915* (Washington, D.C.: U.S. Government Printing Office, 1918, pp. 32—33, 51, 68); William C. Holley, Ellen Winston, and T. J. Woofter, Jr., *The Plantation South, 1934—1937* (Washington, D.C.: U.S. Government Printing Office, 1940, pp. xii—xiii).

4. Charles E. Hall, *Negroes in the United States 1920—1932* (New York: Arno Press and *The New York Times*, 1969, pp. 5, 25).

5. *Ibid.*, p. 27; Lyonel C. Florant, "Negro Internal Migration," *American Sociological Review*, Vol. 7, No. 6, 784 (December 1942).

6. Harry A. Ploski and Roscoe C. Brown, Jr., *The Negro Almanac* (New York: Bellwether Publishing Co., 1967, p. 244).

7. T. Lynn Smith, "The Redistribution of the Negro Population," *The Journal of Negro History*, Vol. II, No. 3 163 (July 1966).

8. Ploski and Brown, *op. cit.*, p. 243.

9. United States Department of Labor, Bureau of Labor Statistics and United States Department of Commerce, Bureau of the Census, *The*

Social and Economic Status of Negroes in the United States, 1969 (Washington, D.C.: Current Population Reports, Series P-23, No. 29, U.S. Government Printing Office, 1969, pp. 3, 7).

10. Samuel Bryan, "Mexican Immigrants in the United States," in Wayne Moquin and Charles Van Doren, eds., *A Documentary History of the Mexican American* (New York: Bantam Books, 1972, pp. 333—334).

11. Gamio, *op. cit.*, p. 13.

12. José Hernández Álvarez, "A Demographic Profile of the Mexican Immigration to the United States," *Journal of Inter-American Studies,* Vol. VIII, No. 3, 471 (July 1966).

13. Leo Grebler, Joan W. Moore, and Ralph C. Guzman, *The Mexican-American People* (New York: The Free Press, 1970, p. 40).

14. *Ibid.,* p. 64; Carey McWilliams, *North From Mexico* (New York: Greenwood Press, 1968, p. 163).

15. Grebler, *op. cit.*, pp. 118—119.

16. McWilliams, *op. cit.*, p. 57.

17. Álvarez, *op. cit.*, p. 489.

18. Ernesto Galarza, *Merchants of Labor* (Santa Barbara: McNally & Loftin Publishers, 1964, p. 52).

19. Ernesto Galarza, Herman Gallegos, and Julian Samora, *Mexican-Americans in the Southwest* (Santa Barbara: McNally & Loftin, 1969, pp. 15, 20).

20. Stan Steiner, *La Raza: The Mexican Americans* (New York: Harper & Row Publishers, 1970, p. 135).

21. Ernesto Galarza, *Merchants of Labor, op. cit.*, p. 59.

22. Grebler, *op. cit.*, p. 64.

23. Galarza, *Mexican-Americans in the Southwest, op. cit.*, p. 15.

24. Grebler, *op. cit.*, p. 113.

25. Frederick G. Tyron and Bushrod W. Allin, "The Southern Appalachian Coal Plateau," in Carter Goodrich, et. al., eds., *Migration and Economic Opportunity* (Philadelphia: University of Pennsylvania Press, 1936, pp. 44—45).

26. James S. Brown and George A. Hillery, Jr., "The Great Migration, 1940-1960," in Thomas R. Ford, ed., *The Southern Appalachian Region* (Lexington, Kentucky: Kentucky Paperbacks, 1967, p. 59); James S. Brown, "Southern Appalachian Population Change, 1960—1970: A First Look at the 1970 Census" (unpublished mimeograph).

27. Brown and Hillery, *op. cit.*, p. 63.

28. Allison Davis, Burleigh B. Gardner, and Mary R. Gardner, *Deep South*

(Chicago: University of Chicago Press, 1941, pp. 268, 271).

29. Holley, *op. cit.*, p. xii.

30. Claude O. Brannen, *Relation of Land Tenure to Plantation Organization* (Fayetteville, 1928, pp. 8—9).

31. *Negro Population 1790—1915, op. cit.*, p. 610; Holley, *op. cit.*, p. 7.

32. Brannen, *op. cit.*, pp. 29—38.

33. *Ibid.*, p. 42

34. Davis, *op. cit.*, pp. 92—95.

35. Holley, *op. cit.*, p. 26.

36. Davis, *op. cit.*, pp. 351—352.

37. Victor Perlo, *The Negro in Southern Agriculture* (New York: International Publishers, 1953, p. 26).

38. Stewart Udall, "Introduction" to Harry M. Caudill, *Night Comes to the Cumberlands* (Boston: Little, Brown and Co., 1963, p. vii).

39. Caudill, *op. cit.*, pp. 5—6.

40. Arnold J. Toynbee, *A Study of History* [abridged] (New York: Oxford Press, 1947, pp. 148—149).

41. Caudill, *op. cit.*, p. 69.

42. *Ibid.*, p. 75.

43. Quoted in Caudill, *op. cit.*, pp. 308—309.

44. Tyron and Allin, *op. cit.*, pp. 91—97.

45. Caudill, *op. cit.*, p. 93.

46. *Ibid.*, pp. 112—115, 125.

47. Quoted in Steiner, *op. cit.*, p. 12.

48. McWilliams, *op. cit.*, p. 30.

49. Frank Tannenbaum, *The Mexican Agrarian Revolution* (Archon Books, 1968, pp. 2—3, 13—14).

50. *Ibid.*, p. 32.

51. *Ibid.*, pp. 30—32.

52. *Ibid.*, pp. 113—114.

53. Galarza, *Merchants of Labor, op. cit.*, p. 18.

54. Tannenbaum, *op. cit.*, pp. 120—121.

55. *Ibid.*, p. 122.

56. *Ibid.*, p. 399

57. *Ibid.*, p. 400.

58. John Womack, Jr., *Zapata and the Mexican Revolution* (New York: Vintage Books, 1970, pp. 165—170).

59. Tannenbaum, *op. cit.*, p. 404.

60. Gamio, *op. cit.*, pp. 164—169.

61. Caudill, *op. cit.*, pp. 188—205.

62. *Ibid.*, pp. 229, 247.

63. *Ibid.*, pp. 260—261.

64. Harold A. Gibbard, "Extractive Industries and Forestry," in Ford, *op. cit.*, p. 110.

65. Quoted in Todd Gitlin and Nanci Hollander, *Uptown* (New York: Harper Colophon Books, 1971, p. 195).

66. Edward E. Lewis, *The Mobility of the Negro* (New York: Columbia University Press, 1931, p. 116); R. H. Leavell, T. R. Snavely, T. J. Woofter, Jr., W. T. B. Williams, and Francis D. Tyson, *Negro Migration in 1916—1917* (Washington, D.C.: U.S. Government Printing Office, 1919, pp. 78—82); John William Fanning, *Negro Migration* (Athens, Georgia: Bulletin of the University of Georgia, 1930, p. 22).

67. Fanning, *op. cit.*, p. 29.

68. *Ibid.*, p. 16.

69. Quoted in St. Clair Drake and Horace R. Cayton, *Black Metropolis, A Study of Negro Life in a Northern City* (New York: Harper Torchbooks, 1962, p. 59).

70. Quoted in Arna Bontemps and Jack Conroy, *Anyplace But Here* (New York: Hill and Wang, 1966, p. 158).

71. Leavell, *op. cit.*, pp. 123—124.

72. Drake, *op. cit.*, p. 59.

73. Clyde Vernon Kiser, *Sea Island to City* (New York: Columbia University Press, 1932, p. 158).

74. Harry K. Schwartzweller, James S. Brown, and J. J. Mangalam, *Mountain Families in Transition* (University Park, Pennsylvania: The Pennsylvania State University Press, 1971, pp. 153—154).

75. Galarza, *Merchants of Labor, op. cit.*, p. 47.

76. *Ibid.*, p. 72.

77. *Ibid.*, p. 156.

78. For those who live in San Jose the name "Gardner" refers to a specific area; the analysis here encompasses the core area and contiguous residential blocks that share the same politics, the same deterioration, and the same population pressures. We took similar liberties when defining the boundaries for each of the five neighborhoods.

79. Eugene T. Sawyer, *History of Santa Clara County* (Los Angeles: Historic Research Co., 1922, pp. 35—36).

80. Robert James Claus, *The Fruit and Vegetable Canning Industry in the Santa Clara Valley* (M.A. Thesis, San Jose State College, August, 1966, pp. 46–48); *Directory of Manufacturers, Santa Clara County* (San Jose, California: Santa Clara County Chambers of Commerce, Inc.).

81. *San Jose: Sprawling City* (Stanford Environmental Law Society, March 1971, p. 6).

82. Joan W. Moore, and Frank G. Mittelbach, "Residential Segregation in the Urban Southwest," *The Mexican American Study Project* (Los Angeles, California: The University of California, pp. 10–12).

83. *Demographic Data, Model Cities of San Jose* (San Jose, California: Diridon Research Corporation, November 12, 1971, p. 50).

84. Robert R. Cotant, *A Socio-Economic Profile of Santa Clara County* (Santa Clara, California: Social Planning Council, 1970).

85. *Neighborhood Analyses* (San Jose City Planning Department, 1968, p. 17).

86. *Ibid.*, p. 47.

87. This account relies on personal observation and Raymond Hutchens, *Kentuckians in Hamilton: A Study of Southern Migrants in an Industrial City* (M.A. Thesis, Miami University, Oxford, Ohio, 1942, pp. 58–59).

88. Samuel F. Hunt, "The Miami Valley, 1791–1891," in Col. D.W. McClung, ed., *The Centennial Anniversary of the City of Hamilton, Ohio* (Cincinnati: The Lawrence Printing and Publishing Co., 1892, p. 93).

89. Alta Harvey Heiser, *Hamilton in the Making* (Oxford, Ohio: The Mississippi Valley Press, 1941, p. 94); Richard V. Smith, *An Economic Study of the Ohio-Kentucky-Indiana Metropolitan Region* (The Hamilton County Regional Planning Commission, 1969, pp. 4, 12).

90. Smith, *op. cit.,* p. 12; *Industrial Survey of Hamilton, Ohio* (Owensboro, Kentucky: The Community Development Section of the Sales Department, Texas Gas Transmission Corporation, October, 1968, p. 8).

91. *Comprehensive Plan: Peck's Addition and Environs* (Hamilton, Ohio: City Planning Department, November, 1968, p. 5).

92. Smith, *op. cit.,* p. 95.

93. Melvin G. Holli, *Reform in Detroit* (New York: Oxford University Press, 1969, p. 4); *The Detroit Free Press, Centennial Edition* (May 10, 1931, p. 9); Arthur Pound, *The Automobile and an American City* (Detroit: Wayne State University Press, 1962).

94. Glen E. Carlson, *The Negro in the Industries of Detroit* (Ph.D. Dissertation, University of Michigan, December, 1929, p. 94).

95. Hall, *op. cit.,* p. 34.

96. Bontemps, *op. cit.*, p. 291; Carlson, *op. cit.*, pp. 52—61.

97. Katherine DuPre Lumpkin, "The General Plan Was Freedom," *Phylon*, Vol. XXVIII, No. 1, 65 (Spring 1967).

98. *The Nonwhite Population of Metropolitan Detroit* (Detroit: United Community Services of Metropolitan Detroit, 1955).

99. The surge came in the war years when Italian and Polish immigration had come to a halt (Carlson, *op. cit.*, p. 49).

100. *The Nonwhite Population of Metropolitan Detroit, loc. cit.*

101. Ann Ratner Miller, *Net Intercensal Migration to Large Urban Areas of the United States 1930—1940, 1940—1950, 1950—1960* (Philadelphia: Population Studies Center, May, 1964, pp. 25—27).

102. Quoted in Carlson, *op. cit.*, pp. 80—82; see also "Negro Migration of 1916—18," *Journal of Negro History*, Vol. VI, No. 4 (October 1921).

103. Pound, *op. cit.*, p. 17.

104. Carlson, *op. cit.*, p. 72.

105. Robert Mowitz and Deil S. Wright, *Profile of a Metropolis, A Case Book* (Detroit: Wayne State University Press, 1962, p. 17).

106. Even in this eastern segment of the neighborhood, however, housing is worse than housing generally in the city; almost one in four houses is in deteriorating or dilapidated condition compared to one in ten for Detroit.

107. *Detroit Free Press* (September 1968); *Report to Mayor Jerome P. Cavanaugh* (Detroit: Mayor's Development Team, October, 1967, p. 791).

108. "Summerhill" for this analysis includes both Summerhill and Mechanics-ville.

109. Elton Morris, *The Rehousing of Non-Whites Displaced by Urban Renewal in Atlanta, Georgia* (M.A. Thesis, Atlanta University, January, 1964, p. 37).

110. *Planning Atlanta* (Atlanta, Georgia: Department of Planning, April, 1970).

111. Franklin M. Garrett, *Atlanta and Environs* (New York: Lewis Historical Publishing Co., Inc., 1954, pp. 25—26); Claudia M. Turner, *Changing Residential Patterns in Southwest Atlanta From 1960 to 1970* (M.A. Thesis, Atlanta University, July, 1970, p. 23).

112. Garrett, *op. cit.*, pp. 213—214.

113. Before 1900 movement along the tracks brought small concentrations of blacks to the "Pittsburgh" area bordering Summerhill.

114. *A Report of Public School Facilities for Negroes in Atlanta, Georgia*

(Atlanta, Georgia: Atlanta Urban League, 1944).

115. *Planning Atlanta, loc. cit.*

116. *Planning Atlanta, loc. cit.;* and *Social Report on Neighborhood Analysis* (Atlanta, Georgia: Atlanta Community Improvement Program).

117. *Report of the Atlanta Commission on Crime and Juvenile Delinquency, Opportunity for Urban Excellence* (Atlanta, Georgia: February, 1966, pp. 5—7, 121).

118. W. E. B. DuBois, *The Philadelphia Negro* (New York: Schocken Books, 1967, p. 25).

119. *Ibid.,* pp. 49—53.

120. E. Digby Baltzell, "Introduction" to DuBois, *op. cit.,* p. xxix.

121. *Bulletin Almanac 1972* (Philadelphia: *The Evening and Sunday Bulletin,* 1972, p. 206).

122. Hall, *op. cit.,* p. 34; and Baltzell, *op. cit.,* p. xxix.

123. Baltzell, *op. cit.,* p. xxix; Martha Lavell, *Philadelphia's Non-White Population 1960, Report No. 1* (Philadelphia: Commission on Human Relations, City of Philadelphia, November, 1961, p. 3).

124. DuBois, *op. cit.,* pp. 99—102.

125. Baltzell, *op. cit.,* p. xxxviii.

126. In 1917, the "North Carolina gang" was used to bust an IWW strike at a sugar refinery and a strike of foreign workers at the oil refineries (Leavell, *op. cit.,* pp. 129—130, 136).

127. Bontemps, *op. cit.,* p. 310.

128. Martha Lavell, *Philadelphia's Non-White Population 1960, Report No. 3* (Philadelphia: Commission on Human Relations, City of Philadelphia, December, 1962, Table 6).

129. DuBois, *op. cit.,* pp. 37, 58.

130. John T. Emlen, "The Movement for the Betterment of the Negro in Philadelphia," in Miriam Ershkowitz and Joseph Zikmund II, eds., *Black Politics in Philadelphia* (New York: Basic Books, forthcoming).

131. *Population of Philadelphia Sections and Wards 1860—1960* (Philadelphia: Philadelphia City Planning Commission, December, 1963); Lavell, *Philadelphia's Non-White Population 1960, Report No. 1, op. cit.,* p. 14.

132. Almost 10,000 units have been built by the Public Housing Authority and 1,000 by nonprofit sponsors [*Low and Moderate-Income Housing Production in Philadelphia* (Philadelphia: Philadelphia City Planning Commission, June, 1970, p. 16)].

133. Conrad Weiler, *Philadelphia: An Urban Profile* (New York: Praeger, forthcoming).

134. Lenora E. Berson, *Case Study of a Riot* (New York: Institute of Human Relations Press, 1966, p. 33).

135. *Public Information Bulletin* (Philadelphia: Philadelphia City Planning Commission, June, 1969).

136. Lavell, *Philadelphia's Non-White Population 1960, Report No. 3*, op. cit., Table 12.

137. *Statistical Report* 1968 (Philadelphia: Police Department, 1968).

Chapter Three: The Political Permutations of Poor Neighborhoods

1. Among their goals is a commitment to "uphold and maintain loyalty to the Constitution and Flag of the United States," and to "preserve and defend the United States from all enemies." [Kaye Briegel, "The Development of Mexican-American Organizations," in Manuel P. Servin, *The Mexican-American: An Awakening Minority* (Beverly Hills: Glencoe Press, 1970, p. 170)].

2. The description of events in the period January, 1967 to June, 1972, is drawn primarily from the *San Jose Mercury* and personal interviews.

3. Miguel David Tirado, "Mexican-American Community Political Organization," *Aztlan*, Vol. I, No. 1, 66 (Spring 1970).

4. *Ibid.*, pp. 63—64.

5. *San Jose Mercury* (March 26, 1970).

6. Ralph M. Kramer, *Participation of the Poor* (Englewood Cliffs, N.J.: Prentice-Hall, Inc., 1969, pp. 85—86).

7. Statements by community leaders were ascertained during interviews with the author. They appear in the text without further citation. Interviewing is described in Appendix A.

8. Margaret Clark, *Health in the Mexican-American Culture* (Berkeley and Los Angeles: University of California Press, 1959, p. 21).

9. Clark, *loc. cit.*

10. Kramer, *op. cit.*, pp. 80, 104.

11. *San Jose Mercury* (August 1970). The article was drawn from a clippings file; a more precise date was not available.

12. The Charter of the City of San Jose states, ". . .the members of the Council including the member who is also to be Mayor, shall be elected. . . at General Municipal Elections from the City at large. The office of each member of the Council . . . shall be deemed to be a separate office to be separately filled."

13. Norman Mineta received 59 percent of the votes in Gardner, compared

to a citywide percentage of 61 percent.

14. Kramer, *op. cit.,* p. 80.

15. *San Jose Mercury* (September 4, 1970).

16. This information was made available to me by Nancy Ward of the Planned Parenthood Association.

17. *Hamilton Journal-News* (March 15, 1968).

18. Allyn Ronfor Frueh, *The Socio-Economic Characteristics and Political Attitudes of the Political Leadership of Butler County, Ohio* (M.A. Thesis, Miami University, Oxford, Ohio, 1963, pp. 32—35).

19. *Hamilton Journal-News* (April 19, 1968).

20. *Hamilton Journal-News* (July 15, 1966).

21. *Hamilton Journal-News* (September 16, 1971).

22. William D. Worley, *Social Characteristics and Participation Patterns of Rural Migrants in an Industrial Community* (M.A. Thesis, Miami University, Oxford, Ohio, p. 61).

23. Alfred McClung Lee, *Race Riot* (New York: Dryden Press, 1943).

24. David J. Greenstone, *Labor in American Politics* (New York: Vintage Books, 1969, pp. 256—259).

25. Denise J. Lewis, *Black Consciousness and the Voting Behavior of Blacks in Detroit 1961—68* (M.A. Thesis, Wayne State University, August, 1969, p. 87).

26. *Ibid.,* p. 88.

27. *Ibid.,* pp. 130, 146.

28. Arna Bontemps and Jack Conroy, *Anyplace But Here* (New York: Hill and Wang, 1966, pp. 296—297).

29. Mel J. Ravitz, "The Sociology of the Block Club," (mimeograph, November 20, 1959, p. 4).

30. *The Detroit Free Press* (December 19, 1968; August 6, 1969; August 24, 1969).

31. Charles E. West, *The Role of Block Clubs in the Detroit Civil Disorder of July, 1967* (M.A. Thesis, Wayne State University, May, 1970, p. 18).

32. *The Detroit Free Press* (May 4, 1969).

33. *Ibid.*

34. *Report of the National Advisory Commission on Civil Disorders* (New York: Bantam Books, 1968, p. 99).

35. Augustus Alven Adair, *The Political History of the Negro in Atlanta, 1908—1953* (M.A. Thesis, Atlanta University, August, 1955, p. 56).

36. Francena Edwina Culmer, *Changing Patterns of Leadership in the Black*

Community of Atlanta, Georgia: 1960—1969 (M.A. Thesis, Atlanta University, August, 1971, p. 17).

37. Edward C. Banfield, *Big City Politics* (New York: Random House, 1965, p. 30).

38. Quoted in Julian Bond, *Black Candidates* (Atlanta, Georgia: Voter Education Project, Southern Regional Council, Inc., May, 1969, p. 43).

39. Jack Walker, "Negro Voting in Atlanta: 1953—1961," *Phylon,* Vol. 24, 382—383 (1963).

40. Jack L. Walker, *Sit-Ins in Atlanta* (New York: McGraw-Hill Book Co., 1964, pp. 8—9).

41. Culmer, *op. cit.,* pp. 26—29.

42. *Ibid.,* p. 36.

43. Pat Watters and Reese Cleghorn, *Climbing Jacob's Ladder* (New York: Harcourt Brace and World, Inc., 1967, p. 79).

44. Numan V. Bartley, "Atlanta Elections and Georgia Political Trends," *New South,* Vol. 25, No. 1, 23 (Winter 1970).

45. *The Atlanta Voice,* Vol. 7, No. 11 (March 11, 1972).

46. Benjamin J. Davis, *Communist Councilman from Harlem* (New York: International Publishers, 1969, pp. 147—148).

47. Eula Mae Jones, *Voluntary Associations in the Atlanta Negro Community* (M.A. Thesis, Atlanta University, August, 1952, pp. 16—30).

48. *Atlanta Constitution* (November 10, 1970 and November 11, 1970).

49. *The Atlanta Voice,* Vol. 7, No. 7 (February 12, 1972).

50. *Atlanta Model Cities,* Vol. 3, No. 2 (February 1, 1972).

51. Robert L. Freedman, *A Report on Politics in Philadelphia* (Cambridge, Massachusetts: Joint Center for Urban Studies of the Massachusetts Institute of Technology and Harvard University, 1963, pp. II—39).

52. Carl Gilbert, *From Integration to "Black Power": The Civil Rights Movement in the City of Philadelphia, 1960—1967* (M.A. Thesis, Temple University, pp. 59, 95).

53. *Ibid.,* pp. 67—85.

54. Dennis Clark, "Urban Blacks and Irishmen: Brothers in Prejudice," in Miriam Ershkowitz and Joseph Zikmund II, eds., *Black Politics in Philadelphia* (New York: Basic Books, forthcoming).

55. John Hadley Strange, "Blacks and Philadelphia Politics: 1963—1966," in Ershkowitz and Zikmund II, *op. cit.*

56. *Ibid.*

57. Conrad Weiler, *Philadelphia: An Urban Profile* (New York: Praeger, forthcoming).

58. Kenneth B. Clark, *A Relevant War Against Poverty* (New York: Metropolitan Applied Research Center, Inc., 1968, pp. 112, 119).

59. AWC was a broad coalition of community organizations, representing all the poverty groups in North Philadelphia.

60. Sherry Arnstein (told to), "Maximum Feasible Manipulation," *City* (November 1970).

Chapter Four: Lower Class Culture and Political Response

1. Herbert J. Gans, *The Urban Villagers* (New York: The Free Press, 1965, pp. 230–234).

2. Oscar Lewis, *La Vida* (New York: Random House, 1966, p. xliii).

3. *Ibid.,* p. li.

4. Seymour Martin Lipset, *Political Man: The Social Bases of Politics* (Garden City: Anchor Books, 1963, p. 112).

5. Ulf Hannerz, *Soulside* (New York: Columbia University Press, 1969, p. 179).

6. Lee Rainwater, "The Problem of Lower-Class Culture and Poverty-War Strategy," in Daniel P. Moynihan, ed., *On Understanding Poverty* (New York: Basic Books, Inc., 1969, pp. 240–241).

7. Lewis, *op. cit.,* p. xliv.

8. Oscar Lewis, "The Culture of Poverty," in Louis A. Ferman, Joyce L. Kornbluh, and Alan Haber, eds., *Poverty in America* (Ann Arbor: The University of Michigan Press, 1968, pp. 408–409).

9. Edward C. Banfield, *The Unheavenly City* (Boston: Little, Brown and Co., 1970, p. 217).

10. Edward C. Banfield, *The Moral Basis of a Backward Society* (New York: The Free Press, 1967, pp. 140, 142).

Where farmers cultivated large tracts of land and operated on a rental basis—in the Po Valley, for example—there were incentives to expand family size, consequently increasing the number of laborers. But a variety of circumstances in southern Italy, including the relatively late breakup of feudalism and the growth of petty proprietors, fostered a large number of small tracts, operated primarily by wage laborers rather than renters. "The peasants. . .," Banfield writes, "had neither incentive or opportunity to organize a family to provide labor and management for the enterprise. Meanwhile population increased rapidly and small farms became smaller by inheritance. For more than a generation there have been few farms in Montegrano large enough to support more than a small, nuclear family" (*ibid.*, p. 145). The tenuous living provided by the land thus created a marginal peasant population, insecure in life and precariously dependent on the nuclear family.

11. Charles A. Valentine, *Culture and Poverty* (Chicago: The University of Chicago Press, 1968, p. 119).

12. S.M. Miller, Frank Riessman, and Arthur A. Seagull, "Poverty and Self-Indulgence: A Critique of the Non-Deferred Gratification Pattern," in Ferman, *op. cit.*, p. 432.

13. Gans, *op. cit.*, pp. 166—167.

14. Lewis, *La Vida, op. cit.*, p. xliv.

15. Robert K. Merton, *Social Theory and Social Structure* (New York: The Free Press, 1968, p. 200).

16. The Eskimo, an example cited by Valentine, is illustrative of a distinctive culture that has responded to the arctic habitat and to European intervention (Valentine, *op. cit.*, p. 5).

17. Herbert J. Gans, "Culture and Class in the Study of Poverty: An Approach to Anti-Poverty Research," in Moynihan, ed., *op. cit.*, p. 211.

18. *Ibid.*, p. 211.

19. Hyman Rodman, "The Lower-Class Value Stretch," in Raymond W. Mack, ed., *Race, Class, and Power* (New York: American Book Co., 1968).

20. Walter Miller, "Focal Concerns of Lower Class Culture," in Ferman, *op. cit.*, pp. 398—403.

21. Lewis, *La Vida, op. cit.*, pp. xlvi—xlviii.

22. Gabriel Almond and Sydney Verba, *The Civic Culture* (Boston: Little, Brown and Co., 1965, pp. 11—30).

23. Gans, *Urban Villagers, op. cit.*, pp. 245—246.

24. *Ibid.*, p. 90.

25. *Ibid.*, p. 91.

26. Banfield, *The Moral Basis of a Backward Society, op. cit.*, pp. 83—97.

27. Banfield *The Unheavenly City, op. cit.*, p. 53.

28. Elliot Liebow, *Tally's Corner* (Boston: Little, Brown and Co., 1967, p. 17).

29. *Ibid.*, pp. 20—21.

30. *Ibid.*, p. 23.

31. *Ibid.*, p. 31.

32. St. Clair Drake and Horace R. Cayton, *Black Metropolis, A Study of Negro Life in a Northern City* (New York: Harper Torchbooks, 1962, p. 600).

33. Kenneth B. Clark, *Dark Ghetto, Dilemmas of Social Power* (New York: Harper Torchbooks, 1967, p. 27).

34. During the hot summer months when school is out, the street life that thrives all year round in the commercial sections of the neighborhood spreads to almost every residential block. A middle-aged man explained to Kenneth Clark his presence outside a home: "We can't go back in the house because we almost suffocate. So we sit down on the curb, or stand on the sidewalk, or on the steps, things like that, till the wee hours of the morning, especially in the summer when its too hot to go up" (Clark, *op. cit.,* p. 5).

Gerald Suttles has described a similar development in a neighborhood of mixed ethnic origins: "During the summer months the streets in the Addams area are thronged with children, young adults, and old people. Street life is especially active in the afternoon after school or work. The front steps are crowded with old people chatting back and forth between households while some occasionally bring out chairs when sitting space gets scarce. Young girls stand in clusters a little distance from the 'stoop-sitters,' giggling, squealing, and glancing at the passerby. Young unmarried men seem to occupy every street corner or unused doorway. Small two- and three-year olds stumble, crawl, and toddle along the sidewalks in front of their homes" [Gerald D. Suttles, *The Social Order of the Slum* (Chicago: The University of Chicago Press, 1968, p. 74)].

The streets of low income urban neighborhoods have not always been the exclusive domain of blacks, Puerto Ricans, and Mexican-Americans. In fact, it is among first and second generation Italian immigrants that a rich street life first achieved social prominence. The early travelers to America from Southern Italy not only brought their own persons and their families, but also travelled with many of their fellow villagers, thus reestablishing their communities—or *paesani*—here in the United States [William Foote Whyte, *Street Corner Society* (Chicago: The University of Chicago Press, 1955, p. xvii)]. The Italian community provided the rich street life for William Whyte's discussion of the North End in Boston and Frederic Thrasher's study of 1313 gangs in Chicago [Frederic M. Thrasher, *The Gang* (Chicago: The University of Chicago Press, 1936)].

The younger population in the North End was divisible into two groups, the college boys and the street corner boys. The latter centered "their social activities upon particular street corners, with their adjoining barbershops, lunchrooms, poolrooms, or clubrooms" (Whyte, *op. cit.*, p. xviii). Although not formally organized, these groups developed a fairly stable set of rules for regulating social interaction among members, and between members and the middle class institutions operating in the neighborhood (Whyte, *op. cit.*, p. 104). The young men who joined the corner life usually maintained membership from their early teens until their late twenties or early thirties (Whyte, *op. cit.*, p. 255). Throughout this period, the street is more important than the home: "Except when he eats, sleeps, or is sick," Whyte writes, "he is rarely at home, and his friends always go to his corner first when they want to find him" (Whyte, *op. cit.*, p. 255).

35. Liebow, *op. cit.*, pp. 61–65.

36. *Ibid.*, p. 57.

37. *Ibid.*, p. 214.

38. Hannerz, *op. cit.*, p. 117.

39. *Ibid.*, p. 112.

40. *Ibid.*, p. 111.

41. Albert K. Cohen, *Delinquent Boys* (New York: The Free Press, 1955, p. 121).

42. *Ibid.*, p. 129.

43. Whyte, *op. cit.*, p. 40.

44. David Matza, *Delinquency and Drift* (New York: John Wiley & Sons, 1964, p. 49). Street corner men rarely indicate that they deserve their position in society, but they infrequently consider their position just.

45. Thrasher, *op. cit.*, p. 26.

46. *Ibid.*, p. 35.

47. Matza, *op. cit.*, pp. 28, 33, 59–60. The combination of spontaneity, flux and flow, intermittent criminal behavior, informal leadership, and impermanence of structure suggests what Lewis Yablonsky calls the "near group" [Lewis Yablonsky, "The Delinquent Gang as a Near Group," *Social Problems*, Vol. 7, No. 2, 109 (Fall 1959)].

48. Saul Bernstein, *Youth on the Streets* (New York: Association Press, 1964, p. 47).

49. Hannerz, *op. cit.*, pp. 38–39.

50. *Ibid.*, p. 42.

51. *Ibid.*, p. 46.

52. Whyte, *loc. cit.*; Gans, *The Urban Villagers*, *loc. cit.*; Hannerz, *loc. cit.*; Liebow, *loc. cit.*

53. Whyte, *op. cit.*, p. 35.

54. Liebow, *op. cit.*, p. 143.

55. Thrasher, *op. cit.*, p. 228.

56. Gans, *The Urban Villagers, op. cit.*, p. 30.

57. Hannerz, *op. cit.*, p. 95.

58. Donald J. Bogue, Bhaskar D. Misra, and D. P. Dandekar, "A New Estimate of the Negro Population and Negro Vital Rates in the United States, 1930–1960," *Demography,* Vol. I, No. 1 (1964).

59. Angus Campbell and Howard Schuman, "Racial Attitudes in Fifteen American Cities," in the *Supplemental Studies for the National Advisory Commission on Civil Disorders* (Washington, D.C.: U.S. Government Printing Office, 1968, p. 65).

60. A discussion of site sampling appears in Warren D. Ten Houten, "Site Sampling and Snowball Sampling in Biased Nets: Methodology for the Study of Community Organization," (Los Angeles: University of California, May 19, 1969), a report prepared for the Office of Economic Opportunity under subcontract to Barss, Reitzel and Associates.

61. Street corner population refers to those individuals *not* located in the following sampling sites: residential inside day and residential inside night.

62. The distinctive responses of the five communities are unaffected by controls for sex, education, age, length of community residence, or size of street corner population. At every educational level, in every age bracket, for both men and women, the differences between the neighborhoods are maintained, with only the barest reduction in margin. Although only four street corner respondents were interviewed in Belmont, the level of present-oriented community response is equalled only by that in Summerhill. Length of residence was unrelated to any of the questions and therefore could not be expected to affect the intercity differences.

63. Samuel Ramos, *Profile of Man and Culture in Mexico* (Austin: University of Texas Press, 1962, pp. 64–65).

64. Loyal Jones, "Appalachian Values" (unpublished mimeograph, Berea College, p. 2).

65. Nikos Kazantzakis, *The Last Temptation of Christ* (New York: Bantam Books, 1961, pp. 1–2).

66. Jack E. Weller, *Yesterday's People* (Lexington, Kentucky: University of Kentucky Press, 1965, p. 34); Thomas R. Ford, "The Passing of Provincialism," in Thomas R. Ford, ed., *The Southern Appalachian*

Region (Lexington, Kentucky: Kentucky Paperbacks, 1967, p. 22).

67. Weller, *op. cit.*, p. 36.

68. Harry K. Schwartzweller, James S. Brown, and J.J. Mangalam, *Mountain Families in Transition* (University Park, Pennsylvania: The Pennsylvania State University Press, 1971, p. 137).

69. Todd Gitlin and Nanci Hollander, *Uptown* (New York: Harper Colophon Books, 1971, pp. 170, 319).

70. Weller, *op. cit.*, p. 53.

71. Jones, *op. cit.*, p. 4.

72. Valentine, *op. cit.*, p. 7.

Chapter Five: The Alienated Politics of Poor Neighborhoods

1. C. Vann Woodward, *Tom Watson* (New York: Rinehart and Co., 1938, pp. 380–403).

2. Gunnar Myrdal, *An American Dilemma* (New York: Harper Torchbooks, 1969, pp. 721–722).

3. Allison Davis, Burleigh B. Gardner, and Mary R. Gardner, *Deep South* (Chicago: University of Chicago Press, 1941, Part II).

4. Harry M. Caudill, *Night Comes to the Cumberlands* (Boston: Little, Brown and Co., 1963, pp. 240–241).

5. Paul W. Wager, "Local Government," in Thomas R. Ford, ed., *The Southern Appalachian Region* (Lexington, Kentucky: Kentucky Paperbacks, 1967, p. 154).

6. Todd Gitlin and Nanci Hollander, *Uptown* (New York: Harper Colophon Books, 1971, p. 142).

7. John Womack, Jr., *Zapata and the Mexican Revolution* (New York: Vintage Books, 1970, pp. 41–54).

8. *Ibid.*, pp. 167–169.

9. Kenneth Keniston, *The Uncommitted, Alienated Youth in American Society* (New York: Delta Books, 1965, p. 452).

10. *Report of the National Advisory Commission on Civil Disorders* (New York: Bantam Books, 1968, pp. 284–285). The commission found that rioters were angrier than nonparticipants with politicians and the police and showed greater contempt for the country (*ibid.*, p. 178).

11. Georg Wilhelm Friedrich Hegel, *The Philosophy of History* in Carl J. Friedrich, *ed.*, *The Philosophy of Hegel* (New York: The Modern Library, 1954, pp. 11, 16); Karl Marx, *Economic and Philosophical Manuscripts*,

in Erich Fromm, *Marx's Concept of Man* (New York: Frederick Ungar Publishing Co., 1961, p. 191).

12. Robert E. Lane, *Political Ideology* (New York: The Free Press, 1967, pp. 161–162).

13. Gabriel Almond and Sydney Verba, *The Civic Culture* (Boston: Little, Brown and Co., 1965, p. 16).

14. David A. Easton, *A Systems Analysis of Political Life* (New York: John Wiley & Sons, 1965, pp. 343–350).

15. David A. Easton, *A Framework for Political Analysis* (Englewood Cliffs: Prentice-Hall, 1965, p. 50).

16. An analysis of survey data for five nations confirms that in evaluating political institutions, citizens distinguish between "input" and "output" processes. See Stanley B. Greenberg, "Systems Theory and Attitude Formation" (unpublished manuscript, Harvard University, May, 1968).

17. The notion of sensed inefficacy developed in the previous section is rooted in existing political arrangements. It is an assessment not of generalized political effectiveness but of the responsiveness of the regular or normal political channels. Of course, violent political behavior might well be tempered by calculations of another form: will violence destroy or radically alter the system? This calculation reflects an assessment of comparative "military" power and bears little relation to a consideration of governmental responsiveness.

18. Theodore Roszak, *The Making of a Counter Culture* (Garden City: Anchor Books, 1969, pp. 206–207).

19. Albert Camus, *The Rebel* (New York: Vintage Books, 1956, pp. 16–22).

20. *Ibid.*, pp. 150–151.

21. Rebellion predicated on a fundamental opposition to the political order might well be tempered by a consideration of likely success—particularly for the leadership—but is very often sustained by less rational concerns. Combatants enter the field of battle certain of triumph, a delusion that is more a part of their apocalyptic assessment of events than of their consideration of objective probabilities. Sorel writes, "The myth must be judged as a means of acting on the present; any attempt to discuss how far it can be taken literally as future history is devoid of sense. It is the myth in its entirety which is alone important" [Georges Sorel, *Reflections on Violence* (New York: Peter Smith, 1941)]. Many a millenarian movement is driven by "a profound and total rejection of the present, evil world, and a passionate longing for another and better one. . ." [E.J. Hobsbawm, *Primitive Rebels* (New York: W.W. Norton and Co.,

1965, p. 57)]. Its revolution will "make itself," for somehow it *must* happen (*ibid.*, p. 59).

22. Talcott Parsons, *The Social System* (New York: The Free Press, 1964, pp. 259—260).

23. Kenneth Keniston, *Young Radicals* (New York: Harcourt, Brace and World, Inc., 1968, pp. 308—310).

24. See note 26 below.

25. The notion of sensed effectiveness as a mediator in political action is not new to this study of alienation for it is also important to Murray Levin's work on political alienation [Murray Levin, "Political Alienation," in Eric and Mary Josephson, eds., *Man Alone* (New York: Dell Publishing Co., 1962)] and Franz Neumann's discussion of the democratic and authoritarian state (Franz Neumann, *The Democratic and the Authoritarian State* (Glencoe, Illinois: The Free Press, 1957)]. Levin suggests, for example, that the essential difference between "rational activism" and "political withdrawl" is whether an individual believes his actions have a reasonable chance of bringing about a change in conditions (Levin, *op. cit.*, pp. 235—236). In one case an individual makes a reasonable calculation that if he acts, it is likely to have some bearing on his situation; in the other, he feels "any political effort on his part has little chance of producing an effect" (Levin, *op. cit.*, p. 235). Levin also suggests a third possible response to feelings of alienation, that of identification with a charismatic leader. This last category of analysis is really a simplified presentation of what Neumann considers man's response to civilization and anxiety. Neumann believes, as does Freud, that one of the essential characteristics of civilization is anxiety, and that anxiety tied to a feeling that there is no possibility for change through individual effort produces a need for concreteness. Some individuals seek certainty through conspiracy theories of politics; others turn to Caesarist movements (Neumann, *op. cit.*, p. 290).

26. Selected survey results are presented below:

(1) Percentage who believe police rough up people unnecessarily

Blacks, males, Watts, 1965	74%
Blacks, females, Watts, 1965	58%
Blacks, Houston, 1966	31%
Blacks, Watts, 1967	36%
Blacks, Oakland, 1967	56%
Blacks, fifteen cities, 1967	35%
Whites, fifteen cities, 1967	10%

(2)   Percentage who are dissatisfied with local schools

Blacks, Houston, 1966	42%
Blacks, Oakland, 1967	73%
Blacks, Watts, 1967	53%
Blacks, fifteen cities, 1967	36%
Blacks, national, 1968	29%
Whites, males, fifteen cities, 1967	22%
Whites, females, fifteen cities, 1967	25%
Whites, national, 1968	14%

(3)   Percentage who feel country is not worth fighting for

Blacks, national, 1963	9%
Blacks, urban, 1964	11%
Blacks, New York, 1964	15%
Blacks, Chicago, 1964	14%
Blacks, Atlanta, 1964	8%
Blacks, Birmingham, 1964	7%
Blacks, national, 1966	6%
Blacks, Detroit rioters, 1967	39%
Blacks, Detroit nonrioters, 1967	16%
Blacks, Newark rioters, 1967	53%
Blacks, Newark nonrioters, 1967	28%

(4)   Percentage who believe riots have helped black people

Blacks, national urban, 1964	41%
Blacks, New York, 1964	39%
Blacks, Chicago, 1964	55%
Blacks, Atlanta, 1964	63%
Blacks, Birmingham, 1964	52%
Blacks, Watts, 1965	38%
Blacks, national, 1966	34%
Blacks, Houston, 1966	30%
Blacks, Oakland, 1967	51%
Blacks, fifteen cities, 1967	34%
Whites, Los Angeles, 1965	19%
Whites, fifteen cities, 1967	14%

(5)   Percentage who believe government officials don't care about us

Blacks, national, 1966	32%
Blacks, national, 1968	52%
Whites, low income, national, 1966	50%
National, 1966	28%
National, 1968	39%

These results were drawn from the following works: Raymond J. Murphy and James M. Watson, "The Structure of Discontent" (Los Angeles: Institute of Government and Public Affairs, University of California); Angus Campbell and Howard Schuman, "Racial Attitudes in Fifteen American Cities," in *The National Advisory Commission on Civil Disorders, Supplemental Studies* (Washington, D.C.: U.S. Government Printing Office, July, 1968); William McCord and John Howard, "Negro Opinions in Three Riot Cities," in Louis H. Masotti and Don R. Bowen, eds., *Riots and Rebellion* (Beverly Hills: Sage Publications, Inc., 1968); William Brink and Louis Harris, Black and White (New York: Simon and Schuster, 1967); Gary T. Marx, *Protest and Prejudice: A Study of Belief in the Black Community* (New York: Harper Torchbooks, 1969); *The Negro and the City* (New York: Time-Life Books, 1968); Jay Schulman, "Ghetto-Area Residence, Political Alienation and Riot Orientation," in Masotti, *op cit.;* T.M. Tomlinson and David O. Sears, "Los Angeles Riot Study, Negro Attitudes Toward the Riot" (Los Angeles: Institute of Government and Public Affairs, University of California); *Report of the National Advisory Commission on Civil Disorders, op. cit.;* Harris Survey (April 15, 1968); CBS News, *White and Negro Attitudes Towards Race Related Issues and Activities* (Princeton: Opinion Research Corporation, 1968).

27. Campbell and Schuman, *op cit.,* p. 40.

28. CBS News, *op. cit.,* p. 9.

29. Murphy and Watson, *op. cit.;* Campbell and Schuman, *op. cit.*

30. See note 26 above.

31. *National Advisory Commission on Civil Disorders, op. cit.,* p. 178.

32. Brink and Harris, *op. cit.,* p. 135; Harris Survey, *op. cit.*

33. Stanley B. Greenberg, *People, Violence and Power* (Ph.D. Dissertation, Harvard University, 1971, p. 49).

34. Robert E. Lane, *Political Life: Why and How People Get Involved in Politics* (New York: The Free Press, 1965, p. 150).

35. V.O. Key, Jr., *Public Opinion and American Democracy* (New York: Alfred A. Knopf, 1964, p. 327).

36. Wayne E. Thompson and John E. Horton, "Political Alienation as a Force in Political Action," *Social Forces,* Vol. XXXVIII, 192 (March 1960).

37. Norman H. Nie, G. Bingham Powell, Jr., and Kenneth Prewitt, "Social Structure and Political Participation: Developmental Relationships, II," *American Political Science Review,* Vol. LXIII, No. 3, 817 (September 1969).

38. Nearly all communities, poor and nonpoor, provide culturally oriented groups that provide a distraction from, or alternative to, conventional politics.

39. Bryan T. Downes, "Social and Political Characteristics of Riot Cities: A Comparative Study," *Social Science Quarterly*, Vol. 49, No. 3, 509 (December 1968).

40. Robert M. Fogelson and Robert B. Hill, "Who Riots? A Study of Participation in the 1967 Riots," in *National Advisory Commission on Civil Disorders, Supplemental Studies, op. cit.*, p. 231.

41. Marx, *Protest and Prejudice, op. cit.*, p. 19.

42. The intercity differences for sensed inefficacy are smaller than for any of the other alienation measures.

43. Caudill, *op. cit.*, p. 164.

44. Jack E. Weller, *Yesterday's People* (Lexington, Kentucky: University of Kentucky Press, 1965, pp. 114–115).

45. Eldridge Cleaver, *Soul on Ice* (New York: McGraw-Hill Book Co., 1968, p. 133).

46. Wager, *op. cit.*, p. 166.

47. Charles E. Hall, *Negroes in the United States 1920–1932* (New York: Arno Press and *The New York Times*, 1969, pp. 34–39).

48. The revolutionary discontent that racked the Mexican countryside in the early part of this century was not widespread in central Mexico. The path of violence traveled from north to south, from the border states to Mexico City. The Central Mesa, the principal source of Mexican migrants, was "far less revolutionary, more sluggish, more content with bad conditions. . ." [Manuel Gamio, *Mexican Immigration to the United States* (Chicago: University of Chicago Press, 1930, pp. 160–161)]. The central populations were battered by revolutionary violence, government repression, and the shattering of the hacienda economy. They did not create these forces, however. Their flight to the southwestern United States was as refugees, not as a revolutionary army.

49. Stan Steiner, *La Raza: The Mexican Americans* (New York: Harper & Row, Publishers, 1970, p. 194).

50. *Ibid.*, p. 251.

51. *San Jose Mercury* (September 4, 1970).

52. Independent confirmation of these attitudes was provided in a survey by the Diridon Research Corporation. They found Gardner residents less critical of the educational system and police practices than other San Jose residents and other Mexican-Americans residing elsewhere in the city *[Demographic Data, Model Cities of San Jose* (San Jose, California:

Diridon Research Corporation, November 12, 1971, pp. 40, 53)].

53. Since no measure of "cultural response" was available in the survey data, the analysis only incompletely tests the model proposed earlier.

54. Hubert M. Blalock, Jr., *Social Statistics* (New York: McGraw-Hill Book Co., 1960, p. 345).

55. This discussion relies on Otis Dudley Duncan, "Path Analysis: Sociological Examples," *American Journal of Sociology,* Vol. 72, No. 1 (July 1966); Otis Dudley Duncan, "Inheritance of Poverty or Inheritance of Race?," in Daniel P. Moynihan, ed., *On Understanding Poverty* (New York: Basic Books, 1969); Hubert M. Blalock, Jr., "Causal Inference, Closed Population, and Measures of Association," *American Political Science Review,* Vol. LXI, No. 1 (March 1967); Raymond Boudon, "A Method of Linear Causal Analysis: Dependence Analysis," *American Sociological Review,* Vol. 30, No. 3 (June 1965).

56. Hubert M. Blalock, Jr., *Causal Inference in Nonexperimental Research* (Chapel Hill: University of North Carolina Press, 1964, pp. 12–30, 46–47).

57. The Appalachian white migrants were not included in these calculations because most questions on political protest and violence were incomprehensible or offensive to them. This is due in part to contextual factors (no riots, no protest in Belmont), but due as well to the nature of their alienation—little policy discontent, for example. These attitudes would suggest few political protest or violence. The pattern of the alienation model, however, is confirmed empirically for participation in community organizations (where data were available). Fully 44 percent of those scoring high on policy dissatisfaction, but low on feelings of inefficacy, belong to an organization, as opposed to just 9 percent of their opposite number (low policy dissatisfaction, high sense of inefficacy). This pattern holds for all five neighborhoods surveyed.

58. *The Detroit Free Press* (May 4, 1969).

59. An extrapolation of belief in Belmont using the regression equations from Figure 5.2 indicates that the level of receptivity to politics would exceed that of Gardner.

60. Although sensed inefficacy is essential to understanding the individual calculations that produce politics or violence, it plays only a limited role in distinguishing between the politics of various neighborhoods. Sensed inefficacy does not vary among the black neighborhoods, whether in the North or South, and is less useful in distinguishing the other communities than the two remaining measures of estrangement.

Chapter Six: The Politics of Collective Understanding

1. W.E.B. DuBois, *The Souls of Black Folk* (Greenwich: Fawcett Publications, Inc., 1961, p. 23).

2. Vincent Harding, "Black Power and the American Christ," in Floyd B. Barbour, ed., *The Black Power Revolt* (Toronto: Collier Books, 1969, p. 100).

3. Stokely Carmichael, "Power and Racism," in Barbour, *op. cit.*, p. 66.

4. National Committee of Negro Churchmen, "Black Power," in Nathan Wright, Jr., *Black Power and Urban Unrest* (New York: Hawthorn Books, 1967, p. 191).

5. Oscar Handlin, *Boston's Immigrants* (Cambridge: Harvard University Press, 1959, pp. 167—169).

6. Samuel Halperin, *The Political World of American Zionism* (Detroit: Wayne State University Press, 1961).

7. We cannot begin to explain the methodology of factor analysis in this chapter, but it should be sufficient to note that where several questions have a high factor loading on a factor, the responses are intercorrelated and reveal, perhaps, an underlying theme. For a simple, straightforward explanation of factor analysis, see Hubert M. Blalock, Jr., *Social Statistics* (New York: McGraw Hill Book Co., 1960, pp. 383—389). For a more thorough presentation, see Harry H. Harmon, *Modern Factor Analysis* (Chicago: The University of Chicago Press, 1967).

8. Stokely Carmichael and Charles V. Hamilton, *Black Power* (New York: Vintage Books, 1967, pp. 44—45).

9. These findings are similar to those observed by Aberbach and Walker for their Detroit sample. They found that those respondents who react favorably to the term "black power" do so for two basic reasons: the stated need for "racial unity" and a demand for a "fair share." [Joel D. Aberbach and Jack L. Walker, "The Meanings of Black Power: A Comparison of White and Black Interpretations of a Political Slogan," *American Political Science Review*, Vol. LXIV, No. 2 (June 1970)]. The latter response suggests that black people deserve a share of the wealth which is unfairly denied by white society, perhaps an elaboration of the concept that the roots of disadvantage are in the larger society.

It is interesting that Aberbach and Walker attain results similar to those presented above using the term "black power." We might account for this coincidence in their use of an open-ended schedule, allowing respondents to reveal a comprehensive account of their views rather than a simple approval or disapproval, as was the case in this study.

10. Quoted in Charles E. Silberman, *Crisis in Black and White* (New York: Vintage Books, 1964, p. 186).

11. Barbour, *op. cit.* p. viii.

12. Malcolm X, *Malcolm X Speaks* (New York: Grove Press, Inc., 1965, pp. 4—5).

13. *Ibid.*, p. 196.

14. Quoted in C. Eric Lincoln, *The Black Muslims in America* (Boston: Beacon Press, 1961, p. 3).

15. Carmichael "Power and Racism," *op. cit.*, p. 71.

16. Carmichael and Hamilton, *op. cit.*, p. 47.

17. LeRoi Jones, "The Need for a Cultural Base to Civil Rites and Black Bpower Mooments" in Barbour, *op. cit.*, p. 141.

18. Lincoln, *op. cit.*, p. 67.

19. E. U. Essien-Udom, *Black Nationalism, A Search for an Identity in America* (New York: Dell Publishing Co., 1964, p. 276).

20. Systematic surveys of poor neighborhoods, including this one, have not grappled very successfully with this issue. National surveys discussed by Gary Marx and William Brink and Louis Harris show minimal support in the black community for the Black Muslims and Elijah Muhammed. Expressions that they are helping black people or doing a "pretty good job" rarely exceed 10 percent [Gary T. Marx, *Protest and Prejudice: A Study of Belief in the Black Community* (New York: Harper Torchbooks, 1969, p. 25); William Brink and Louis Harris, *Black and White* (New York: Simon and Schuster, 1967, pp. 248, 254)]. In the three black neighborhoods in this study, slightly more than 10 percent support the notion of a "separate black nation"; just under 15 percent consider their nationality "Afro-American."

21. Stanley M. Elkins, *Slavery, A Problem in American Institutional and Intellectual Life* (Chicago: The University of Chicago Press, 1968, p. 101).

22. *Ibid.*, pp. 101—102.

23. Arnold Rose, *The Negro's Morale, Group Identification and Protest* (Minneapolis: The University of Minnesota Press, 1949, p. 76).

24. Melville J. Herskovits, *The Myth of the Negro Past* (Boston: Beacon Press, 1958, pp. 148—149).

25. *Ibid.*, pp. 213—219.

26. *Ibid.*, pp. 280—291.

27. Claude M. Lightfoot, *Ghetto Rebellion to Black Liberation* (New York: International Publishers, 1968, p. 129).

28. Frantz Fanon, *The Wretched of the Earth* (New York: Grove Press,Inc., 1968, p. 216).

29. E. David Cronon, *Black Moses: The Story of Marcus Garvey* (Madison: The University of Wisconsin Press, 1969, p. 128).

30. Malcolm X, *The Autobiography of Malcolm X* (New York: Grove Press, Inc., 1966, p. 7).

31. W. E. B. DuBois, *The Autobiography of W. E. B. DuBois, A Soliloquy on Viewing My Life From the Last Decade of Its First Century* (New York: International Publishers Co., 1968, p. 289).

32. Ulf Hannerz, *Soulside* (New York: Columbia University Press, 1969, p. 153).

33. Charles Keil, *Urban Blues* (Chicago: The University of Chicago Press, 1966, pp. 165—166).

34. *Ibid.,* pp. 167—181.

35. Ralph Ellison, *Invisible Man* (New York: Signet Books, 1952, p. 496).

36. Carmichael, "Power and Racism," *op. cit.,* p. 64.

37. Cesar Chavez, quoted in Peter Matthiessen, "Profiles Organizer—II," *The New Yorker* (June 28, 1969).

38. Stan Steiner, *La Raza: The Mexican Americans* (New York: Harper and Row Publishers, 1970, p. 114).

39. Eliu Carranza *Pensamientos on Los Chicanos: A Cultural Revolution* (Berkeley: California Book Co., Ltd., 1969, p. 1); James A. Kelso, *Mexican Americans in a Middle Class Anglo American Society, A Study of Intergroup Value Conflict* (Berkeley: California Book Co., Ltd., 1970, pp. 13—15).

40. See Rodolfo Gonzales, "I am Joaquin."

41. *Ibid.*

42. Joan W. Moore and Frank G. Mittelbach, "Residential Segregation in the Urban Southwest," *The Mexican American Study Project* (Los Angeles: The University of California, pp. 16—18).

43. In Los Angeles only 13 percent of Mexican-American respondents found marriage with Anglos distasteful, but 85 percent found marriage with a black person distasteful [Leo Grebler, Joan W. Moore and Ralph C. Guzman, *The Mexican-American People* (New York: The Free Press, 1970, p. 392)].

44. Miguel David Tirado, "Mexican American Community Political Organization," *Aztlan,* Vol. 1, No. 1, 57 (Spring 1970).

45. Grebler, *op. cit.,* p. 381.

46. Steiner, *op. cit.,* p. 55.

47. Quoted in Steiner, *op. cit.*, p. 296.

48. Helen Rowan, "A Minority Nobody Knows," in John H. Burma, ed., *Mexican-Americans in the United States: A Reader* (Cambridge: Schenkman Publishing Co., Inc., 1970, p. 299).

49. A number of Mexican-American community leaders in Gardner returned to Mexico after losing control of the Model Cities program.

50. Eighty-four percent of Mexican-Americans in Los Angeles and 91 percent in San Antonio are fluent in Spanish (Grebler, *op. cit.*, p. 424).

51. See Nathan Glazer and Daniel P. Moynihan, *Beyond the Melting Pot* (Cambridge: The M.I.T. Press, 1963, pp. 241–243). Mexican-Americans are the only immigrant group in the United States whose interests are protected in a treaty signed by the leaders of this nation and those of a foreign power and supervised by a foreign embassy [Ruth D. Tuck, *Not With the Fist* (New York: Harcourt, Brace and Co., 1946, p. vii)].

52. Quoted in Carey McWilliams, *North From Mexico* (New York: Greenwood Press, 1968, p. 41).

53. *Ibid.*, p. 39.

54. Tuck, *op. cit.*, pp. 16–19.

55. Only 10 percent of Mexican-Americans can reasonably be typed as pure Spanish-European (Jack D. Forbes, "Race and Color in Mexican-American Problems," *Journal of Human Relations*, Vol. 16, No. 1, 57 (1968).

56. Tuck, *op. cit.*, p. 134.

57. Rudolfo Gonzales, "What Political Road for the Chicano Movement?," in Wayne Moquin, ed., *A Documentary History of the Mexican Americans* (New York: Bantam Books, 1972, p. 491).

58. Thomas R. Ford, "The Passing of Provincialism," in Thomas R. Ford, ed., *The Southern Appalachian Region* (Lexington, Kentucky: Kentucky Paperbacks, 1967, p. 33).

59. Jack E. Weller, *Yesterday's People* (Lexington, Kentucky: University of Kentucky Press, 1965, pp. 80–81).

60. Todd Gitlin and Nanci Hollander, *Uptown* (New York: Harper Colophon Books, 1971, p. 242).

61. Harry K. Schwartzweller, James S. Brown, and J. J. Mangalam, *Mountain Families in Transition* (University Park, Pennsylvania: The Pennsylvania State University Press, 1971, p. 140).

62. It is important to note that this desire, attributed to all Appalachian migrants, is pronounced only for men. Schwartzweller and his associates found that 60 percent of the men, but only 22 percent of the

women, want to return to Kentucky. Approximately half of both the men and women, however, consider Kentucky "home" (Schwartzweller, *op. cit.*, pp. 140—141).

63. See Frank H. Smith, "Dances and Singing Games," in Ford, *op. cit.*, pp. 271—278.

64. Margaret Clark, *Health in the Mexican-American Culture* (Berkeley and Los Angeles: University of California Press, 1959, p. 21).

65. Although anti-Anglo sentiments are not central aspects of Mexican-American identity in this research, there are exceptions and recent changes that should be noted. First, this research focuses on the poorest neighborhood in San Jose. Antipathy toward whites was increasingly evident, however, in the somewhat more prosperous neighborhoods to the east. Support for the *la Raza Unida* Party, though very weak, comes largely from these more easterly areas. Second, although anti-Anglo feelings never dominated interpersonal contact in Gardner, these sentiments were more often expressed in my last trip to San Jose than in the first. Together these two observations very likely suggest an increasing concern with the issue of responsibility, particularly among those who have escaped the poverty of Gardner. But even in these latter cases, the concern with oppression does not remotely approach that evident on the East Side, or even North Central.

66. Morton Grodzins, *The Loyal and the Disloyal, Social Boundaries of Patriotism and Treason* (Cleveland and New York: The World Publishing Co., 1966, p. 106).

67. *Ibid.*, p. 117.

68. *Ibid.*, pp. 120—121.

69. *Ibid.*, p. 127.

70. Rose, *op. cit.*, p. 5.

71. *Ibid.*, p. 6.

72. Hubert Blalock, *Social Statistics* (New York: McGraw-Hill Book Co., 1960, p. 345).

73. Otis Dudley Duncan, "Path Analysis: Sociological Examples," *American Journal of Sociology*, Vol. 72, No. 1 (July 1966).

74. Estrangement is defined by the three alienation questions. Because sense of inefficacy plays a mediating role in political expression, its impact on involvement is opposed to that of other alienation measures. The coefficient with receptivity to politics, therefore, is smaller than would be expected given the results of Chapter Five.

75. Roland L. Warren, *The Community in America* (Chicago: Rand McNally, 1963, pp. 13—16).

76. John Walton, "The Vertical Axis of Community Organization and the Structure of Power," *Social Science Quarterly,* Vol. 48, No. 3, 365 (December 1967).

77. James Q. Wilson, *Negro Politics, The Search for Leadership* (New York: The Free Press, 1965); Carmichael and Hamilton, *op. cit.,* p. 11.

78. Saul D. Alinsky, "The War on Poverty—Political Pornography," in Chaim I. Waxman, ed., *Poverty: Power and Politics* (New York: Grosset and Dunlap, 1968, p. 173).

Chapter Seven: The Politics of Class

1. Pamphlet of the National Association of Manufacturers, quoted in Ely Chinoy, *Automobile Workers and the American Dream* (Garden City: Doubleday and Co., 1955, pp. 6—7).

2. Chinoy, *op. cit.,* p. 19.

3. Elliot Liebow, *Tally's Corner* (Boston: Little, Brown and Co., 1967, p. 63).

4. Morris Rosenberg, "Perceptual Obstacles to Class Consciousness," *Social Forces,* Vol. 32 (October 1953); Daniel Bell, *The End of Ideology* (New York: The Free Press, 1965); Seymour Martin Lipset, *Political Man: The Social Bases of Politics* (Garden City: Anchor Books, 1963).

5. Arthur Kornhauser, *Mental Health of the Industrial Worker* (New York: John Wiley and Sons, 1965, pp. 129—131).

6. Robert Blauner, "Work Satisfaction and Industrial Trends in Modern Society," in Reinhard Bendix and Seymour Martin Lipset, eds., *Class, Status, and Power* (New York: The Free Press, 1966, pp. 478—483).

7. Chinoy, *op. cit.,* pp. 67, 133.

8. Robert E. Lane, *Political Ideology* (New York: The Free Press, 1967), pp. 65—67.

9. Louis Hartz, *The Liberal Tradition in America* (New York: Harcourt Brace and World, 1955, pp. 3—7, 203—227).

10. David Apter, *Choice and the Politics of Allocation* (New Haven: Yale University Press, 1971, p. 61); see also T. B. Bottomore, *Classes in Modern Society* (New York: Vintage Books, 1966, pp. 86—90).

11. The decomposition of labor is discussed by Ralf Dahrendorf, *Class and Class Conflict in Industrial Society* (Stanford: Stanford University Press, 1959, pp. 48—51).

12. *Ibid.,* pp. 51—52.

13. Apter, *op. cit.,* pp. 87—88.

14. This view does not emerge simply from Marx's analysis of class, for he granted considerable importance to theory and perspective in the formulation of a class position [Karl Marx, *German Ideology* (New York: International Publishers, 1970, pp. 83—89)]. But even Marx assumed that the working class condition—its misery and special relation to production—provided a singular basis for consciousness and understanding in bourgeois society (Georg Lukács, *History and Class Consciousness* (Cambridge: The M.I.T. Press, 1971, p. 19)].

15. C. Vann Woodward, *Tom Watson* (New York: Rinehart and Co., 1938, pp. 217—242).

16. Wilson Record, *The Negro and the Communist Party* (New York: Atheneum, 1971, p. 15).

17. Quoted in August Meier and Elliot Rudwick, "Attitudes of Negro Leaders Toward the American Labor Movement from the Civil War to World War I," in *The Negro and the American Labor Movement,* edited by Julius Jacobson. Copyright © 1968 by Julius Jacobson. Reprinted by permission of Doubleday & Company, Inc.

18. Marc Karson and Ronald Radosh, "The American Federation of Labor and the Negro Worker, 1894—1949," in Jacobson, *op. cit.,* pp. 155—156, 181.

19. *Ibid.,* p. 181.

20. *Ibid.,* p. 187.

21. Thomas R. Brooks, *Toil and Trouble* (New York: Delta Books, 1964, pp. 243—244).

22. Irving Bernstein, *Turbulent Years* (Boston: Houghton Mifflin Co., 1969, p. 353).

23. *Ibid.,* p. 454.

24. *Ibid.,* p. 744.

25. Sumner M. Rosen, "The CIO Era, 1935—55," in Jacobson, *op. cit.,* p. 190.

26. Benjamin J. Davis, *Communist Councilman from Harlem* (New York: International Publishers, 1969, p. 27).

27. Woodward, *op. cit.,* pp. 220—221, 241—242.

28. *Ibid.,* p. 241.

29. *Ibid.,* p. 371.

30. E. Franklin Frazier, *Black Bourgeoisie* (New York: Collier Books, 1962, p. 132).

31. *Ibid.,* pp. 137, 150—151.

32. Meier and Rudwick, *op. cit.,* p. 34.

33. Quoted in Meier and Rudwick, *op. cit.,* p. 38.

34. *Ibid.*, p. 30.
35. Record, *op. cit.*, p. 22.
36. *Ibid.*, p. 108.
37. *Ibid.*, p. 143. The CIO might have made these efforts in any event, given the difficulties in restricting employment in large scale industry. Sumner Rosen believes that the effort to include black workers would have occurred even without Communist party participation. "But wherever Negro workers formed a significant fraction of the labor force, intensive, persistent efforts were expended to secure their support. This was true whether Communists played a subordinate role or held the key positions of leadership" (Rosen, *op. cit.*, p. 195).
38. Harold Cruse, *The Crisis of the Negro Intellectual* (New York: William Morrow and Co., 1967, pp. 171−177).
39. *Ibid.*, pp. 207−224.
40. Record, *op. cit.*, p. 15.
41. *Ibid.*, pp. 53−56.
42. *Ibid.*, p. 65.
43. *Ibid.*, p. 97.
44. *Ibid.*, p. 135.
45. Julius Jacobson, "Union Conservatism: A Barrier to Racial Equality," in Jacobson, *op. cit.*, p. 7.
46. Brendan Sexton and Patricia Cayo Sexton, "Labor's Decade—Maybe," *Dissent*, 369 (August 1971).
47. Bernstein, *op. cit.*, p. 736; "Industries," *The Negro in Detroit* (Detroit: Mayor's Inter-Racial Committee, 1926, p. 4).
48. Arna Bontemps and Jack Conroy, *Anyplace But Here* (New York: Hill and Wang, 1966, pp. 296−297).
49. Glen E. Carlson, *The Negro in the Industries of Detroit* (Ph.D. Dissertation, University of Michigan, December, 1929, pp. 188−189).
50. "Community Organizations," *The Negro in Detroit, op. cit.*, p. 12.
51. Carlson, *op. cit.*, p. 201.
52. Bontemps, *op. cit.*, p. 297.
53. Bernstein, *op. cit.*, p. 744.
54. Thomas R. Brooks, "Workers, Black and White, DRUMbeats in Detroit," *Dissent*, 17 (January-February 1970).
55. *Ibid.*, p. 19.
56. Woodward, *op. cit.*, p. 379.
57. Franklin M. Garrett, *Atlanta and Environs* (New York: Lewis Historical Publishing Co., Inc., 1954, p. 502).

58. *Ibid.,* p. 500.

59. Woodward, *op. cit.,* p. 379.

60. *Ibid.,* p. 379.

61. Augustus Alven Adair, *The Political History of the Negro in Atlanta, 1908–1953* (M.A. Thesis, Atlanta University, August, 1955, pp. 42–56).

62. Sheila Jackson, *Black Political Power in the Deep South* (unpublished senior essay, Yale University, New Haven, Conn., May, 1972, p. 118).

63. Edward C. Banfield, *Big City Politics* (New York: Random House, 1965, p. 23).

64. Francena Edwina Culmer, *Changing Patterns of Leadership in the Black Community of Atlanta, Georgia: 1960–1969* (M.A. Thesis, Atlanta University, 1971, p. 36).

65. Carey McWilliams, *North From Mexico* (New York: Greenwood Press, 1968, pp. 190–192).

66. Ronald W. Lopez, "The El Monte Berry Strike of 1933," *Aztlan,* Vol. 1, No. 1 (Spring 1970).

67. Stan Steiner, *La Raza: The Mexican Americans* (New York: Harper and Row Publishers, 1970, pp. 294–295).

68. Bernstein, *op. cit.,* p. 155.

69. Lopez, *op. cit.,* pp. 105, 111.

70. McWilliams, *op. cit.,* p. 189.

71. Leo Grebler, Joan W. Moore, and Ralph C. Guzman, *The Mexican-American People* (New York: The Free Press, 1970, pp. 86–89).

72. Steiner, *op. cit.,* p. 306.

73. Grebler, *op. cit.,* p. 91.

74. The automobile plants at Milpitas employ many Mexican-Americans, though very few live in Gardner. Mexican-Americans are substantially represented in the hierarchy of the UAW.

75. Joan W. Moore and Frank G. Mittelbach, "Residential Segregation in the Urban Southwest," *The Mexican American Study Project* (Los Angeles: University of California Press, p. 16).

76. Grebler, *op. cit.,* pp. 392–393.

77. Harry M. Caudill, *Night Comes to the Cumberlands* (Boston: Little, Brown and Co., 1963, p. 167).

78. Todd Gitlin and Nanci Hollander, *Uptown* (New York: Harper Colophon Books, 1971, p. 87).

79. John C. Leggett, *Class, Race and Labor, Working Class Consciousness in Detroit* (New York: Oxford University Press, 1968, p. 8).

80. *Ibid.*, pp. 62—75.

81. E. P. Thompson, *The Making of the English Working Class* (New York: Vintage Books, 1963, p. 549).

82. *Ibid.*, p. 712.

83. *Ibid.*, p. 807.

84. *Ibid.*, p. 814.

85. The depression led many of the miners in Appalachia, for example, to question the motivations of the President. Caudill writes, "None of them could make it quite clear what Mr. Hoover expected to gain by bringing this singular tragedy down upon the millions of Americans who had honored him with their votes, but it's accepted as a verity that he planned and executed these hard times for the benefit of the rich" (Caudill, *op. cit.*, p. 183). Mexican farm workers who pondered membership in the Cannery and Agricultural Workers Union witnessed first hand the violence and hatred of the growers. And when in Atlanta "push came to shove," the poor blacks of Summerhill supported the pickets and the boycotts, endangering the good will of the liberal businessmen who ran the ruling coalition.

86. Karl Marx and Friedrich Engels, "The Manifesto of the Communist League" in Dan N. Jacobs, ed., *The New Communist Manifesto* (New York: Harper Torchbooks, 1965, pp. 44—54); Marx, *German Ideology, op. cit.*, p. 82.

87. Bottomore, *op. cit.*, pp. 16—18.

88. Apter, *op. cit.*, pp. 64—65.

89. Lukács, *op. cit.*, p. 76.

90. *Ibid.*, pp. 162—163.

91. *Ibid.*, p. 69.

92. *Ibid.*, p. 22.

93. Cruse, *op. cit.*, p. 57.

94. *Ibid.*, p. 299

95. *Ibid.*, pp. 137—138.

96. Claude M. Lightfoot, *Ghetto Rebellion to Black Liberation* (New York: International Publishers, 1968, p. 45).

97. Leggett. *op. cit.*, p. 106.

98. Ben W. Gilbert, *Ten Blocks from the White House, Anatomy of the Washington Riots of 1968* (New York: Frederick A. Praeger, Publishers, 1968, p. 21).

99. Leggett, *op. cit.*, p. 5.

100. T. M. Tomlinson, "Riot Ideology Among Urban Negroes," in Louis H. Masotti and Dan R. Bowen, *Riots and Rebellion, Civil Violence in the Urban Community* (Beverly Hills: Sage Publications, 1968, p. 421).

101. Richard Centers, *The Psychology of Social Classes* (New York: Russell and Russell, 1961, p. 46).

102. Oscar Glantz, "Class Consciousness and Political Solidarity," *American Sociological Review*, Vol. 23, 380–381 (1958).

Chapter Eight: Conclusion: Radical and Liberal Political Man

1. The unique variance of group consciousness is 8 percent. Sensed inefficacy, the next most important determinant, accounts for 4 percent of the variance.

2. We might argue that calculations of this kind are even more important to the poor since they have fewer resources to expend, are apt to get less from politics, and can less afford to view politics as leisure or a luxury.

3. The measure of political expression is not very strong in this case and the original average difference of 6 points not very great. These differences understate the real disparity of politics between these neighborhoods because (1) qualitative indicators confirm great differences, and (2) the types of organizational membership are sharply contrasting (e.g., service oriented in Belmont and politically oriented in the East Side). Nonetheless, it is difficult to rely on these figures for anything but clues to likely disparities and convergence.

4. Angus Campbell, Philip E. Converse, Warren E. Miller, and Donald E. Stokes, *The American Voter* (New York: John Wiley and Sons, Inc., 1960, pp. 24–37).

Appendix A

The Data Base
. . . .

I SURVEY DATA

The survey data used in this report were gathered during January and February, 1969, in five inner city poor neighborhoods. Sampling areas encompassed (OEO) neighborhood center jurisdictions selected in a stratified procedure that ensured the inclusion of black, Mexican-American, and Appalachian white respondents. These areas were drawn from a list of neighborhood center jurisdictions in fifty cities (more than 50,000 population) compiled by the Office of Economic Opportunity; the cities themselves were selected on a weighted probability basis from the (NORC) permanent community sample. The final neighborhood sample included Gardner (San Jose, California), Belmont (Hamilton, Ohio), East Side (Detroit, Michigan), Summerhill (Atlanta, Georgia), and North Central (Philadelphia, Pennsylvania).

Because of the special characteristics of poor neighborhoods (including "street culture" and the high incidence of families headed by women) we used a unique field procedure called "site sampling" (Warren TenHouten, *Site Sampling and Snowball Sampling in Biased Nets: Methodology for the Study of Community Organization,* Los Angeles, California, University of California, May 19, 1969). Each community was divided into sampling areas based on the combination of three dichotomized variables: commercial or residential establishments, inside or outside these establishments, and daytime or nighttime interviewing. These combinations of time and space form eight sites that exhaust the logical disposition of those living within the neighborhood. Using initial estimates by field supervisors and later information gathered from the interviews, we were able to estimate the population of each site and draw a sample that reflected the actual population distribution. The sample distribution is presented in Tables A.1 and A.2.

By using site sampling rather than a conventional residential sample, we were able to minimize the underrepresentation of individuals who visit a residence infrequently. Conventional sampling procedures typically underenumerate young black males living in central cities, a disastrous bias in a study limited to urban poor communities (Donald Bogue, Bhaskar D. Misra, and D. P. Dandekar, "A New Estimate of the Negro Population and Negro Vital Rates in the United States, 1930–1960," *Demography,* Vol. I, No. 1, 1964). The site sampling procedures used in this report, however, substantially increase the number of interviews with young black and Mexican-American males. The representativeness of the sample can still be questioned. Fifty-five percent of the respondents are women; the predominance of young males in the nonresidential sample, however, indicates that the bias is less than would have been produced by an exclusively residential sample.

II OBSERVATION

During the summer of 1969, I began personal observation in these five poor neighborhoods. I first visited Gardner for a brief time in August, 1968, and in January, 1969, completed short inspection trips to North Central Belmont, and Summerhill. In the summer of 1970 I revisited Gardner and Belmont, and made my first observation trip to the East Side. Later in the year, I spent two weeks in

Table A.1   Sampling Sites

			Neighborhoods		
	Gardner	Belmont(i)	East Side	Summerhill	North Central
Residential, inside, day	44%	79%	40%	52%	47%
Residential, inside, night	43%	20%	22%	22%	42%
Residential, outside, day	2%	0%	1%	2%	0%
Residential, outside, night	1%	0%	0%	0%	0%
Commercial, inside, day	3%	2%	20%	15%	6%
Commercial, inside, night	3%	0%	12%	7%	5%
Commercial, outside, day	3%	0%	4%	2%	0%
Commercial, outside, night	1%	0%	2%	0%	0%
Number of interviews completed	153	178	280	251	250

(i) Because these percentages were rounded off, column totals sometimes do not equal 100%.

Table A.2   Characteristics of Residential and Nonresidential Samples

Characteristics	Residential	Nonresidential [i]
Under 36 years of age	47% (703)	64% (218)
Male	40% (689)	67% (210)

[i] Excludes day and night, inside residential interviews.

Summerhill and North Central. I resumed these observation visits almost a year later, devoting a month to eastern Kentucky, Belmont, and the East Side. During the spring and summer of 1972, I completed the field work with one week excursions to Summerhill, North Central, and Gardner.

In each community, I began by examining back issues (microfilms) of a citywide circulation newspaper and clippings files (if they were available). After completing this review, I conducted a similar inquiry into local community newspapers if they were political in content and if back issues were available. General source material on the city and community were acquired from central branches of public and university libraries, redevelopment agencies, boards of elections, planning boards, and information clearinghouses (e.g., the Southern Regional Council).

I began actual interviewing with perhaps the most accessible respondents, university faculty or graduate students who had done research in the area and newspaper staff who had reported on the neighborhoods under study. These initial contacts provided names of informed or politically active community residents. Drawing on these suggestions and material from the newspapers, I constructed a list of potential interviewees. These usually included members of the Human Relations Commission, local elected officials, employees of a neighborhood antipoverty office or Model Cities program, a leader of a Welfare Rights Organization, union officials, personnel managers in local industry, ministers active in social service agencies, and leaders of prominent community organizations. Barring a few individuals in the latter category, respondents were generally accessible and receptive to my inquiries. As a matter of course, I also contacted the district office of the congressman or state representative and community organizers in the local poverty program.

Whenever possible, I conducted an unsystematic walking survey of the neighborhood—talking to residents, visiting storefront operations (religious, social, and political) and other establishments or offices seemingly frequented by neighborhood residents or remotely concerned with neighborhood politics.

Appendix B
Derivation of Measures

. . . .

I LOWER CLASS CULTURE

Present Orientation

Respondents were asked whether they "agreed" or "disagreed" with the following statement:

"The wise person lives for today and lets tomorrow take care of itself."

Distrust

Respondents were asked the following question:

"Do you think people who live in this neighborhood can generally be trusted?"

II POLITICAL ALIENATION

Policy Dissatisfaction

Policy dissatisfaction is a summation of scores on the three items indicated below:

1. One point is accorded for a negative ("no") answer to the question, "Do you think that the children in the schools around here get a good education?"
2. One point is accorded for a positive ("yes") answer to the question, "Some people say that the police rough up people unnecessarily when they are arresting them or afterwards. Do you think this happens to people in this neighborhood?"
3. One point is accorded for listing government policies as one of the major problems in the community or if, in defining the term "political," a negative reference is made to specific government policies.

Scores range between zero and three, from the least policy dissatisfaction to the most pronounced. For portions of this analysis, these categories are collapsed so that 0 or 1 is "low" and 2 or 3 is "high."

Sense of Inefficacy

A Guttman scale was formed using the following items:

1. "People like me don't have any say in what the government does." (strongly disagree, disagree, agree, strongly agree)
2. "Are there any government officials in this city who really care a lot about what people in this neighborhood want?" (yes, don't know, no)
3. A situation involving discrimination in hiring was described and respondents were then asked, "Do you think it would help to complain to a public official?" (yes, don't know, no)

Scores were scaled from one to six so that a score of one is least inefficacy and six most inefficacy. The coefficient of reproducibility is .88. For portions of this analysis 1, 2, or 3 is "low" inefficacy and 4, 5, or 6 is "high."

Political System Rejection

A Guttman scale was formed using the following items:

1. "Do you personally feel that this country is worth fighting for, or not?" (no, don't know, yes)
2. "Some people say that things will never get better for poor people without major changes in the way the country is run. Do you think this is true?" (yes, don't know, no)
3. "How do you think the U.S. Government feels about poor people? Would you say it is trying to help poor people, or is it doing very little to help poor people, or is it trying to keep poor people down?" (keep down, very little, help)

Scores were scaled from one to five, from lowest system rejection to highest. The coefficient of reproducibility is .93. For portions of the analysis these categories are collapsed so that a score of 1 or 2 is "low" system rejection; 3, 4, or 5 is "high" system rejection.

III GROUP CONSCIOUSNESS

Group Blame

Respondents are given one point each time they respond "strongly disagree" or "disagree" to each of the following statements:

1. "Black people (Mexican-Americans) who want to work hard can get ahead just as easily as anyone else."
2. "Black people (Mexican-Americans) blame too many of their problems on whites (Anglos)."

A score of 0 means inner-directed hostility, 1 reflects ambivalence on the two items, and 2 means outer-directed hostility.

Group Autonomy

Group autonomy is a summation of scores on three items. One point is given each time a respondent indicates "strongly agree" or "agree" on each of the following statements:

1. "Stores in a black (Mexican-American) neighborhood should be owned and run by black people (Mexican-Americans)."

2. "Black people (Mexican-Americans) would do better if they only voted for blacks (Mexican-Americans)."
3. "Black people (Mexican-Americans) will have very little say in the government unless they all decide to vote for the same candidates."

Scores were scaled from zero, least autonomy, to a possible score of three, the strongest commitment to autonomy. For portions of this analysis 0 or 1 is "low" and 2 or 3 is "high" group autonomy.

Group Consciousness

Group consciousness is a summation of scores on all group autonomy and group blame items. Scores range from zero, minimal group consciousness, to five, strongest group consciousness. For portions of the analysis a score of 0, 1, or 2 is "low" group consciousness and 3, 4, or 5 is "high."

IV   CLASS IDEOLOGY

Class Ideology

Respondents are given a point for each "class" oriented response ("yes" or "good idea") on the following questions:

1. "Do you think all people have the right to have enough money to live on, whether they are working or not?"
2. "How would you feel if everyone got paid the same amount of money, no matter what his job was?"

Scores range from zero, mimimal class ideology, to two, the highest indication of class ideology.

V   POLITICAL EXPRESSION

Receptivity to Violence

Receptivity to violence is a summation of the following scores:

1. One point is accorded for a negative response ("no") to the question, "Do

you think that black people (Mexican-Americans) today can win their rights without using violence?"

2. One point was accorded if a respondent indicates he would "join in" when asked, "If a disturbance like the ones that occurred after the assassination of Martin Luther King broke out here, do you think you would join in, or would you try to stop it, or would you stay away from it?"

3. One point is accorded if respondent answers "helped" when asked, "On the whole, do you think the disturbances have helped or hurt the cause of rights for black people, or would you say they haven't made much difference?"

Scores range from zero, least receptivity, to three, most receptivity to violence. For portions of the analysis the above categories are collapsed so that a score of 0 is "low" receptivity and a score of 1, 2, or 3 is "high."

Receptivity to Politics

After being told of a hypothetical case of job discrimination, each respondent was asked whether he would be willing to:

1. Complain to the manager of a store
2. Complain to a public official
3. Picket a store
4. Join a boycott

Their responses form a Guttman scale; the coefficient of reproducibility is .93. Scores ranged from one, least receptive, to five, most receptive. For portions of this analysis 1, 2, or 3 is "low" receptivity to politics, and 4 or 5 is "high."

Membership in Community Organizations

Respondents were asked the following question:

"What are the most important groups or organizations that people in this neighborhood belong to?"

Of those who named an organization, the following question was asked: "Do you belong to any of them?"

Index

Africa, 142, 143–145, 146, 156, 172
Agricultural Workers Industrial Union, 190
Alabama, 15, 16, 34
Alienation, 107–130, 141, 159, 162, 163, 164, 165, 165, 167, 178, 198, 200, 204, 205, 211–212
  political, 4, 5, 52, 89, 94–95, 107–130, 141, 162, 198, 208, 209–210, 211–212, 215, 217, 224–225
Alinsky, Saul, 169–170
Almond, Gabriel, 109
American Federation of Labor, 180, 181, 185, 187, 191
Analysis, Factor, 133–138, 157, 162
Anomie, 79–80
Apathy, 51–52, 62, 75–76, 111, 115–116, 125, 130, 209–210
Apolitics, 107
Appalachia, 18, 20, 25–26, 33, 168
  whites, 19, 22–23, 25–26, 49–53, 97, 99–100, 105, 107, 120, 121–122, 123, 133, 150–153, 159, 178, 179, 192–193, 197, 209, 210, 214, 225, 226, 227
Apter, David, 175
Area Service Centers, 45, 47
Area Wide Council, 70
Assimilation, 46, 48
Atlanta, 36, 59–64, 106, 122–123, 158, 188–189, 193
Atlanta Negro Voters League, 60, 61, 189
Atlanta Stadium, 36, 122, 204
Austin, Richard, 57

Autonomy, 55, 62, 66, 82, 135, 141, 154, 158, 163–164, 165, 171, 198, 199, 200, 202, 205, 210

Banfield, Edward, 77, 78–79, 83–84, 94, 158
Barrios, 31
Belief, 3, 4, 5, 73, 75–76, 77–103, 112–113, 116, 118, 120–121, 124, 130, 134, 147, 208–209, 211, 213, 214, 215–229
Belmont, 7, 32–34, 49–53, 71, 72, 86, 97, 98, 99, 100, 102, 106, 119, 120, 121, 122, 124, 130, 133, 151, 159, 168, 172, 176–177, 194, 208, 209, 212, 213, 214, 215, 220–221, 225
Bernstein, Saul, 90
Black Belt, 14, 15, 20–22, 26, 27, 29, 34, 39, 41, 104, 106, 206, 207
Blacks, 15–16, 20–21, 26–27, 34–40, 53–71, 92, 104–105, 115, 116–117, 118, 120–121, 122–123, 124, 128–129, 130, 131–132, 133, 134, 135–137, 139, 141–146, 151, 152, 153, 156–159, 160, 162, 163–164, 166, 167, 168, 169–172, 178, 179–185, 186–189, 193–194, 196–197, 198, 199, 200, 201, 202–203, 204–205, 210, 211, 212, 213, 214, 215, 217–226, 227, 228
Black Muslims, 142–143
Black Nationalism, 142–143
Black Power, 68, 131–132, 134, 135, 137, 142, 147, 153

Block Clubs, 58, 59
Boll Weevil, 26, 34, 122
Bracero, 17, 18, 29
Business, 59–60, 173–178

California, 15, 16, 17, 18, 29, 30–31
Camus, Albert, 113
Cannery and Agricultural Workers Union
    (C & AW), 190
Carmichael, Stokely, 131, 135, 142, 144,
    146, 169
Caudill, Harry, 120, 192
Cavanaugh, Jerome, 129–187
Cayton, Horace R., 87
Central Mesa, 16, 24, 25, 27, 41, 105, 206,
    207
Chamber of Commerce, 61–62, 189
Champion Papers, 33, 185, 192–193, 228
Chavez, Cesar, 44–45, 48, 123, 149, 191
Chicago Defender, 27–28, 145
Chicanos, 46
Chrysler, 187
Church, 55–56, 57, 58, 59, 60, 63, 65, 68,
    97, 99, 144, 149, 151, 184, 186
Churches on the East Side for Social Action,
    59
City-Wide Tenants Council, 67, 68
Class, 173–205, 209, 210
    consciousness, 193–196
    ideology, 4, 5, 199, 209, 210, 212, 213,
        214, 215
    working, 228–266
Cleaver, Eldridge, 121
Coal, 22–23, 25–26
Cohen, Albert, 89
Communist Party, 179–180, 183–185, 190,
    194, 196–198
Community, Sense of, 112, 122, 123, 124
Community Service Organization (CSO),
    44–45, 46, 148, 191
Confederation de la Raza Unida, 45, 46,
    47, 147–148, 150, 154, 172, 205
Congress of Industrial Organizations (CIO),
    180–181, 183, 185, 193–194
CORE, 68
Cotton, 19–22
Crime, 36, 37–40, 52, 58, 89–90, 106
    East Side, 36
    North Central, 39–40
    Summerhill, 37–38

Crocket, Judge, 56, 58
Cruse, Harold, 196
Culture, 4, 5, 9, 75, 76–77, 77–104, 107,
    111, 112, 113–115, 118, 122, 123–
    124, 140, 142–149, 153–157, 159–
    161, 168, 198, 205, 208, 209, 210,
    211, 214, 215, 216
    "Lower Class," 9, 75, 76–104, 107, 208,
        209, 210, 215
Cumberland Plateau, 15, 18, 20, 22–23, 24,
    25, 27, 29, 41, 105, 192, 206

Debt Peonage, 24–25
Delta Region, 15, 21, 22, 27, 29, 34
Democratic Party, 51, 55–56, 57–58, 66–
    67, 68–69, 187–189, 200
Dependency, 169–170, 178
Deportation, 18
Despair, 78, 111, 113–114, 116, 118
Detroit, 35–36, 53–59, 63, 128–129, 156–
    158, 170–171, 181, 186–188, 193,
    214–215
Diggs, Congressman, 56–57
Disloyalty, 161–162, 163
Distrust, 209, 210–214
Dodge Revolutionary Union Movement
    (DRUM), 187
Drake, St. Clair, 87
Dream, American, 172–174, 179
DuBois, W. E. B., 38, 131, 145

East Los Angeles, 44, 48, 147
Easton, David, 109, 110
East Side, 6, 34–36, 53–59, 71, 72, 86, 97,
    98, 99, 106, 119, 120–121, 124, 128–
    129, 130, 133, 154, 155, 156–158,
    159, 162, 166, 170–171, 172, 176,
    186–188, 201, 204, 208, 212, 213,
    214, 215, 216, 217, 218–219, 220–
    222, 224–225, 226, 229
Economic and Social Opportunities (ESO),
    43, 45, 47
Ellison, Ralph, 146
Embourgeoisement, 174–175
Employment, 31–32, 32–34, 38–39, 42,
    87–88
    Belmont, 32–34
    Gardner, 31–32
    North Central, 38–39
Essien-Udom, E. U., 143

Ethnicity, 132, 135, 139–140, 149, 210, 224

Fairfield Township, 52–53
Family Heritage, 27–28, 45–46, 52–53, 82–83, 91–93, 99, 114, 120, 151–153, 190–191
Fanon, Frantz, 144
Fatalism, 75–76, 81–82, 84–85, 99–100, 101, 102, 209, 211
Ford Motors, 34–35, 41, 57–58, 181
Ford, Thomas R., 121–122
Free Villages, 24
Fundamentalism, 99

Gans, Herbert, 76, 79, 80, 82–83, 92–93
Gardner, 7, 30–32, 43–48, 71, 72, 86, 96–97, 98, 106, 119, 120, 121, 123–124, 130, 133, 147, 148, 153, 154–156, 159, 166, 171, 176, 186, 201, 204, 205, 208, 211–214, 215, 216, 218–219, 220–223, 225, 226, 228–229
Gardner Assembly, 45, 47
Georgia, 16, 21, 28, 34, 38, 122–123
G. I. Forum, 44, 45, 148
Grodzins, 161
Group Blame, 155, 163–164, 172, 199, 224
Group Consciousness, 5, 48, 133–134, 135–136, 140–172, 175, 178, 195, 197–198, 201, 202–205, 209, 210–211, 212, 213, 214–216, 217
Group Solidarity, 178, 196, 204, 205
Growers, 190
Guanajuato, 16

Haciendas, 24, 25, 105
Hamilton, 32, 49–53, 99, 122
Hamilton, Charles, 135, 144, 169
Hannerz, Ulf, 88, 91, 93
Harlem, 13, 31, 63, 87
Hegel, 108–109
Highways, 30, 32, 35–36, 36–37, 106, 158, 204
Belmont, 32
East Side, 35–36
Gardner, 32
Summerhill, 36–37
Hillbillies, 150–153
History, 6, 8, 113, 140, 142, 143–145, 146, 147–150, 159, 160, 171–172, 198, 205, 208, 210, 211, 226, 227, 228, 229
Horton, 118
Housing, 31, 32, 35–36, 37, 39–40, 40–41, 63, 106, 122
Belmont, 32
East Side, 35–36
Gardner, 31
North Central, 39–40
Summerhill, 37
Human Relations Commission, 57

Identity, 132, 135–153, 156–157, 158–159, 160–168, 191–192
group, 161–162, 209, 210, 211–214, 215–216
Ideology, 174, 175–178, 179, 185, 195, 196–200, 208, 210, 212, 213, 214, 215
Immediacy, 83–86, 94–96, 97, 98, 99–100, 107
Income, 175, 195, 200, 201
Industry, 2, 14, 22–23, 26, 27, 28, 31, 33–34, 35, 42, 52, 60, 105, 112, 173–174, 178, 180–181, 184–194, 207
automobile, 34–35, 41, 57, 182, 185, 186, 187
Inefficacy, sense of, 110, 111, 112, 113–114, 115–116, 117–118, 119, 124, 125, 126–127, 128–129, 130, 163–164, 199, 202–203, 209, 212, 213, 214, 215–216, 217

Jalisco, 16
Jones, LeRoi, 142

Kazantzakos, Nikos, 99
Kenison, Kenneth, 108, 114–115
Kentucky, 14, 18, 19, 20, 22, 26, 34, 52, 152, 159
Key, V. O., Jr., 118

Labor, 25–26, 44–45, 55–57, 178, 179–181, 182–183, 184–185, 185–188, 189–193, 200–201
Agents, 27, 28
Agricultural, 2, 14, 20–22, 23–25, 28–29, 189–190
Land, 148–149
Lane, Robert, 109–110, 117
Latin American Citizens Association, 191

Leggett, John, 194–195, 197
Lewis, John L., 26, 181, 183
Lewis, Oscar, 76, 77, 78, 79, 82, 83
Liberals, 55, 56
Liberal Political Man, 3
Liebow, Elliot, 86–87, 88, 90, 173–174
Lightfoot, Claude, 144, 197
Lincoln, C. Eric, 143
Lipset, Seymour Martin, 77

McWilliams, Cary, 150, 190
Mainstreamers, 91, 93
Malcolm X, 141, 142, 145
Marginality, 20–21, 21–22, 23–25, 27, 78, 82, 106–107, 175, 178, 195, 197, 198, 200, 201, 204–205
Marx, Karl, 108–109, 195, 197–198, 200
Men, 85, 86, 87–88, 90, 91, 93, 94, 95, 209
Merton, Robert, 79
Mexican-Americans, 31, 43–48, 120, 121, 123–124, 133, 134, 135, 137–138, 139–140, 141, 146–150, 151, 153–156, 160, 162, 163–164, 165, 166, 167, 168, 171, 178, 179, 186, 189–192, 193–194, 197, 198, 199, 201, 202, 205, 210, 211–212, 216, 218–224, 225, 226–227, 228
Mexican-American Community Organization, 47
Mexican-American Political Association, 45, 46, 148
Mexico, 16–18, 19, 23–25, 147, 149–150, 153–154, 210
  culture, 147, 149–150, 153–154
  Indians, 24
  migration, 16–18, 19
  people, 23–25
  Revolution, 17, 25
Michoacan, 16
Migration, 2–3, 15–20, 24, 28, 30, 32–33, 42, 122–123, 149
  Appalachian white, 18, 19, 20, 33
  Black, 19, 32–33, 37, 38–39
  Mexican, 16–18, 19
Miller, Walter, 81, 82–83
Mills, C. Wright, 5–6
Mining, 17, 18–20, 22–23, 25–26, 174
Ministers, 179, 186–187, 189
Mississippi, 15, 16, 21, 34

Mobility, 40
Model Cities, 36–37, 43, 45, 47, 58, 62, 63, 64, 69, 70, 71, 97, 106, 120, 170, 171
Modernization, 3, 8, 11
Moore, Cecil B., 66, 68
Myths, 88, 89, 90

National Advisory Committee on Civil Disorders, 13
National Association for the Advancement of Colored People (NAACP), 66, 68, 90, 118, 184
Negro Voters League, 106
New Detroit Committee, 58–59
New Mexico, 16, 17, 25
Nix, Robert, 66, 69
Nonviolence, 43–48, 71, 208, 211–212, 228–229
North Carolina, 21, 38
North Central, 6, 38–40, 64–71, 85–86, 87, 96–97, 98, 106, 119, 120, 124, 128, 130, 154, 155, 157, 158, 159, 162, 166, 170, 171, 172, 176–177, 186, 188, 201, 204, 208, 212–213, 215, 217, 218–219, 220–221, 222–223, 224, 225, 226

Ohio, 20, 32
Organizations, community, 43–47, 49–51, 54, 58–59, 60–61, 63, 64–65, 67, 68–71, 75, 85, 95–96, 97, 99, 100–102, 128–130, 165, 166, 167, 169–170, 191, 214, 220, 225, 228
  Belmont, 49–51
  East Side, 54, 58–59, 60–61, 63, 64
  Gardner, 43–47
  North Central, 64–65, 67, 68–71
  Summerhill, 60, 61, 63–64
Orientation, personal, 82–83, 84–85, 101, 102–103, 152–153, 209, 212, 213, 214, 217
O'Tuck, 50–51, 159

PAAC, 69–70
Parsons, Talcott, 114
Patrick, William, 55
Path Analysis, 125–126, 162–165
Patron, 123
"Peck's Addition," 32–33, 34, 49, 71, 122
Philadelphia, 38–39, 64–71, 188

Philadelphia Welfare Rights Organization, 67
Plantation System, 21
Police, 48, 58, 116–117, 120–122, 124, 129, 130, 156, 162, 169, 200, 224
Policy, 110, 111, 112, 113, 114, 119, 120–121
  Dissatisfaction, 110, 111, 112, 113, 114, 119, 124, 125, 126, 127, 128, 129–130, 163–164, 199, 202–203, 209–210, 212, 213, 214, 215, 216, 217
Politics, 3, 4–5, 11, 43–93, 109, 110, 121, 132–172, 206–230
  Belmont, 48–53, 71–72
  East Side, 53–59, 71–72
  Gardner, 43–48, 71–72
  North Central, 64–71, 72
  Summerhill, 59–64, 71–72
  conventional, 44, 50–52, 54, 55–56, 61–62, 65, 66–67, 70–71, 72, 76–77, 83, 84, 90, 100–103, 104–105, 111, 113, 115–116, 118, 125, 126–127, 128, 129, 130, 134, 135, 160, 162, 165, 166, 167, 168, 169–171, 172, 200–201, 205, 207, 209–210, 211, 212, 213, 214, 215, 216, 217, 224, 225, 227, 228, 229
  electoral, 44, 47–48, 50, 51, 52, 53–57, 58, 59–60, 61–62, 64–67, 68–69, 96–97, 100–101, 117–118, 120, 130, 157, 159, 162, 181–182, 188, 189, 200–201, 227–228
    Belmont, 50, 51, 52
    East Side, 53–57, 58
    Gardner, 44, 47–48
    North Central, 64–67, 168–169
    Summerhill, 59–60, 61–62
Poverty Programs, 44–46, 51–52, 58, 63–64, 69–70, 169–171
  Belmont, 51–52
  East Side, 58
  Gardner, 44–46
  North Central, 69–70
  Summerhill, 63–64
Protest, 48, 59, 61–62, 63–64, 76–77, 85, 96–97, 108, 111, 114–115, 118, 127, 129, 151, 158–159, 174, 184, 188, 224, 228

Racism, 131, 134, 141–142, 149, 151–152, 171–172, 180–181, 182, 191–192, 197
Radical Political Man, 2, 3
Railroads, 16, 28, 37
Ralph Bunche Community Council, 58
Randolph, A. Phillip, 180, 184
Rebellion, 2, 111, 113–115
Reconstruction, 55
Record, Wilson, 184
Rejection, system, 110, 111, 112, 113, 114, 117, 119, 124, 125, 126–127, 128, 130, 163–164, 199, 202–203, 209, 212, 213, 215
Republican Party, 51, 68
Responsiveness, Government, 110, 114–116, 117, 119, 126–127, 128–129, 130
Revolution, 113, 118, 174, 228
Rio Grande Valley, 17
Riots, 13, 14, 53, 59, 63–64, 108, 115, 118, 133–134, 181, 187, 188–189, 198, 200, 204–205
Rizzo, Frank, 66
Robles, General, 25, 105
Rose, Arnold, 161
Roszak, Theodore, 112–113
Rural Society, 14, 20, 42, 104–105

San Jose, 30–31, 44, 45, 120, 148, 153, 190, 191
Schools, 48, 52–53, 116–117, 120, 121–122, 123, 124, 129, 130, 134, 162, 169, 224
Segregation, 147–148
Sharecropping, 21–22, 24
Site Sampling, 94–95, 96, 98
Slavery, 21, 22, 143–144
Social Deviance, 79–80, 89–90, 92
Socialism, 179–180, 183, 184–185, 196
Sociological Imagination, 5–6
"Soul," 145–146
South, 15–16, 20–22, 27–28, 104–105, 122–123
South Carolina, 15, 16, 38
Southwest, 16, 29, 105, 148, 149, 150, 189–190, 191
Spanish Domination, 23–24
Steel, 28
Steiner, Stan, 123
Streetcorner Society, 76, 85–96, 209
  Gangs, 68, 81–82, 89–90, 92

Strikes, 39, 180–181, 183, 187, 189–190
Student Nonviolent Coordinating Com-
    mittee, (SNCC), 64
Summerhill, 6–7, 36–38, 59–64, 71, 72,
    86–87, 97, 98, 102, 106, 119, 121,
    122–123, 130, 154, 155, 158, 159,
    162, 165, 166, 172, 176–177, 188–
    189, 201, 202–203, 204, 208, 212,
    213, 214–215, 218–219, 220–221,
    222–223, 224, 225
Survey, 6–7, 48, 93–95, 98, 117–118, 191
Swingers, 91

Tally's Corner, 87, 89, 90, 92
Texas, 14, 16, 17, 18, 25, 26
Thompson, E. P., 118, 194–195
Thrasher, Frederick, 90, 92
Timber, 22, 105
Time, 75, 76, 81, 95, 99, 101, 102
Tomlinson, T. M., 200
Trade Union Leadership Conference, 187
Transcendence, 195–196, 197, 198

Udall, Stewart, 22
United Automobile Workers, 55–56, 57–
    58, 186–187
United Farm Workers Organizing Com-
    ittee, 45
United Latin-Americans of America, 46
United Mine Workers, 26, 161, 192
United Tenants for Collective Action, 58
Unions, 25–26, 45, 56, 57–58, 178, 179,
    180–181, 183, 184–185, 186–188,
    189–193, 200
Urbanization, 4–5, 7, 8–9, 13–14, 17–18,
    27–29, 32, 34, 35–36, 36–37, 75,
    85–87, 106, 108, 118, 120, 195
    Urban League, 186
    Urban Renewal, 32, 34, 35–36, 36–37,
        40–41, 106, 120, 122
        Belmont, 34
        East Side, 35–36
        Gardner, 32

Summerhill, 36–37
Valentine, Charles, 79, 102–103
Vaughn, Jackie, 55, 58
Verba, Sidney, 109
Vietnam War, 14
Violence, 2, 13–14, 43, 44, 48, 50, 54, 59,
    61, 63–64, 68, 72, 76–77, 81, 95,
    101, 102, 105–106, 108, 109, 110–
    116, 118, 124, 125, 126, 127, 128,
    130, 141, 160, 162–163, 165–166,
    167, 168, 171–172, 198, 201, 202–
    203, 205, 208, 209–210, 211, 213,
    214, 215, 216, 217, 218–219, 220–
    221, 222–223, 224–225, 226,
    227–229
    Belmont, 50
    East Side, 54, 59
    Gardner, 43, 44, 48
    North Central, 64, 65, 68
    Summerhill, 61, 63–64
Virginia, 15, 22, 38

"War on Poverty," 13, 49–50, 156
Warren, Roland, 169
Washington, Booker T., 182–183
Watson, Tom, 188–189
Watts, 13, 48, 63, 117
Welfare Rights Organization, 59
West Virginia, 18
Whyte, William, 92
Wilson, James Q., 169
Witt, Frank, 49, 51
Women, 92–93, 126, 209
Woodward, C. Vann, 181–182, 189
Working Class, 228–266
WWI, 15, 18, 26, 34, 35, 38, 122, 161, 184
WWII, 16, 17, 18, 22, 29, 38, 39, 123, 160,
    180, 184, 193

Young, Coleman, 56, 58, 157

Zionism, 132